WAITING

Mastering the UnAvoidable

WAITING

Mastering the UnAvoidable

Dr. Tuesday Tate

Waiting: Mastering the UnAvoidable

Published by:
Professional Woman Publishing
www.pwnbooks.com

ISBN: 978-0-578-14515-0

Dedication

This study of "Waiting" is dedicated to God and the people and things in my life that taught me how to wait and to wait right. I thank God for His voice and the Word that has led and comforted me many hours, days, weeks, months, and years. It was and is Your presence, Your peace, and Your assurance that I find and hold to. It is Your Word Father God that has kept me. It is to You I give the glory, honor, and praise. To You Holy Father, I am grateful. To my dear sweet precious loving mother Martha J. Tate who never judges and always encourages. How I appreciate and love you. To my Pastor, A. Thomas Hill, not enough space or time to express my gratitude for your encouragement, correction, wisdom, and shepherd's heart. Thank you for your patience and guidance in my spiritual and natural life and development. Thank you for listening to my many ideas, for helping, teaching, and guiding me. While I bless God for and love all my siblings (Brenda Taylor, Jean, Columbus and Gardus Tate), I must give a special acknowledgement to my sister Markeelie Goff, who first hand witnessed my pilgrimage and me waiting on God to do His will in His time. You have been a trooper and to you I say thank you a 1000 times over.

Contents

Foreword

How refreshing it is when a voice emerges and gives fresh insight to a universal dilemma. This is a hot button subject. We live in an age where access to information and resources is moving at a fast pace. Thus, waiting is somewhat archaic in the culture in which we live. Where everything we do is quick fast and in a hurry: instant coffee, tea, and even marriage. The world gets frustrated more and more about waiting.

I'm excited about this book as Dr. Tate masterfully teaches us how to master the unavoidable reality of waiting. You will find strategies within these pages on how to wait right. I applaud her for addressing this subject and giving practical strategies to an age-old problem that will never go away. The ready are moved to understand completely the purpose of waiting and not demonize the process but see it as a providential part of God's plan for their life. The bewildered, frustrated, and weary will find comfort and hope within the pages of this book.

Dr. Tate shares her wealth of personal experiences, testimonies, and presents this book with great transparency as she brings to light revelations that will change your perspective. This book literally shows us how to embrace the waiting process and pay attention to the valuable lessons God teaches us while we wait. It pushes the reader to self-reflection ultimately evolving into self-discovery.

Pastoring over 20 years, I have seen many people frustrated by waiting. I am very excited that now I can share with them a tool;

this book *Mastering the UnAvoidable* that can assist them in the reality of waiting. There is a purpose that God has for all of our lives and to fulfill it waiting will be a part of it. When we truly understand that purpose it makes waiting easier.

This book contains great research, both biblical and practical. What is taught is backed by Scripture as well as a wealth of life experiences. It's a serious attempt to share knowledge and experience to give others hope. It shows people how to embrace the process of waiting and focus on their God given purpose and in turn motivate them to help others accomplish the same. What a great service to the Body of Christ!

I'm so thankful for Dr. Tate for writing this amazing book. You hold in your hands a great book, written masterfully to help others. My prayer is that God will use it to transform your life and the lives of others you engage daily. Waiting is inevitable, but this book reveals "how" you wait is a choice – your choice.

Thank you Dr. Tate for showing us how to wait right.

BISHOP JOSEPH WARREN WALKER, III
SENIOR PASTOR, MOUNT ZION BAPTIST CHURCH—NASHVILLE
PRESIDING BISHOP-ELECT, FULL GOSPEL BAPTIST CHURCH FELLOWSHIP INTL

Comments

"I am convinced that the most valuable of teaching resources, whether verbal or written, are derived from authors who have personally experienced what they have chosen to communicate. As her pastor, teacher, and mentor of over 12 years, I can honestly attest to the fact that Dr. Tate has given us a resource that she has not only researched through others and the Word, but has lived out herself. Her invaluable experiential knowledge on the subject of "waiting" contained in this book is worth much more than you paid for the pages you're about to ingest. I hope you enjoy her story as much as I have enjoyed observing her innate ability to wait without wavering and finish without quitting."

A. THOMAS HILL
SENIOR PASTOR, HEALING STREAMS WORD AND WORSHIP CENTER

"Waiting is a discipline that each of us must learn, but few have mastered. Dr. Tuesday Tate gives us insight and strategy on how to do it God's way in order to achieve His perfect Will. Powerful and insightful. This book is a *must read*, especially if you have ever grown weary while waiting."

DR. DORA SANDERS HILL
FOUNDER, VICTORY TO GLORY MINISTRIES INTERNATIONAL

"Tuesday has lived life to its fullest and brings so much wisdom from her experience in waiting to this book. She has taken every experience of her life and used it as a puzzle piece, building something beautiful. So many passages will stir your soul and speak to you. Yes, we all are in the waiting place."

LINDA TOUPIN
NATIONAL SALES DIRECTOR, MARY KAY

Introduction

One afternoon, I was sitting with my great-niece who loves to read. She was about eighteen months old at the time and she said in her very special voice, "Let's read this one Auntie, I like this one." I really thought, "Let us read? Won't I be the one reading and you will be listening? But ok, let's read." It was a Dr. Seuss poem, *The Waiting Place* written by Theodor Geisel. I proceeded to open the book and what I read quickly captured my attention! There was a truth that Dr. Seuss' words had hit upon. These words resonated deeply in my soul and caused my mind to do a few cartwheels. Why? At that time, this 'truth' was exactly where I was in my life. It was exactly how I was feeling…waiting…moving, or at least taking steps, but not really going anywhere. I realized I had picked up a Dr. Seuss treasure. At forty and two, I had never read the book *Oh the Places You will Go*. Certainly and like most, *Green Eggs and Ham*, but never *The Waiting Place*.

This caused a stirring thought, "Waiting is something that everyone must do in one way, time, or another…but why is waiting so dang-gone hard!" I wondered if waiting on people was easier than waiting on God or vice-versa. So, I surveyed (see attached) over 50 individuals, male, female, old, and young. I was surprised to discover that 76% of those surveyed said that waiting on God was not as challenging as waiting on people. With nothing else beyond the natural or their understanding to compare to God, they saw their ability to wait on God to be easier. Yet, when asked to consider how they had handled waiting on God, the overwhelming response was that 98% had waited impatiently. Perhaps this flip flop demonstrates an initial religious response to the first question. The realization of these outcomes resulted in participants reconsidering just how "easy" waiting on God really is. All people; not just Christians and people of faith, will experience waiting. It is a discipline that is necessary for a mature life and Christian walk.

Though discipline is not something that most of us like; when it is practiced and demonstrated, it can be an equipper for life. Hebrews 12:11 says, "No *discipline seems pleasant at the time, but painful. Later on, however, for those who have been trained by it, it produces a harvest of righteousness and peace.*" As I began to study this unavoidable life discipline, I took note of the spiritual disciplines that were most often studied and taught, but waiting was not one of them. I became more and more convinced that waiting is quite possibly the most difficult discipline a person will face and the most challenging to master.

It is my hope that by reading this book you will be helped in some way. The truth is everyone has to wait. You probably picked up this book because you are in a waiting place or a state of waiting now. Some of you just left a waiting place. And some of you are about to go into one. Whatever the state or status, I am confident that you will gain great insight and understanding of the necessity of waiting and waiting right. You will receive valuable instruction and tools to help you navigate through your waiting place and seasons; and seek to master this most unavoidable discipline. On your journey and the places you will go, I encourage you to be strengthened, encouraged, comforted, and enlightened. I invite you to take this journey with me. Mastering your waiting place is possible and available to you. Welcome to *Waiting*. Mastery awaits you.

Oh, the Places You'll Go!

by Dr. Seuss

*"You can get so confused that you'll start in to race...
headed, I fear, toward a most useless place.
The Waiting Place...for people just waiting.*

*Waiting for a train to go
or a bus to come, or a plane to go
or the mail to come, or the rain to go
or the phone to ring, or the snow to snow
or waiting around for a Yes or a No...*
Everyone is just waiting...

NO!
That's not for you!
*Somehow you'll escape all that waiting and staying.
You'll find the bright places..."*

Dr. Seuss, Dr. Seuss, Dr. Seuss! Dr. Seuss nailed it. Yes, everyone is waiting for or on something or someone. Unfortunately, I must disagree with his assertion that you will escape the waiting and staying. The truth is everyone has to wait! So often it is that we wait, we may not even realize that we are waiting. Everyone is either currently waiting, will wait or is about to wait. Whether waiting for a relationship to reconcile, a call to come, a sickness to leave, a prayer to be answered, a business deal to go through, help to come, a problem or challenge to end, a child to return, a spouse to change or your chance to come; waiting to wait, then only to wait some more. Everyone is waiting on someone or for something. Sorry, Dr. Seuss, until we leave this earth we will find ourselves waiting and staying. It is at the mention of the reality called the "waiting place" that I write this book and have come to realize and accept that waiting is unavoidable. It is a discipline we cannot escape. And since we cannot get through life without experiencing it, I submit to you that being tooled to maneuver in it and through it successfully is important.

Consider all things that you or someone you know may have or are currently waiting on:

to be healed or to be delivered from a vice
for bitterness to abate
for loneliness to wash away or sadness to subside
to get married or to be free from marriage
for a need to be met or an issue to be resolved
for the pain of a lost to end
for your heart to mend
fighting to win
for the right opportunity to come along or a connection to collide
to give a response or receive an answer
for help to come

to get right to receive Christ – not necessary but many wait
anyway to know
and accept the purpose for their life
for peace to come or joy to reside
for things to get better
for you or someone else to get it together
for change to come
for your turn
for your name to be called
for someone to grow up and just stop it
for fear to go
to be whole again
to take a chance
to make a stance
to live again
to love again
to learn
to know
to stop something
to be free again and live without
for the tears to stop and know beyond a shadow of a doubt
for everything to be 'just right'
for light to overcome the night
for near perfect before you make a move - go forward or take flight
for the ball to drop
praying but still waiting
wondering and wandering while waiting
just to wait and wait some more
Waiting…waiting…waiting

This was just a rough list of places, times, and seasons where you will wait. Did you find yourself or someone you know on this list? You could probably add to it. The objective of recognizing your waiting place is for you to consider and accept that you will wait. And identify how you wait when you are called to wait. Now, let's go together on this journey of learning how to find, apply, and practice peace, patience, and purpose in the waiting place.

ONE

"Wait On..."

Wait

A study in the United Kingdom in 2010, found that the average person throughout his or her lifetime spends five years waiting in lines and roughly six months waiting at traffic lights. Wow! Five years of our life is spent doing nothing but waiting. Certainly, we as a society of 21st Century, fast pace, social media, need to stay connected people have found a way to multi-task and fill every bit of our time doing what we would say is "being productive." Not so much. With every text in line, checking the email at the light, responding to a message at dinner, we prove that we don't know how to wait. Remind me, what did we do before cell phones, tablets, etc.?

So, what does it mean "to wait"? Probably, the most well-known and quoted waiting scripture is found in Isaiah 40:31, *"But they that wait upon the LORD shall renew their strength; they shall mount up with wings as eagles; they shall run, and not be weary; and they shall walk, and not faint."* Strong's Hebrew and Greek Dictionary defines 'waiting' as, "to bind together, by twisting, to expect, to look (for)". The Children of Israel were charged by God in Proverbs 3 to bind (twisting securely) the Word to their necks. By doing this, they would be able to do what

1

verses 5 and 6 instructs them to do, *"Trust in the LORD with all your heart, And lean not on your own understanding; In all your ways acknowledge Him, And HE shall direct (make) your paths."* They that wait would be able to wait to hear and receive what they need from the Lord and trust Him while they wait. They would be able and ready for flight.

The World Book Dictionary defines waiting as to:

1   *stay* in place in expectation of
2   *delays* in serving
3   wait as *a serv*ant or a waiter ready serve
4   remain stationary in readiness or expectation
5   pause for another to catch up
6   look forward expectantly – eagerly
7   hold back expectantly <waiting for a chance to strike>
8   be ready and available
9   *remain temporarily* neglected or unrealized

Isn't it intriguing to discover that waiting stays in place in expectation of something? Wow! What a revelation; waiting, delays (its self) in serving – in coming. Waiting waits to deliver. It remains stationary – holding back, but ready, available, expecting - looking forward to an opportunity to serve. Like a servant, it seeks and looks for a way to supply a need or attend to another. This sounds like Jesus to me! It reminds me of when HE waited to go and see about Lazarus. Waiting can be polite. It pauses for another to catch up. It looks forward, not back. What? Waiting has a personality. It has a look – a way about it. These definitions support that there is a right way to wait. Interestingly, I have yet to come across a definition or description of waiting that suggests that waiting has a mouth to speak – murmurs or complains. Waiting has no voice. It just waits. I would suggest to those who have a tendency to murmur and complain in their waiting to quiet yourself as my pastor's wife says. Like Jesus did according to

Philippians 2, take on the disposition and position of a servant in the waiting place.

Over 12-years ago, Acts 1 verse 4 spoke directly to me and started my journey of waiting. Jesus tells His followers "do not depart from Jerusalem, but to wait for the Promise of the Father..." This was the scripture that the LORD gave me when I was feeling the urge – the pull – to leave Corporate America in 1998. I was working for a Fortune 500 company. I had recently purchased my first home at 27-years old. I was driving my 'Z', traveling, and living well. Still in Indiana with the same company, I had been promoted to oversee all Year 2000 System Quality Audits for North America. I was traveling across the country and to other countries. I had racked up so many frequent flier miles and hotel points that I was able to travel to Hawaii, Vegas, New York and a few other places after leaving my job. Making very, very good money, my life was grand. Then one day in 1998, I started feeling a pull to leave my job. Wait a minute. Leave?! Leave this to do what. Leave my position. Leave my status. Leave my title. Leave my benefits – my bonuses. Leave my almost 6 figure salary at 30 years old. Leave…to do what? My job gave me a great deal of autonym, liberty, and delegated authority. I was riding high.

Because of my success as the lead auditor over all Year 2000 processes and system qualification; nearing the conclusion of the assignment, I receive another promotion that included a move to Atlanta. With this job came a mentor. Their assignment was to prepare me for my next promotion. I was placed on a 3-year fast track plan to Vice President. Though I just listed all these great things about this season of my life, something happened. It seemed like overnight, I started to lose my zeal for the ladder. I became tired of being on the road, staying in 5-Star hotels, calling my hotel room "home", eating at the finest restaurants, having lower level seats to the professional ball games, side tripping to exotic islands at very little cost. Life was exciting and amazing for this little Benton Harbor girl. Yet, something was different. I started to feel uncomfortable. Restless would be a good word to describe this season of my life. Those feelings brought with them a sense of urgency that I could not shake.

The pull to do something was gravely increasing and intense. But what was it...Leave...To do what...To go where? I questioned if this could really be God. I mean really...this was crazy? Now only 29 years old and rounding 30, a little girl from Benton Harbor, youngest of six, with no advance degree at the time, parents who went no further than high school...Was I really considering leaving my job and walking away from all of this. I thought, "Wait a minute girlie, have you lost it, you must be crazy - what is wrong with you?"

To my dismay, not only did my desire towards the upward mobility of corporate start to change, so did all that was being offered with the promotion. From the point of my accepting the position to move to Atlanta and signing the transfer letter, not only did the title and level change but so did the pay and bonus. The pull to leave came from the inside. Soon, the push came from the outside. These were signs that I tried to ignore. Challenged with these uncertainties, I was due to report to Florida for training for my new job in Atlanta and to meet my staff. I found myself wavering on if I should go or just walk away from it all; but to what for what? So I went to Florida.

Several days prior to my trip; with all this swirling in my mind, I had a dream. In the dream, I heard the name Paul, and I saw a 3 and a 1. To my recall prior to this time, I had never had a dream that I knew meant something. But this time, I knew there was something to this one. I was certain there was a message in it. With mixed feelings of leaving and staying; wanting to hold on to what I knew while being drawn to do something I had not a clue, I began to seek God through prayer and fasting. I believe this was the first time I had fasted as well. I asked two other sisters to join me. I was about three days into my fast; denying myself food, treats, and television - only drinking water and praying that I had the dream. I called a 'mother'; one of my mentors (Shirley Alexander) to tell her about the dream. She instructed me to fast, seek God, and read Acts. Though I said OK, I put it off until I was in the airport headed to Florida to meet my staff.

Still feeling perplexed, still unsure, I waited in the boarding area. The call to board the plane for Tampa came. Prior to the first call to board, I was sitting, waiting anxiously, wondering, thinking, I opened my Bible and began to read Acts Chapter 3. I remember at that moment I thought, "What does this have to do with me? This is about the crippled man at the Gate Beautiful. This has nothing to do with me." The call to board came again. I gathered my things and boarded. It was a small jumper plan that went from Indianapolis to Cincinnati. I took my seat, belted myself in, and again opened my Bible. With all my travel, this had become common practice for me to read and study the Bible 30,000 feet in the air. I had every intention of going back to Chapter 3, but found myself starting to read Acts Chapter 1. And there it was.

As I read Acts 1, my heart seemed to stop. My stomach dropped. My eyes became enlarged and watery. My breaths became long, deep, full, and short all at the same time. My mouth became dry and I swallowed hard. There was my answer in Acts Chapter 1 starting in verse 3 through 8, "*After his suffering, he presented himself to them and gave many convincing proofs that he was alive. HE appeared to them over a period of forty days and spoke about the kingdom of God. On one occasion, while he was eating with them, he gave them this command: "Do not leave Jerusalem, but wait for the gift my Father promised, which you have heard me speak about. For John baptized with water, but in a few days you will be baptized with the Holy*

Spirit.".... HE said to them: "It is not for you to know the (set) times or (appointed) dates the Father has set by his own authority. But you will receive power when the Holy Spirit comes on you; and you will be my witnesses in Jerusalem (local city), and in all Judea (state) and Samaria (country), and to the ends of the earth (world)." Trying to take it in, I read it a few more times. By now I was perspiring, and tears were flowing. My heart was beating exceptionally fast. I knew the guy next to me could not only hear my deep breathes and see my tears, but I am certain he could also hear and see my heart racing and about to jump out of my chest. I wanted to get out of my seat and run, but I couldn't do a thing on that little jumper plane. All I could do was sit there and humbly accept what I was hearing the Lord say.

Immediately, the 40-days jumped out at me. I quickly turned and asked the man sitting next to me if he had a calendar. He did not. I began to count from the date I had the dream to the date I was due to report to Atlanta to start the new position. It was exactly 40-days. I knew I was to not leave, but wait until God showed me what I was to do next. Thus began my life's journeys (that I can remember) of waiting on the Lord. When I arrived in Cincinnati, before connecting, I called Mother Alexander and today her words still ring very true and apropos. She said, "Just be still, wait to hear what the Father is saying." During that week in Tampa, after each meeting, I would return to my room – pray, read, and re-read this scripture, be still and wait to hear. I can't tell you how many journals I started and finished in that season. From that time until now, journaling has helped save my life and kept my sanity in my waiting seasons. Each morning I would awake and ask God, "What am I to do?" What became clear during that week was that I was to leave corporate. I was to leave my job, but not leave Indianapolis, but for what? To do what? I had not a clue. The question now was when, why, and how? Though I never thought I would be called to the service of ministry, I somehow knew that day that I would be used by God for His glory and to the world. It was about 3-years later that I heard, received, and accepted "the call" to ministry. And to this day, I have not looked backed. It took several agonizing years before I fully accepted who God said I was and walked without self imposed or religious constraint in my calling and purpose.

Waiting on God in prayer and fasting led me to my purpose and sealed my destiny. Even today, people often ask me why am I still in Indianapolis. They speak of how I could do this or that if I was elsewhere, but God has not told me to leave. I jokingly, but seriously say, "I will leave when my husband comes and gets me." With great expectation, I joyfully and purposefully wait on God to do all that HE has promised.

Ecclesiastes 11 tells us because we do not know the path of the wind, or how the body is formed in a mother's womb; we certainly cannot understand the work of God, the Maker of all things (verse 5). Yet, we can ask Him anything. In some way, shape, or form you have a concern about waiting; or else you would not be reading this book. So I encourage you to ask God to teach you how to wait and give you understanding for the necessity and value of waiting. I have come to a place where I appreciate and respect the waiting process. I may not like it or want to do it, but I have learned it is good to wait. There is always a message – a lesson - a testimony that comes from waiting; particularly when you wait right.

Waiting requires faith for the thing(s) we desire to come to pass. It is the hope that comes by faith while you wait for the substance and the evidence of thing(s) not (yet) seen (Hebrews 11:1). Waiting expects. It anticipates and it trusts. Faith houses both trust and belief. Trust is found in our heart and based on our emotions; how we feel about a thing or person based on past experiences or knowledge. Belief is how we think about a thing or person based on past experiences, what we have been told and or our personal knowledge. Those who are expecting, dream and those anticipating, dream BIG with excitement and prepare. If you let it, waiting can build and add to your faith (2 Peter 1:4-6). The Word warns us in Isaiah 64 to not count our works as accomplishments to gain reward and favor from God. It is our work done by faith through His grace that is necessary for us to please Him and to complete the purpose that HE has for us (verse 6). When we learn to wait, wait patiently, and wait right, we get bragging rights from the Lord.

As we consider Scripture there are numerous times where expectation and or anticipation are mentioned or inferred. One of the most significant Scriptures that speaks to this is Romans 8 starting in verse 18 that says, *"I consider that our present sufferings are not worth comparing with the glory that will be revealed in us. For the creation waits in eager expectation for the children of God to be revealed."* The entire chapter will bless you when you seek to understand waiting and suffering in hope to receive the promise.

Throughout this book, I will use the words expect and anticipate quite often. I thought it was important that I define them. Though both are by faith, and often used interchangeably, they are different. Let's use a pregnant mother. She conceives and though development begins immediately, she will not feel movement or start showing until the second trimester. She may wait to tell people she is expecting until then. Sharing the promised expectation may occur simply because others see it or her personal excitement and confidence motivates the confession. In this season without fully showing, people may ask out of curiosity and uncertainty, "Are you expecting." However, once it is evident she is pregnant with a promise, the question slightly changes from "are you" to "when are you due". That is anticipation. Anticipation sees the promise, hopes, and declares the arrival. The feelings that are attached to the promise are the hope of our one day (soon) seeing it, touching it, holding it, smelling it – having it. You see it already done. You see it here – in the now in the present. Great outward expressions arise when the hope of a promise becomes real to the once expecting. This is anticipation. Transitioning from expecting to anticipating involves preparing for the promised arrival. Expectation waits whereas anticipation acts. As the expectant mother begins to feel the excitement of life growing in her; she moves from not only seeing, but feeling. As she goes in her anticipation, the outward expression grows and change occurs. These changes can and do affect her physically, psychologically, mentally, and emotionally.

As development continues, there is an opportunity to be told the sex of the baby. Some choose to know others elect not to know. The choice is theirs. In your waiting seasons and in life; while expecting and anticipating, you will be presented with options and choices. You will be called to make decisions. I encourage you to not allow emotions or others to cause you to make them in haste or waste. Some will be important and need to be decided now, others can wait, and still others are not for you to address. Whether the parents choose a name in advance or the day of arrival; not choosing a name prior will not stop the promise from coming. Yes, most promises require preparation before manifestation, learning when to rest and when to prepare will help you immensely to get to the end and not be too tired to enjoy the blessing. Preparation is one of the purposes of the waiting place. When ordered by God resting is preparation. Both resting and preparing are acts of you working your faith.

Like this mom, anticipation moves you into action. This is where excitement builds and is elevated. They go beyond discussing a theme for the baby's room to purchasing and preparing the room for the arrival. Anticipation encompasses movement and goes beyond expecting to a confident knowing. It is going from just a thought or consideration and talking about it to action(s). Movement occurs in preparation to receive what they are anticipating. Expectation is hoping and believing. Think about when you are waiting; expecting to see someone, you check your lips, adjust your tie before you see them, but when they are in view coming your way, there is a shift. As they draw near, anticipation causes you to stand up to greet and receive them. Your heart may race, palms may sweat, and you start to move in their direction. That is anticipation. It is the story of the Lost Son in Luke 15. His father saw him coming a far off (returning home from living with and caring for pigs) and he ran to him and hugged him. For the father to be outside and see him coming, he had to be waiting with expectation with hope; anticipating his arrival…his return.

1 Kings 18 tells the story of Elijah's servant who was sent by him (his master) to go and look for something in the sky. With expectation, seven times he went to look. Now, if he did not believe (expect) there was something he would see, he would not have continued to trust his master and go back in obedience to look (anticipate) and certainly not seven times. Waiting right includes both expectation (*a belief*) and anticipation (*a trust that looks for*).

Wait Upon

So what does it mean to "wait upon?" The World Book Dictionary makes a very profound statement in defining "wait upon." It says, "Wait can wait upon." I pondered this for some time. Then it hit me. Here waiting is used as a noun. It has a look to it – a personality with defined characteristics. It is meant to be a positive experience. Consider the nine definitions mentioned early. Only one has even somewhat of a negative connotation… "to remain temporarily neglected or unrealized." Waiting is not always about sitting or standing still. Waiting upon is active.

The waiting that God calls us to is active. It is not an inactive state. It is not sitting or standing still. It is sitting with a purpose and a plan or listening to get one or creating one. This type of waiting is what God showed me was "active waiting." Most often waiting will require us to do something. No matter how subtle or simply, we will often be charged to "keep it moving" while we wait. It is not busy work. It is a purposeful work. It is the working of our faith. Remember, faith without works is dead. We are required to do our part in cooperation with the plan and will of God for our lives.

"Waiting upon" speaks to and through our actions.

- It attends to
- Serves as a servant
- Formally calls on to check in or on
- It supplies the wants and needs of

When you "wait upon" God, you have defined and affirmed your place. You place yourself where HE is. You operate from an elevated place of strength, power, understanding, and peace. Isaiah 40 verse 31 tells us that when you wait upon the Lord, your strength is renewed and you soar on wings like an eagle. Waiting upon takes Chronos or chronological time out of it. There is a dependence on God. It is the waiting that says, "I trust His timing." An anonymous writer on the web writes, "This waiting on the Lord is a matter of continuity, something that one is regularly doing without extended interruption or lapse." Hosea 12 says, *"Therefore turn thou to thy God: keep mercy and judgment, and wait on thy God continually (verse 6)."* It is not a seasonal, sporadic, or spasmodic thing; neither is it unique. Waiting on someone or something is a choice and time influences it. However, "waiting upon" is neither a choice, nor is it impacted by time. Another anonymous writer wrote that "Waiting on the Lord is as embedded in the life *(of a believer)* as breathing." In other words, you can't avoid times and or season of waiting.

The discipline of waiting has a goal – a purpose. We wait because there is something we or someone else needs to know, learn, or gain through waiting. It comes to perfect – mature us. While we wait, waiting is used to teach and equip us to press, to not give up, but to move forward. Waiting upon the Lord will ready you to receive what HE has for you on the other side of your waiting place.

WHAT I LEARNED

Waiting stays in a place of expectation. Waiting is active. It speaks through and to me in my waiting. Waiting is meant to be a positive experience. It has a goal – a purpose. We wait because there is something we or someone else needs to know and learn through this (our) experience. I must make a choice to wait and an even greater choice to wait patiently. Lord, help me to wait and wait on you patiently. Expectation believes and anticipation acts.

I have learned that...

_____

_____

_____

_____

Scripture or Statement for Meditation

_____

What waiting means to me...

_____

_____

_____

_____

TWO

Wait for It

God or Man

In my life, I have seen two states of waiting: waiting on man and waiting on God. I surveyed (see attached) over 100 individuals male and female and was surprised that 76% said that waiting on God was less challenging – easier for them. So, I pose this question to you, "Which is easier or less challenging for you - waiting on man or waiting on God." For me, waiting on man has been easier.

Does that surprise you? Let me explain. When I consider David Timms statement regarding waiting on man, he says, "Waiting on others isn't about achieving and end of our own, rather, it positions us to serve the other end." Though waiting on others can present its own set of issues; for the most part, this is not where I face the biggest challenge in waiting. Why? Whether leading or a participant on the team, I can wait on a person to accomplish a common goal and still go forth and do my part of the goal or project. If they do not do their part (drop the ball or lag behind), I can find someone to assist. If graced to know and do, I can do their part and complete the task on my own. To some, this may seem like control and at one time it may have been, but as I grew and matured, I was enlightened that everyone's commitment level is different and that was ok. Life happens and peoples circumstances change.

I have learned (and still learning) the skill of separating without regret or grudge. It is the ability to separate the person and personality from the mission and objective to ensure that success is achieved and the goal is accomplished. Appreciate and value them, but ultimately the show must go on and if you are the lead, the buck stops with you. The people factor in waiting right can be a challenge, but it is expected. With people; when it is necessary or possible, we can go ahead of each other, around, or leave them behind, but with God these approaches would not be beneficial to us.

It is the reality and truth of His "Omni" existence, His providence, and sovereignty that we should acknowledge and respect. The church, people in general…have lost their fear – the reverence of God. Reverence is not being scared when HE brings correction, but appreciating and being confident of His love for us because HE corrected us. Hebrews 12 verse 6 says, "…*the Lord disciplines those HE loves.*" My simple interpretation of reverence is to have a perfect fear where the foundation is love, respect, and honor. When we refuse to wait on God, we are communicating our lack of reverence of Him. We dishonor and give no importance to the truth that HE knows all; HE is and has all power and is all wise. We disrespect Him and the plan HE has mapped out for us when we choose to not listen, not obey, and not wait.

God over Man

Waiting on God has still been the most challenging spiritual discipline for me. Simply because, with Him, I can't just move on, go around, or leave Him behind. HE is the beginning, the middle, and the end of the matter. I reverence Him. I have a holy fear of Him. It would behoove us all to seek to have a holy fear of God and His sovereignty. A great deal of what our society and nation are facing is that people in general; not just the church, do not fear or reverence God. Though we are a nation that currently has on their money, "In God We Trust" and songs that ask God to bless it, we have moved so very far from the reverence God. There is no real, consistent, or holy respect for God, His Word, Will, or Way. Even more shameless is that reverence of the Creator is not a teaching that is coming from our pulpits.

Today, people and our nation are excessively greedy, selfish, careless, devaluing, disrespectful, disobedient, and rebellious. Impatience, entitlement, and pride fuels these behaviors. We see it in our children, youth, and adults; old and young, black and white, in the church and outside, in the government; self-appointed, elected leaders, and everything in between. From the pulpit to the parking lot to the parks to our schools and sporting arenas, there are Christians and non-Christian who dishonor God and devalue His worth and existence daily. Our reverence and love for God should grow. It is our love and reverence of Him that will keep and sustain you. Our appreciation of Him should expand every time HE forgives us, gives us another chance, we awake to another day, and HE bestows the blessing of mercy on us. In our life waiting place, I believe, no, I implore you to consider and grasps the importance; whatever your belief, to have a holy, healthy, justifiable love, fear – reverence of the Creator – Elohim – God – Jehovah – The Great I AM! It is and will always be God over man. Remind yourself, teach it to your children, and tell it to your friends. It is HE who has made us, not ourselves. Boot straps my foot! You couldn't pull your boots up without Him giving you your hands, thumbs, strength to pull, a mind to know to pull, a leg with a foot attached to even be able to wear a boot. HE is GOD and never shall any man, women, person or being ever be GREATER than or equal to Him!

Only God can heal, restore, set-free, make whole, create something from nothing, or release me and you from and into all at the same time. Whatever the pain, it is still by His stripes we are healed; healed by and through His love. HE formed you on purpose, for purpose and placed destiny in you. And put you in your waiting place to birth something in you and bring that out of you. Neither you nor any man can do one of these things for me or you. Now armed with this knowledge and truth, I pray you are compelled to get to know God and learn to wait Him. Even when you do not want to wait; when you want to run or escape the wait – wait anyway and wait even the more – learn to wait right – suffer to wait right! Your reward shall be greater than you could dream or image. I charge you to use this tool – this book to learn the benefits of waiting and more over to learn to wait on Him.

God's Word tells us that no one who waits, believes, and trusts in Him will be put to shame. So, I have learned to wait. Despite what others said or thought, I had to wait on God to do what others have said could not and would not happen. I had to learn to stand and wait on His clearance. In obedience to God, sometimes against the advice of others whom I respected and love; I have waited on God to instruct me in the "how" and "when" of matters. Though I didn't always know how it would turn out, I had to trust and obey God. Sometimes it took much longer than I would have liked and others wanted or I wanted, but in the end, HE spoke and HE did not lie. The outcome was good and good for me.

HE has promised us good things when we wait on Him. A short list goes something like this... *Those who put their trust in the LORD will: receive renewed strength, never to be put to shame, strengthen our heart, HE will incline His ear and hear their cry and petition.* We can wait in full expectation and anticipation of what God can, will, and is able to do. We can believe and daily grow in trusting in HIM to do what HE has said and promised.

From the moment a promise; a word from the Lord is spoken, heard, and received by you, there begins the waiting process of manifestation.

I have waited on God wondering and wandering, annoyed, angry, confused, frustrated, and in tears, but I waited. I waited for His direction, His peace, His voice, and in time, HE responded. Sometimes HE responded quickly and other times not so quickly. Even as I write this, I am in a waiting place; to do or not to do, to move forward, continue, or walk away, to let go or try again. Sometimes, the choices are too many for us and we are too emotionally or psychologically attached to know with certainty what to do. So, why not wait to hear and avoid another mishap or delay. It is in these times and situations that you realize that your waiting place may be your protective place and you too will say, "It was good for me to wait on the Lord." Though it may feel like and appear that you are waiting on a person or a circumstance to change; as long as you know you are waiting on God for His voice, His direction, His release; be at peace, be still, and wait. Even when it is not what you want to hear or do, still wait. His Word will make all things clear and will allow you to proceed with a knowing that cannot be taken or shaken. Knowing that you have waited on Lord and His instruction makes it easier when the internal and external questions arise challenging on if you should or should not have waited.

Our ability to wait (on God) is a sign and demonstration of our obedience and trust. God says, if you love Me (if you trust ME) you will obey Me and obey me even when it hurts. Waiting becomes easier, when you learn to trust God fully with your life, in every area of your life and with the process. Until you learn to trust Him, waiting will remain a difficult discipline for you to face and conquer. Do you believe HE knows what is best for you? Do you believe HE has a plan for you? Answering these questions in the affirmative will make trusting and obeying Him easier and waiting less difficult. Beloved, life is not always about knowing or getting the answers, but living with the questions. My God. Thank you LORD. As a believer in Jesus Christ, it is also about trusting and resting in God whether you receive the answer or not.

So often in scripture we find that questions were asked but no answer to the question was given. Two examples that come to mind are Jacob in Genesis 32 where he asked the Angel of the Lord "What is your name?" And the Angel asked him why did he need to know His name and the next sentence says, "And he blessed Jacob there." No answer to Jacob's question but a blessing anyhow. My God. Thank you LORD! Paul in 2 Corinthians 12 where he asked God to remove the thorn (the challenge from his life) from his flesh and God said, "My grace is sufficient for you, for my power is made perfect in weakness." Paul goes on to say, "Therefore I will boast all the more gladly about my weaknesses, so that Christ's power may rest on me." Here Paul show us that even when we don't get what we want or the answer we are seeking, it can draw us closer to God and waiting on Him brings power and reward. Charles Nichols poem *Questions* speaks to this perfectly,

> *"Can a word ever hold*
> *What a soul feels within?*
> *Can passions be freed*
> *Through the voice of the pen?*
> *Can a longing so wide,*
> *Or the wish for a look,*
> *Or the turmoil for truth, Be fit, in a book?*
> *Can the oceans of love,*
> *Be divided and claimed?*
> *Can life direct onward,*
> *And love still remain?*
> *Can 'obey' be ignored*
> *And pride be made safe?*

Or can knowledge and courage,
Be taken, for faith?
Will not God, Who knows all,
In His loving way, offer?
In our need, and His time,
A most perfect answer?"

As I read this piece, I naturally ended it with "I pray." I have discovered in this life journey that not all my questions will be answered on this side of Glory and on the other side; in heaven with God and Jesus, I will probably not care. Desiring to know, but not unto worry is okay. But seeking and learning to trust Him to lead you without all the answers is crucial and necessary for a peaceful and restful pilgrimage.

Breathe Through It

Recently, I went to the dentist and the optometrist in the same day. What was interesting is that they both said the same thing, "Be still, and breathe through it. It will only take a few minutes, and you will be done." I really didn't want to go. I had other things to do, but I needed to get this done. I didn't want to be the cause of any delay, decay, or setback, so I made the appointments and went. Once there, I had to listen, follow the instructions, and do what I was told. I followed the directions and was done – out of there and on my way in a short time. It was over quickly and I was out of there and on my way to my next destination. I had to trust that they knew what they were doing and was fully equipped with knowledge and training to handle my tooth and correct my vision. Now, if I can trust these doctors, I certainly can trust the Great Physician who formed and created me before the foundations of the world with these eyes and teeth. The challenge is that we find it difficult in the wait to relax, sit still, and just breathe through it.

I have a friend who teases me about how I breathe when the Spirit of the Lord is speaking, moving, or I am being challenged with something: a person's behavior, what someone is saying, when I want to say something but am trying to be patient, quiet, and thinking through it, giving myself time to choose my words carefully or not do anything at all. I breathe while I listen and wait to hear to speak or not to speak. Breathing through it works. It is a different type of breathing. In times past, my passion to teach, instruct, and for all to have understanding; I was guilty of not always waiting my turn to speak or to share. Learning (still learning) to breathe through it; waiting my turn helped me. This has also helped me in relationships; since it is said that men hate to be interrupted. (That was a freebie to all my sisters.) Waiting your turn and being still until, is a sign of our maturity both in spirit and character. It is our submitting to the will and wisdom of God in order to receive His instruction, His words, His peace, and rest. In our waiting place, we are often receiving, conceiving, and for some there will be a birthing of God's will, plan, purpose, the new man for a new life. Learning to breathe in your waiting place will help you to go through it with less stress, impatience, and frustration. Breathing through it is a part of waiting right.

Let's try it. Take a deep abdominal breath where your stomach comes out as you inhale through your nose – hold it – think about something that may have or is bothering you – now release your breath – pulling your stomach in as you exhale out of your nose or mouth. Do this a few times. I promise you, release and peace will come. With every breath, you have the power and potential to change your outlook *(mindset, perspective)* about your current state of waiting.

Obey It

Waiting right certainly includes and requires obedience. The foundation of waiting on God is obedience and trust. I contend that you cannot obey and not also trust. Both obedience and trust are love issues. The act of waiting is a demonstration of our respect and honor of His wisdom and knowledge. Waiting is an act of obedience. How you wait is a demonstration of trust. It is important that we grow to a place that we trust that God really does know what is best for us now and in the future. Our sacrifice is to let go of what we want or think and choose to obey His way and will. This will always be rewarded. Your obedience will not go unnoticed. In your waiting place and seasons, wait. Wait on the Lord to reveal His will to you for your life.

If we let it, the implications and perceptions of waiting can produce negativity, but does not have to. If waiting for you, becomes a place of idle time and negativity, I am here to serve you notice...your wait will be long (or even longer). You must become an active participant. Negative passive waiting cannot be the norm. You do not have to stay there, plant, and grow in the negativities of worry, fear, anxiety, hopelessness, and weariness while you wait. How you wait is up to you. How long you wait; may or may not be up to you, but make sure you are not the reason you remain in the waiting place longer than (God) intended. How do you do that?

Keep your heart and attitude right in the waiting place. Remember, "If I do not faint – lose hope - give up, God has promised me in due season...I will reap if I (obey and) do not faint." Your due season awaits you. And all that God has planned, reserved, and appointed for you will be waiting for you when you come out of your waiting place. Isaiah 40 expresses this so perfectly with these words of encouragement, "...but those who hope in the LORD – who wait on Him, will renew their strength. They will soar on wings like eagles; they will run and not grow weary, they will walk and not be faint." From the entrepreneur to the young lady waiting on that proposal to the person waiting on the lab results, and everyone in between, it is my hope that this Word brings you comfort. Waiting on God produces strength, takes you higher, and brings restoration…if and when you let it.

I have learned (and still learning – being perfected) to stay right where God put me and do the part I know to do, or have been instructed to do - to obey Him even when it hurts. On occasion that included not doing anything but being still and knowing that God's got it and me. The purpose of this was to wait in obedience to hear His voice - His instruction. Waiting in His presence, taught me to distinguish and know the voice of God from my own. The assurance of this helped me to obey and follow Him more closely. To learn and apply this will require that you shut down your own voice; sit and listen – mediate - learn to be still to hear His voice and listen to and for His instruction. All this is active waiting.

Trust It

Undoubtedly, I love God; yet, I had to come to the truth that at times I found myself not trusting Him (totally). At a minimum because I didn't understand the process, I did not trust the process. When we don't trust someone or something, obeying is very difficult. So, we do as asked or expected out of obligation and not love. When we do not trust, we obey out of fear and not from love and faith. I trusted God in most things but when it seemed HE was tarrying or taking too long; when things weren't going my way, my trust of Him would wane. I always believed HE was able to do what I was petitioning Him for; however I had to ask myself if I trusted only in His ability to do or trust Him just because HE is God.

I trusted Him with my past and some of my present, but I did not completely trust Him with my future. I had not surrendered every part of me – my life to Him. The truth was I did not solely trust Him to do what I wanted or what I thought was best for me. Though I told Him I trust you with my life, I was still trying to be in control of parts of my life. This issue of my lack of trust was similar to the revelation HE gave me that His people believe 'in Him' but they do not 'believe Him.' Christians believe unto salvation to get their names written in the Lambs Book of Life and for many that is enough. However, many struggle with believing Him – His Word. They are challenged to believe that what HE said HE meant. That HE can, will, and is able to do ALL that His Word says.

Over time, God revealed to me that I trusted and knew *HE could* (trust in Him), but I struggled with believing and trusting that *HE wanted* too. Until I believed HE wanted too, I could believe HE would. I had a distrust of God. It is even challenging for me to write. I know…wow! How crazy was and is this. I know many others have or do feel this way. The truth is; there are a great number of people…believers who say, *'I love and I believe (intellectually) God can'*, but their heart does not trust that HE will or wants to do it for them. Nothing was or is wrong with God; it is you and me and our lack of understanding and belief. HE is consistent and faithful. The issue is us; our knowledge and understanding or lack thereof of Him is what makes not only believing God difficult but asking and receiving.

When we are with God and are confident that HE is with us, nothing will be impossible for us; including, waiting, trusting, and obeying. You can have the assurance that His promises to you are still 'Yes in Him and Amen, to the glory of God.' (2 Corinthians 1:20). With Him, we can wait confidently in our waiting place no matter how long we are confined there. Take comfort in knowing that God is with you. Be convinced that HE is for you. You cannot go wrong waiting in or on God. HE who promises is faithful (Hebrews 10:23). HE has promised to never leave you or forsake you. What part of never are you not getting? It means...never...at no time, under no condition or circumstances – NEVER! When we consider the meaning of forsake: to overlook, dismiss, abandon, this should give us a better appreciation of God's promise. God has promised that under no conditions, or circumstances; at no time will HE leave, overlook, dismiss or abandon you. That is a good news message in the waiting place. You are never alone because God is always with you. Equally exciting to know is that HE is for you.

Now with all this understanding, we have to still choose to trust and obey. This is the dichotomy that challenges us; the gift of choice and free will, to choose our way over His way. Particularly when our way is not His way or His will. That darn free will. Though I slightly joke, this is what makes the choice and life of Christianity challenging for some. The discipline of waiting, waiting right, and following God's plan and process for our life is a difficult task for most. We thank Him for our free will because we are not robots. But we must learn to learn to submit - surrender our will to His will. This is what Jesus did in the Garden. That is the part we don't like or want to do. Many choose to use that freedom of chose to not accept and receive Him as Savior and Lord. Now how crazy is that. Waiting and waiting right is a learned behavior and attitude. This state of waiting against our free will is often learned through our hardheadedness and free will "my will – my way" decisions and mishaps.

Though my free will wanted to rebel, it took some time and a number of experiences, struggles, losses, and yes, failures, and victories in my waiting place before I learned to be content and obey. I am still being perfected in this. I have grown to understand and trust that no matter the state or place I am in or how long I have been or will be there; I can believe and expect to see the glory of God manifested in my life on this side of heaven. Every obedient response adds to our faith and strengthens our testimony and our trust in Him.

Discipline of It

The discipline of waiting is compounded when the spiritual aspect of waiting on God is added. How do you wait on someone or thing that is invisible or intangible? This can produce a quandary of thoughts and emotions. Do we choose to not wait on Him – The One who knows the way you should take before you take it? Do you not wait on The One who created and formed you – who has and knows the plan for you and your life? The One that the Word says is The Way, The Truth, and The Light. How do I go past or not heed The One who is a lamp to my feet and a light on my path? It is these truths about God, who HE is, and what HE has the capacity and ability to do that makes both waiting and not waiting on Him complex.

The quandary: to wait or not to wait. To wait and possibly have to wait some more and still obey; to trust and wait to receive or not wait at all. Disobey and risk the uncertainty of repercussions and certain delay. Or wait in obedience and demonstrate that we trust God and the process. Your reward is guaranteed. To not wait is to demonstrate that we do not trust Him…at least not totally. I certainly have been there. In time, with practice you will learn how to wait and obey when everything around you and in you says, "Do it your way."

The more I am charged to wait, the more it supports that waiting is probably the most difficult discipline you will face. It is a discipline, that once you surrendered to it, it will develop and solidify you and your character. The discipline of learning to wait and to wait right can perfect or rather mature you and your character. Through the discipline of waiting, we will be forced to self-examine and submit to His will or we will choose to continue on and do it our way. Either way, waiting will be inevitable. A place and choice of surrender is best.

Submit to It – Surrender to It

Waiting is submitting to the will and way of God. It is a surrendering of our will and our way to and for His. Our confession of faith receiving Jesus as Savior is submission. Often we stop at submitting to God and never get to surrender. Surrender goes a step beyond submission. Surrender is turning over our will and our way to receive and do His will His way. Submission is coming under His love of redemption unto salvation. However, when we willingly accept Him and give yourself over to Him as Lord (Master, Adonai, Ruler) of your life that is surrender. Surrendering is recognizing that HE is in control and letting go of 'your way or the highway' and 'gotta-have-it my way'; to now, letting Him have His way in your life. That is surrender.

1 Timothy says, *"Godliness with contentment is great gain."* Contentment is to make or set at ease one's own mind to be at peace, satisfied, or pleased. To be content is to submit to the process and be at peace with it. It is an inward state that manifests outward. Contentment is noticeable and attractive. It carries with it a consistency and confidence. Though it is at ease and easy, it is not complacent or weak. On the contrary, to be content is a sign of strength. Particularly when what you are still waiting on is something you have the ability and free will to make happen on your own. This is meekness; which is power under control. It doesn't mean you like the situation you are in, only that you (have learned) trust God that it will change and the outcome will be for your good. It is the 'never the less' you get in your soul and

spirit to obey God. It helps you to go all the way, and hold-on until your change comes. You may not want to do what God is calling you to do. This is what it means when the Scripture says our obedience to God is better than the sacrifice of our wants and will. When you have a heart to submit to God – His will – the process, contentment comes and allows you to obey Him and the process even when it hurts and your rebellious nature says, "No" because it doesn't want to obey.

What a comfort and pleasant reminder that contentment is learned and not something I come into the world with and therefore should expect myself to have mastering it by now. Submission and surrender brings peace and contentment. I do believe being content is something we need to get assistance from God, His Word, and the Holy Spirit to understand, apply, and live out. "Oh, help us Lord to trust You more and where there is unbelief, uncertainty or hopelessness, strengthen us - your people – teach us how to be content."

As I stated earlier, contentment is not complacency. To be complacent is to be unaware of actual dangers or deficiencies and still choosing to do nothing. Complacencies often come with complaints. Its root is fear, self and an attitude of ignorance (to ignore the truth), and often silence. Some of our waiting seasons have been (or will be) self-induced - caused by us. We are often delayed; simply because we have chosen to lean to our own understanding and delay our progress and release by being complacent and thus disobedient. Proudly we sing, "I did it my way…" and we remain or are set back in the process or brought back to wait. Our way over God's way will never end well.

When we are waiting on God (or say we are) and still choose to do it our way, we cannot be certain what our disobedience to Him or the process and His instruction will afford us. We can be certain of this, when we do it our way there will be loss, setbacks, causalities, and consequences. The internal struggle of your self-will and inability to wait will strangle you and halt the forward movement and advancement of you reaching your goals. It will be derailed or at a minimum delayed when you go off the path designed for you onto your own beaten path. It is important that we recognize the necessity of the process found in waiting. The path and plan set for you before the foundations of the world includes your waiting place. In the long run, the process to get to where and what God has for us will be more valuable and more useful when we surrender to it. In Richard Foster's book "Celebration of Discipline," he states "If all human strivings ends in moral bankruptcy and if righteousness is a gracious gift from God, then is it not logical to conclude that we must wait for God..." The things we experience and learn in the process of waiting on our way to our destiny will become the treasures for life application, jewels in our crown, and hope for others.

As I mentioned, waiting in and on God is active. It submits to the will and way of God. It is a surrendering of our will and our way to and for His will. If what you are called to do is be still – be still. If it is to pray – then pray. If His instruction is to go left – go left. If it is to right – go right. Just do it. Submit and obey. Whatever HE tells you to do, do it. By the way, "just do it" was first said by Mary, Jesus' mother at the wedding where He turned water into wine. When we resist Him, we are demonstrating that there is something that still needs to be worked out of us before we are released into our next level, assignment, or our purpose. When we resist, we run the risk of continuing and remaining in our waiting place, often much longer than we want or God intended.

Be Honest About It

Whether you have all the answers or not or understand it all or not, be upfront with those who are directly or indirectly impacted by your decision to wait on the Lord. Be honest with yourself and others about where God has you. Here are the honest, hard, heart questions you should ask yourself about your waiting season:

1 Was this my decision or God's
2 What evidence do I have that God has instructed me in this (the Word of God or a confirming Word, agreement with loved ones, internal peace, etc.)
3 Am I being lazy, irresponsible
4 Do I procrastinate
5 Am I ready for what I keep asking God for
6 Am I careless with the things – the gifts (of people, talents, abilities) God gives me
7 Am I careless with my life and others
8 Where does waiting put me, my family, and love ones
9 Do I have or has God given me a plan
10 Am I willing to do what it takes in my waiting season to find out the plan and will of God
11 Do I have peace about and in this place
12 Has God told me to do something
13 Am I obedient to Him - the plan – the process
14 Am I open – honest with those who need to know where I am and my next steps

If you cannot answer these questions in the affirmative, your waiting is most likely not from, designed or purposed by God. And therein lies your increased and magnified frustration and conflict that you feel. I submit to you that when God is orchestrating (doing it or allowing it) a thing; even a hard, hurtful, hectic thing, peace can be found in the chaos and the confusion.

However, if your response to these questions is in the affirmative, know that it will work out for your good. God is up to something in you, for you or through you. Get in the Word of

God, stay connected, pray, meditate to hear, and if needed fast. Take time to sit, to listen, and hear from God. Maybe even take a few days and get away to a designated place. Ask God to help your family, friends, and love ones to see and understand as HE sees and shows you and brings you understanding. Hold fast to God. Keep your ears and heart open to Him. Do not allow others to cause you to move out of your place of obedience. Now listen, I am not saying if you are a husband, father, a wife, a mom, etc. and you need to take action; like get a job that you should not do so. However, when you are accountable to and responsible for others, a God led decision (of any kind) to wait, to be still, to seek Him to hear, know, and do will be received. Though it may not be immediate, you working your faith in obedience to God while you wait will find agreement.

Reverence It

For me my reverence (or rather, my fear) of God as a Holy and Sovereign God restrained me to wait. I had to learn to be still and know that HE is God. To trust that HE will come and that His timing was and is perfect. I had to trust that HE would provide. I had to be reminded that HE is Omni; all knowing, all wise, all powerful. HE is ALL God and HE is my Father and my creator. HE loves and cares about me, despite me. That in itself is amazing to me. I had to respect His decision; His will for me to wait. HE knows and desires only what is best for me. I had to learn to be content in my waiting place.

Before God could release me from my waiting place and give me what HE had for me, I had to die to me; what I wanted, expected, and how I thought things should be. I had to let go of a number of things: tradition, religion, materially, psychologically, emotionally, and relationally and focus on my relationship with Him and who HE was. I had to let go of past issues, forgive some folk, and myself. I performed a few burials and eulogies during my many intense and prolonged waiting times and I am sure there are more to come. Most of what I had to die to was self-inflicted and self-imposed mindsets. Including expectations of others who had very little understanding or respect for where I was and what God was requiring of me and doing in me. But really, when you think about it, how could I expect or demand others to honor and respect the process and me, when I didn't respect and honor the process. It required a daily dying. For me, it was to:

- Self – Me – My Way – My Opinions – My will
- Impatience
- Pride
- Greed
- Insecurities
- Jealousy/Envy
- Rejection
- Fear (of: rejection, acceptance, failure, and success)
- Past (unmet needs, unhealed hurts, and unresolved issues)

Good list, right? I had to let these things go. There were also a number of things that I had to resurrect. For example: the vision God had given me, dreams, faith at a new level, acceptance of self and God, His love, and forgiveness. I had to find it in me to forgive and be patient with myself. Let patience have its perfect (maturing) work in me so that I would be mature and lack nothing (have peace). While waiting, I discovered that forgiveness is a necessary process to walk in and must be lived out to have a victorious life. It can be immediate or as you go. It is more for you than for them. We set our hearts to forgive and as we go, it manifests. We ask God for clean hands and a pure heart, but we forgot that we cannot have a pure heart with unforgiveness dwelling in us. From this place of forgiveness, I vigorously sought His peace, confidence, and boldness. I reconnected to the call on my life and accepted it with the full confidence and grace of God. I found His wisdom. I received a new understanding of the necessity of the Fruit and the Gifts of the Spirit. I must admit, I have enjoyed the latter (the reconstruction) much more than the former (burials). I reestablished my hope in the unlimited possibilities of God.

Unfortunately, I had no clue of how to die daily and still hold on, live, and produce while I waited. How to live and walk this out was all foreign and uncomfortable to me. I knew that my sentence in my waiting place was prolonged because I had fought the process. It became clear that I had to let go of everything that was self-focused and full of selfish ambition. With each of these, there had to be surrender, a death, burial, and a committal; ashes to ashes dust to dust. It was here that through pray and reading the Word, I stumbled upon the law of agreement (Matthew 18:20 – see Appendix 2), decreeing, and declaring (Job 22:28).

Agree to It

Agreement is an understanding reached by 2 or more persons. It means to come to or have the same understanding, and to be consistent in all essentials without differences or contradictions. When you are in agreement all parties have the same feeling or opinion about the issue. Being in agreement in its basic sense is good, but being in agreement to do something that God would not have us do is not.

For example, agreement is what was in full operation in Genesis 11 when the people came together to make a name for themselves by building a city and tower that would reach heaven. God said they were one people with one language. HE goes on to say, that they were in agreement saying the same thing and if they were allowed to continue nothing would be impossible for them.

HE said, let Us go down there and confuse their language. The issue was not that they were in agreement that was a good thing. The issue was that it was never God's plan for man to do anything to get to Him. His plan was to come to us. The Word defines what healthy and purposeful agreement looks like in Matthew 18. Jesus says that if any two or three touch and agree upon anything in the earth; not in the sky or heaven that HE would be in the midst of them and our Father (God) in Heaven will answer their prayer. True agreement is what produces God results and welcomes Jesus to be in the midst of you. Agree with God. Welcome Jesus to be with you on your journey and in your waiting place and allow the Holy Spirit to lead you through it all.

In your waiting place it is important that you have someone – the right one(s) to touch and agree with you on the issues that you are waiting on God to direct you in and or resolve. The more critical, important or big the situation; the longer you have been waiting, and the weaker you have become in your waiting the more you need someone to walk with you in and through the process in agreement by faith. I believe it is necessary to have someone to agree with you when it seems as if your prayers and petitions (supplications – definite and clear requests) to God are not being answered. How empowering and comforting it is to have someone to stand in faith with you in agreement in prayer to break through the opposition.

Amos 3 asked, "How can two walk together unless they agree?" Visualize with me, two people walking together. Though they are walking together they may not be in-step with one another. Consider this: a person can walk with you and not be in agreement with you or you with them. They can also walk with and not be "in-step". That denotes the two not being in harmony. As we grow in relationship with those we are in agreement with, the goal is to also be in harmony. What does this look like? Glad you ask. It is when both are stepping on the same step; stepping left together and then stepping right together. This is agreement and harmony. This is symmetry or what someone would call an organic flow. Harmony with those you are in relationship and agreement with makes the journey of life go much smoother...some would say, easier.

As I progressed through this pilgrimage called God's plan, I wrote down everything I needed God to intervene in for my life (see Appendix 2). I recorded my personal declaration and "I Am" statements (see Appendix 1). With these tools, I encouraged myself and I built myself up in my most Holy Faith. I spoke and declared the Word of God from my mouth about me; my desires, dreams, present and future. Psalm 116 says, *"I believe therefore I spoke."* Slowly but surely, my perspective about me, God, and my circumstances changed. The Scriptures were no longer just good words to say or religious colloquialism. They became what I earnestly believed and had faith to wait on God and His timing to do. I had an expectation of what I read, had been spoken, and declared would come to pass. Look, the person whose words and voice we hear the most is our own. It is imperative in your waiting place that you speak in agreement what God's Word says about you and your life. Speak life, hope, and God's Word into your purpose. It is His Word that will not return void (Isaiah 55:11). Once it is spoken (by faith), it most go and accomplish what it is spoken and sent to do.

Moving out in this new revelation of agreement, I identified persons to stand in full agreement with me. My selection of these persons was based on their prayer life and what I had seen God do for them and or through them by prayers and faith. The first time I applied the law of agreement; I was believing God for a debt free, sowed in (someone gives/donates it to me), reliable car. I asked those to pray in agreement with me who had seen God provide the same or similar for them. With them, there would be and was no apprehension, jealousy, or envy to ask God to do this for me and expect it come to pass. They would be willing and able to believe with me, celebrate in advance, and once it came to pass. This prayer focus of "faith in action" through agreement went on for over a year and half. I continued to speak and declare my debt free, sowed in, reliable, suitable (for me) automobile. And guess what…God did it. On my 40th birthday, I joyfully received what I asked for. We stood together in agreement; saying the same thing about the same thing and God did it. The story on how the 'blesser' received the funds to buy the car to give it to me is another spoken word in prayers of agreement. I have seen this Biblical truth prove itself several times. I drove that car for 2-years. On the day it went out on the highway; unbeknownst to me, my brand new Mary Kay car that I earned in 5-months had been delivered 2-days prior to the dealership. All I had to do was go pick it up. God is faithful. HE is a keeper. A sure provider.

Speak to It

I had to speak to my soul and command peace without worry. I had to learn to declare (speak) what I believed. I had to put into practice what I believed and what I taught. I had to speak to my soul in times of despair. I had to call things were not (yet) as though they already were (Romans 4:17) done and in existence. I had to believe and have confidence in my day of breakthrough and deliverance. I learned to renounce and denounce what and where I was at and declare what called me to be and where I was going. I had to be mindful to not cancel out my prayers and supplications with words of doubt, careless questions, and subtle complaints. As many of the Psalms do, Psalm 116 perfectly speaks to the thanksgiving we should give for our deliverance. As David found himself many times in a place of despair and uncertainty, he often concluded and sealed his challenges (before the manifestation) with praise and declaration of belief.

In Psalm 116 the psalmist says *"Gracious is the LORD, and righteous; Yes, our God is merciful. The LORD preserves the simple; I was brought low, and HE saved me. Return to your rest, O my soul, For the LORD has dealt bountifully with you (my soul). For You have delivered my soul from death (despair, loss, emptiness), My eyes from tears, And my feet from falling. I will walk before the LORD in the land of the living. I believed, therefore I spoke..."* (verses 5-10). Please know that whatever you believe; good or bad about yourself, your situation, your present or your future, you will speak. This is why examining your heart is so key. So a man thinks in his heart, so he is and out of – from that heart the mouth will speak (Proverbs 23:7, Matthew 12:34). Even when what you say may not be what you wanted to say and it just slips out, those words - your words still carry life. Retract, retrace, rethink, and recommit to speaking good into your life. You shall have what you say. When we are in prolonged waiting states or we just don't want to wait, we are not too far removed from David who had to speak to himself and command his soul to bless the Lord because it was disquieted.

Build yourself up in your most holy faith – the Word of God (Jude 1:20). Believe and speak what you believe (2 Corinthians 4:13) about God and who you are to Him and who HE is to you. Speak to your insecurities, imperfections, and feelings of inadequacies – not being worthy or good enough and over compensating to convince. Remind them and you that you are blessed and highly favored; you are the beloved, and the apple of God's eye. You are fearfully and wonderfully made...Positive self talk in your waiting place will sustain, encourage, and keep you and your mind.

Going It Alone

Though we have the assurance from the Father that HE will never leave or forsake, there may come a time when you find yourself waiting without human support. There will be times that you will feel alone in your waiting place. Like me, you may be a confident and trusting believer; yet, you find yourself concerned about possibly taking your journey alone. I came to a place in my waiting seasons that I had to be honest that the weight of the waiting on the promise and the promise its' self was one that I did not want to go or do alone. And yet, even this truth was one I had to wait on the Lord to bring to me. Until then, HE allowed me to find others (mature sisters in Christ) to confide in and laugh with.

There will be times when not only your family and love ones do not understand why you are waiting or what you are waiting on. The truth is you may not always be clear. Then to compound your uncertainty, you may experience the questions of others and their judgment of you. You may be accused or be seen as being lazy, complacent, irresponsible, foolish, or unmotivated. It is here that you must know that you know and a resolve that you have been commissioned and ordered by God to wait – to be still, know, and trust. This is where and why it is important that you have a trusted, truthful, and if possible, (at least) a neutral confidant. There were times in my waiting seasons, God drew me away and out from amongst others. I was not released to serve, minister, etc. These were often more consecration times but none the less; they were seasons of quietly waiting. Be sensitive and mindful of what the Lord is requiring of you. HE will favor you and give you a plan – a strategy in the waiting place that will set you up and apart for purpose.

Married or single, it is possible to be surrounded by people and still feel alone. Sometimes, the weight of what you are waiting on and called to do is so big that even those close to you can seem far away. Sometimes God will make you go it alone. I have found that this is the time to draw even closer to God for His peace and direction. The feeling of being alone; yet, surrounded by others is a strange feeling to conquer but often necessary for the journey. Mastering your waiting place will involve you finding peace and hope in the midst of confusion and loneliness. Listen, peace is only needed because you have unanswered questions and unsettled issues; like waiting, confusion, frustration, etc. You are apt to encounter physical, emotional, and or mental bouts of loneliness. It is my hope and prayer that God will allow and guide you to a human resource for support. If HE does supply an encourager; honor and treasure them. But if HE doesn't, either way, I encourage and charge you to run to God. Stay close to Him. Seek His face, His voice to receive your comfort, and to know His will. HE will give you what and maybe who you need when the fear or concern of going it alone tries to plague you.

I had to accept that waiting on the Lord and His will; may cost me something and it did: friends, relationships, opportunities, and "open" doors. Everyone, everything lost, and given up or away in my waiting seasons was not a bad thing. Many, I discovered later were for the best. And what was dead has remained dead. Some was simply that we drifted apart. And it is well. Others, I was released from. In other situations their absence was because they did not know how to support me as a friend in my waiting season. They had deemed it best to move on. Yet, through it all, I was comforted by the Word. No matter what you seemingly have lost, be encouraged. You will never truly lose when you choose to wait on and in God. No matter what it looks like, the truth is that you are winning. When you choose to submit to and trust Him and His will, in the end you will win. I learned it was ok to wait in and on the Lord, even when I had to go it alone. Through every waiting season, I have grown stronger and wiser. Waiting has taught me to not only be patient with others but myself.

Be confident of this, no matter what you deem as a loss, God is your stronghold, your escape, your defense, your rescue, and your restorer. HE is holds your reward. No matter how long it takes to get you ready, to line all things up, or if you have to go it alone; wait on the Lord in obedience. You will see the glory of the Lord on this side of heaven. HE will do all that HE said and promised. HE rises to show compassion towards you. HE does not want you to fail or to fall. HE will come to your aid, to help you in your time of need – in your waiting place - in your loneliness. HE will be and is your comfort.

I know it is difficult to grasp, but you are really never alone, because God is always with you. I recognize that you have been waiting long and human contact and comfort is what you long for; someone who understands and gets you, but be of good cheer and courage. As the song says, "It won't always be like this." God can, is willing, and able to turn it around for you. It won't be much longer. Help is on the way. God will help you in the wait and teach you how to wait. His grace will give you strength and the power to persevere and endure.

Participate in It

Active waiting is similar to faith. Meaning, by faith we do what God tells us to do while we wait. Like faith, in waiting we don't always see or know what we are waiting for and believing God to do. Though some of our actions may not be visible to others, waiting in God is (should be) always forward moving. What a glorious day it will be for those who have watched you and more over for those who have waited with you, when they see the manifestation of your obedience to wait. When it comes to pass, the testimony of your faith will be worth the wait of watching yours and their faith increase.

It is through our learning to wait and how to wait patiently that we will receive the promise. As I have learned to wait on God, my waiting place(s) have become much easier and less complicated. My hope is that by reading this journey of the life lessons that I have encountered and learned from that you will recognize, understand, better appreciate, and seek to rest in God in your waiting seasons and your waiting place.

Let me reiterate, you must know God has called, caused, or placed you here. If you know this, then you can confidently add to your faith knowing that HE has a plan, a purpose, and a time ordained for your release and reward. HE is in control. Without this confidence in and from God, waiting possibly without the support of friends and family will be (more) difficult and maybe even impossible. It is a dangerous day when you start to question or lose sight of God and your hope in Him in the wait. I encourage you even the more to trust God. When you start to feel alone. When the questions come to challenge your faith. When it seems like nothing is going right. When you feel like you have no one in the trenches with you. It is here that your relationship and time with God will be a "must have."

In your waiting, participate in perfecting your waiting. Speak to your soul and command it to believe and trust God. Continue to pray, fast, read, and study the Word. When feasible and possible, surround yourself with like-minded people; those with positive attitudes, and mindsets. Declare His Word and rehearse His promises over my life. Sit still to be still and obey. Use this time to prepare for your next and serve others. Train and renew your mind to expect and receive. In the end, your obedience to wait and to wait right will be greatly rewarded.

Appointed and Set Time for It

The appointed and set times belong to God. They represent different aspects of God's timing. The simplest way for me to define this is to use a doctor's appointment. The set time is the call we make to go to the doctor and set (schedule) a time for an appointment. Once a time is set, you now have an appointment. It is the appointed time that has been set aside for us on that day at that time to see the doctor.

Think of a woman who has conceived and a due date (a set time) is determined. The truth is that your doctor can get close or even an exact date of delivery, but it is God that determines the appointed time. This is the day of breakthrough that the baby will come forth. This is the only time this special event can occur. It is the time that the baby is appointed to come into the world. This is also what can be referred to as the Kairos timing of God. I will give a more detailed understanding of Kairos in a later chapter. I address the set and appointed times because we can start to believe our change will never come. Waiting, knowing, and confidently expecting God to show up and intervene is necessary for you to hold on. Yet, the honest truth is that all this can diminish the longer you are called to wait.

Beloved, there is an appointed time set for your breakthrough, your deliverance, and your reward. In John 2, Jesus told His mother My time has not yet come. Jesus understood that there was a time for His glory and purpose to be revealed. That moment, the appointed time had been set in heaven and at the wedding was not it. Yet, Jesus was moved by Mary's (His mother) confession of faith (as a believer - not because she was His mother) in making her request to Him and belief that HE could and would bring a resolution to the issue. His love and compassion for this believer (who just so happen to be His mother) compelled Him to rearrange not only His plans but God changed His ordained and appointed time. His life purpose was accelerated from then, to not yet, to now. His appointed (*Kairos*) time (*a once in a lifetime unrepeatable moment*) was modified to meet the need and request of a believer. Oh dear heart, be of good cheer. God is not a respecter of person. Jesus did not do this because she was His mother; a relative asking. HE responded because her statement of confession declared she not only knew who HE was but believed in Him and what HE was able to do. This is the same thing HE is asking of us today. To declare that we believe and what we believe about Him and what HE not only is able to do but what HE will do because we believe. And just as Mary's earnest request moved Jesus, so can yours. Believe God.

Let's look at the story of Hezekiah in 2 Kings 20 to support this truth. Be encouraged that your unwavering faith, belief, and trust in God can cause Him to adjust His timing for your life. Hezekiah had an appointed time to die. The prophet came to tell him to get his house in order. Though Hezekiah did not know the appointed time, God did. Hezekiah prayed and God changed his appointed time of death and extended his life 15 years. Oh, created vessels of God, children of the Most High, believe the Lord your God and stand on His Word. HE will hear your earnest hearts cry.

We cannot forget Abraham when we speak of the timing of God. God told Abraham in Genesis 17 that HE would establish His covenant with his son (verse 17). A son he did not have yet. And at the old age of about 75, he certainly could not imagine (and probably had not) that happening without God. A time was set for the birth of the promised child to be born. By chapter 21, Sara had conceived and gave birth to the promise at the appointed time of life. Because time and the times belong to God, HE determines (declares – prophecies) the set and appointed time for every natural and spiritual birthing and breakthrough in our lives. Do not confuse God's patience and His timing with His absence. HE is always there; a very present God, there to help in your time of trouble or need. HE is in control of your time in your waiting place. Yet, I do believe as supported by scripture that we can influence our length.

One of my favorite scriptures is Psalm 105; specifically verses 15-21. I came across it in a study of Joseph some years ago when I was worrying about when, why, how, and if things would (ever) change. In the Message Bible it says, *"HE is the LORD our God; his judgments are in all the earth. Do not touch my anointed ones; do my prophets no harm. Moreover, HE called for a famine upon the land [of Egypt]; HE cut off every source of bread. HE sent a man before them, even Joseph, who was sold as a servant. His feet they hurt with fetters; he was laid in chains of iron and his soul entered into the iron, Until his (Joseph's) word [to his cruel brothers] came true, the Word (prophecy – prophetic dream) of the Lord tried and tested him."*

I was comforted; as I hope you will be, to discover that it was not (just or simply) because Joseph told the dream that he went through all he did. We discover that Joseph's waiting for his dream to come to pass had a purpose. It was *the dream* its self – the promise – the prophecy – the Word of the Lord that tried and tested him to perfect *(ready and mature)* him for the assignment (plan) that God had for him. He had to tell it. Telling it provoked the process that tested and perfected him. This passage also taught me that the full prophecy had to come to pass for the prophecy (dream) to be true. Joseph had to go through all that he went through. His trial and his test prepared, equipped, and authenticated him for his purpose.

So often I have witnessed people who have received a Word from the Lord; a Prophetic Word and they grow weary in waiting for the manifestation. They charge out of their waiting place; their place of preparation and perfecting, without fully understanding and or having (complete) instructions. They allow their anxiousness (zeal without understanding), talents, and impatience to cause them to move and pursue before it's time. For example, let's say the Word they received is a promise without any points of reference or it has three parts or conditions. Another example of this is demonstrated in Abraham's life. We first read of the promise or prophetic Word spoken to him in

Genesis 12. The LORD gives him the promise and instructions saying, *"Go from your country, your people and your father's household to the land I will show you. I will make you into a great nation, and I will bless you; I will make your name great, and you will be a blessing. I will bless those who bless you, and whoever curses you I will curse; and all peoples on earth will be blessed through you. So Abram went, as the LORD had told him; Abram departed, as the LORD had spoken unto him;..."*

This was not a small thing. Abram had to take his family and leave everything that was familiar and comfortable and go where God led him. Headed to Canaan; he left Ur of the Chaldeans where the Tower of Babel was built and landed in Haran and waited there. From there he went to Damascus before entering into to the land of Canaan. God commanded him to leave the place of disobedience; where confusion first began to a place of direction and focus. Be mindful that he did not live to see the full manifestation of the promise. But what if he would have gotten tired, frustrated, angry, or experienced something great while in Damascus and stopped? He would have not experienced his promises and prophecies. God said Canaan not Damascus. Wait! Be still to listen, to hear, to follow the full order and instructions of God. HE comes to lead us into all truth.

God said leave and go all the way...Follow the instructions...The full instruction of the LORD...not part but all. I say and will no doubt say it again, partial obedience is still disobedience. If you follow all and do as the LORD instructions, you like Abraham, Joseph, and many others will receive all. Though time may pass waiting purposefully and strategically on the LORD; you in your lifetime, or through your children's, or your children's children will see the manifestation of the promise. Yes, your promise or prophecy will test you; your character, your faith, your trust, and your patience, but wait for it. Wait for your appointed time. It will come to pass. Do not allow the trails, tests, ignorance, immaturity, fear, zeal, or the trying of your faith to stop you from receiving the full reward of your faith (James 1 and 1 Peter 1). HE who promises is faithful to do just what HE said.

At different points in ministry, I have felt like Peter putting my heart and my foot in my mouth. Then there are the Isaiah moments where God uses me in detail, direct, and powerful prophetic ministry. Yet, still having times that I would feel as if I was not being heard or received. Like Paul with books, teachings, ministry, and revelations for days upon days, I wasn't sure what to do with it all. Then there were times that I could relate to Joseph's plight. With him having all those talents and favor, but having moments where he felt confined, limited, rejected, locked up and locked out.

With each of these, God shows us that HE can, does, and will use people and circumstances; including waiting, jail, loss, accusation, persecution, break-ups, suffering, etc. in our process. I am reminded of Genesis 40 with the Joseph and the cupbearer and baker. Somewhere - somehow over the years, I had forgotten who had dismissed Joseph and his gift and his request. I recalled the baker was killed, but how did the cupbearer story go. Who forgot Joseph? I guess I confused who was killed with who didn't remember.

As I reread this, my eyes were opened to a few key things that I had somehow missed. His gifts had the power to remove him and make room for him. Initially the cupbearer did forget about him, which delayed his release. It was two years later that he remembered Joseph. Though man may forget and confine us, God never forgets. HE will not forsake (forget about) us. Joseph had to go through all that. Yet, through it all, he never forgot who he was or who his God was. He confidently walked in the favor that was on him and with him. He was faithful to his assignment and continued to use his gifts no matter where he was or who he was among. Though limited by location, rules, and guards, he was not limited by God. His gifts really did make room for him and brought him (back) before great men.

When he returned to position after being remembered, recommended, released, and let go to flow, he shaved and changed his clothes. Joseph lived in prison – in one room with an expectation of getting out and going up. For him to shave and change, he had a preconceived thought; an expectation, a hope, an anticipation not to return or go back to what or where he was. He expected that his release would bring him more; bigger, better, greater, more elevation. Though he could not have known to what degree he would have success or the journey to get there, he had to believe and expect. By faith, he held to the vision. Wait on God! HE will give you hope, expectation, and confirm your vision in your waiting place.

The dream (the promise) perfected (matured) and readied him for his purpose. In my study of Genesis Chapters 37-43, I discovered a few things about the perfecting of Joseph that came by way of his promise testing him:

1   Joseph was 17 years old (Genesis 37) when he had the dreams and told his brothers and his father – *immaturity – zeal without wisdom and self control often causes us to get into trouble*

2   He was outwardly stripped of his blessing – promise – dream – *rejected and publically disgraced by those close to him – his brothers – his family*

3   The dream or rather his telling the dream to his brothers and family, placed him in an uncomfortable place – an unused well – a pit – dark, cold, probably damp, empty, fruitless, lonely place – *sometimes – for a time or a season – the purpose on our life will bring with it these challenges – it will cause us to be put in a place we didn't want and certainly didn't ask for or expect – it may separate us from family –*

bring haters, hatred and threats; simply because we have a dream – a vision or a purpose that others do not have or understand - remember Martin Luther King...Remember Jesus

4   From the pit, he was sold into slavery to serve in Potiphar's the palace – *promotion comes with trials and persecution*

5   There he finds himself running things and having to run from the advances Potiphar's wife – who strips him again – *on our journey to purpose you will experience dichotomies of extremes – one minute on top of things then suddenly things are on top of you – you may find yourself facing a similar trail you previously faced to finished what you didn't get the other time or to address another aspect of you but it is all for purpose*

6   From the pit to the palace to Potiphar's wife and now to prison back to the palace – *the roller-coaster of life*

7   Joseph waited close to thirty years to see the full manifestation of his coat of many colors and bowing down of his brothers coming to pass – *despite the challenges – tests – trails that rise against us – we will see the glory (the promise) of the Lord if we do not faint – give up – throw in the towel - God will do exactly what HE has said and promised*

Through it all; you never read where Joseph complained. He remained confident in himself, the promise, and that God was with him (Chapter 40 verse 8). Like Joseph's dream, Paul's conversion and every promise of God; including yours, waits an appointed time. The promises of God are still yes and Amen in Christ.

Even when the cupbearer forgot about him and he remained in prison, he was steadfast. Psalm 105 goes on to say that the king sent for Joseph and set him free. His set time came two years later and at the appointed time. He had an appointment with the governor. This appointment promoted him and took him from prison back to the palace. He became ruler of the people, overseer of all the affairs of the king's house, his substance, and the kingdom. For his trouble, trying, and testing, he was elevated to a position of authority and rule. He waited right without complaint or confrontation, and through that position, he was able to provide for, reconcile, and redeem his family. This is what God can do when we wait on Him and do it His way.

I believe that quit possibly, the greatest test Joseph faced was not waiting to be brought out of the pit or even to get out of prison, but being so close to his family whom he loved and not being able (or ready) to fully express it or receive it. Waiting for the appointed time; the time that God had ordained had to be difficult. Can you imagine the anxiousness of Joseph in this situation? A love lost found but you have to hold back until God says, "Now." Waiting and wanting to be reconciled, for love to come; knowing it is yours to have, to give love whole heartedly, and for it be expressed genuinely or be restored completely, but having to wait had to be extremely difficult. Under any circumstance or situation; not just love and relationship but having to wait knowing that what awaits you is yours to have, but you are not released to go get it, to have it. That would be a challenge for anyone.

Think about it...have you ever wanted to tell someone I forgive you...please forgive me, that you (still) love them, how you really feel; knowing it would bring healing and reconciliation, but God is says, "Not yet...Wait...There is (still) something in you – in them. I Am perfecting... If you go (back) now, say it now, they won't get it or receive it...They will treat you the way they had treated you previously...They do not yet know or understand your worth or the gift you are to them...that I have given you to them as favor as a blessing...They have not yet been humbled...They still think they were justified, etc...No, wait. Hold on. Be still. Be patient. I will perfect them for you and you for them." I can only imagine...No, actually, I can absolutely relate to this. Go back, read Chapters 41 and 42 and see the struggle

Joseph had to say or not say. Like him, we all have said, "I can wait." But unlike him many of us have forged ahead against God's will and not waited and the result was disastrous. Even if the brothers had not returned and followed Joseph's instructions, Joseph still would have received his reward. Like Abraham and Isaac, this too is an awesome testimony of obedience to God being of a greater reward than sacrifice.

Can you wait? In your anxiousness, can you wait? Wait on the Lord. Again I say wait. Hold on. Be encouraged. Your change, release, freedom is coming. You have an appointment with God. There is a set time for your deliverance. Your set time is coming. God has an appointed time for you. Do your part. The part you have been instructed and know to do. Wait right without complaining, fear, worry, or doubt. Expect God. HE is not a man that HE can lie. HE who promises is faithful to His Word to do exactly what HE has promised. HE has to do what HE promised.

WHAT I LEARNED

I couldn't expect my family and friends to understand, support, and or encourage me in my waiting place when I didn't understand it. God had me walk through my seasons of waiting alone because HE needed to me to learn His voice, His ways, and His word. It was here that I accepted my call. It was here that I heard His voice and His confirmation. It was here that I found my identity in Him and my purpose. It was here on my pilgrimage with God that I became confident of who I am in Him. Old things passed and are still passing away and my beholding of who and what HE has created me to be and do was confirmed and is affirmed. It was in this time, place and season, I grew to like me. I learned to love me. I like being with me – hanging out with friends or family or just me – I'm good with me. Whether in a crowd or alone; I have the peace of God and peace with God. It was and is in those waiting times alone with God that I experience His amazing love and peace. I learned that sometimes you have to go it alone and sometimes you have to do it afraid. God has promised to never leave me or cast me assign and forget about me – so I go – staying close to hear.

I have learned that...

_____

_____

_____

_____

_____

_____

Scripture or Statement for Meditation

_____

What waiting means to me...

_____

_____

_____

_____

_____

THREE

Facing Your Waiting

Necessity of It

Consider for a moment that sometimes God brings us to our waiting place not only to perfect and conform us to His will but also to protect us. It is in and through these experiences we will learn to thank and trust Him more. Many stories of heroism, missed trains, plans, and called off sick days came forth after the like 9-11 tragedy. I would like to share a personal testimony of that day with you.

Waiting and Obeying Protected Me

It was the summer of 2001. I had left my corporate job 2-years prior and was moving forward in my call as a minister of the Gospel. I had preached at my local church a few times and had received and accepted a few local engagements. My savings was gone and I had dipped into my 401k and it was nearing or maybe it had already been reduced to $0. At the time, speaking and preaching engagements were not enough to maintain my lifestyle or to meet my basic expenses. I was beginning to doubt if what I had done was what God had said. Was this decision mine or His?

Near the end of the summer, I received a call from a New York Corporation expressing an interest in my project management and process auditing certifications and skills. I recall asking the gentleman how he found me. My name was referred by a staff member that I had met during a Year 2000 Audit training meeting in New York in 1999. He shared how his team member was impressed with my project management and process auditing knowledge. We set up a phone interview for later that week. The phone interview went well. I believe my interviewer was with the Vice President of the department. I recall the position would have been a Director with a staff of 5.

Secretly, I had an unspoken desire to live in New York but always said (to myself) I would only live there for about 3 years, no more than 5. Near the conclusion of the interview, he told me that the project was funded by the government and guaranteed for 5-yrs. However, if the project was not renewed, my contract would guarantee me a third of my current annual salary as a severance package. However, I had to commit to 3-yrs and train someone as a back-up. The starting salary offer was $185,000. The start date was the 1st Monday in September. I remember thinking that would only give me 2-4 weeks to move.

I had sold my home and was living in a 3-bedroom apartment with one of the rooms set apart as my office and prayer room. I sat back in my chair at my desk and shock my head. He was saying everything that I had secretly wanted. The job was in Manhattan. He told me that most of his staff lived in Jersey, not in Manhattan. How amazing was this: New York plays – culture – director – expense account – travel – east coast brothers – love that dialect – amazing benefits – quarterly bonuses – profit sharing with a $185k *salary. I was so perplexed…but why. It was everything I (thought I) wanted. Why was I not jumping on this?*

Had I made the wrong choice 2-years ago? Was God calling me back into the corporate arena? He offered me the job and a visit to their offices. I asked him to give me a few days and I would get back with him. I called my brother Gardus. He said something to me that I have never forgotten "Does this sound like a job that you would get up and do for free. Is this your passion?" No. He asked me the name of the company but I could not remember it. Why that quick…why can't I remember? I remembered praying, but I did not have peace. I thought to do a salary comparison between Indianapolis and New York. I discovered that difference between what I was last making and this job with cost of living only gave me an increase of about $18k. Was that worth moving to NY? Still not at peace; something was telling me, 'be still and wait'.

I waited. Five days passed before I called him back. My decision was no. I know… crazy right. It was 2-3 weeks later that 9/11 happened. As the list of companies scrolled across the screen, the name of the company that had offered me the position was listed. I sat back in my home office chair shaking my head with tears flowing down my face. Oh, the love and protection of God. God blocked it. The unrest of my spirit and lack of peace was my indicator and became my saving grace…my protection.

Often God is causing us to be still and wait. HE sends messages to caution or stop us. It is the yellow and red lights in our life that signal us but we often ignore them. All of us have been guilty of it. That purchase, that relationship, those words, that action, etc., I implore you to pay attention to that gentle voice, indicators, and the abrasive nudges. Note those things that bring an unsettling. Listen to hear the silent promptings cautioning you to proceed with caution or to stop or go no further. Though waiting can be annoying, challenging, frustrating, and the list can go on; I encourage you to learn to appreciate the yellow and red lights. They are there to protect us from what we may not see coming. Now that you are armed with the thought that waiting can come to protect you; take a moment to think of a time that your obedience to wait; consciously or unconsciously saved or protected you from something. Unfortunately, it often takes tragedy for us to grow in patience and appreciate the protection of waiting.

> *I recall several years ago, I had to take my sister to work. It was about 7:45am and I was headed back to the house with my doggie Kain with me. He was shepherd collie mix with a look and bark to intimidate, but really he was simply a precious peaceful protector. As we approached the green light, I remember thinking, "Can I make that light." Then my very next thought was, "No. If something happened with Kain with me what would happen to him. He would go after somebody who he thought was trying to hurt me but was really trying to help me." So I began to slow down. At that very same moment, a late model dusty blue pick-up truck came racing pass me. As the truck approached, the light turned yellow. He sped up to catch the light and plowed right into a small green 4-door car that was turning left. Shocked, I screamed and immediately I began to pray.*

> *Now on the other side of the light, I parked, cracked the windows, exited the car and locked the doors – leaving Kain unattended, barking uncontrollably. I walk up to the small green 4-door car to find 3-young high school students. The 2 in the front were clearly shaken and hurt. The young boy in the back was slumped over with obvious injures. I could hear the driver (female) crying for her mom. Someone somehow*

gets her mother's number from her (who is out of town) and calls her. The driver of the pick-up was a young 20-something young man headed (rushing) to his college class a half block away. The young people were siblings on their way to their high school. Unfortunately, that day, the impatience of one person and their inability to wait caused the loss of a 15 year old young boy's life and left the siblings with serious injuries, grave curdling sounds and memories and a mother without a child.

Whether you are a believer in Jesus Christ or not or believe in the power and urging of the Holy Spirit or you call what you encounter conscious or intuition, I admonish you to respect and honor those times that you have or will sense that you should wait – stop – be still. Obey and adhere to the sense that you should proceed with caution, or not be in a hurry. Proverbs 6:18 reinforces this with *"There are six things which the Lord hates, yes, seven which are an abomination to Him…feet that run rapidly (quickly - without hesitation) into evil (trouble)."* Slow down, be patient, be still, be anxious for nothing, breathe, wait, and again I say wait. Our impatience and urgency cannot only damage us but others.

Purpose of It

What is the purpose of waiting? Well, it has many purposes. As I said in the previous topics, you will either learn to trust Him or thank Him. Trust Him in-spite of or thank Him because of. No matter the purpose, cause, or reason we will all find ourselves in a waiting place. Ultimately, it is for us and for those who will be privileged to watch us wait right. In and through our waiting seasons, we not only learn God, we learn ourselves, and what we believe. As we wait in and on God, God is perfecting the things (including us) that concern us. Life is a series of tests. It is through these tests and waiting for the favorable outcome that we, our waiting skills, and character are developed and perfected. Yes, waiting is a character builder. Waiting will develop and build our patience and add to and or increase our faith. If we allow our life experiences; including waiting to have its perfect work, we will not get to a place where our gifts, talent, abilities, and ambitions have taken us but we cannot maintain or remain. We must go through the waiting place to learn how to die to self, to flesh, to the things that are not God's will for us. The things that will delay our purpose or abort our destiny are what God desires for us to deal with and submit to His work in us in our waiting place. It is in our waiting that the restlessness, fear, and dissatisfaction of our soul can surface and be addressed. The purpose of waiting and learning how to wait is for the perfecting of our character and our faith.

I have found that the best way to submit to this work is to focus on developing and growing in the Fruit of the Spirit. Desire and seek God for the development and blessing of the Fruit of the Spirit more than the Gifts of the Spirit. In this place, want – thirst – hunger for Him more than you want what He can give or use you to do. If we delight *(take great pleasure and joy in Him – just Him being Him – God our Father our Daddy our Creator)* ourselves in Him; HE will give us the desires *(things From Him - the Father - His will for our lives)* of our heart. In the wait, I challenge you to seek, learn, and receive God's love and His ways and practice giving Him away. Wouldn't it be grand, if we found ourselves; more often, asking God to bless us with His love and give us opportunities to be used to give His love away, than asking for stuff. Love is a necessary perfecting in the waiting place. God's perfecting of us is for today and about our tomorrows. Meaning, where you are in your life today is to better you. It is about where God plans to take you to be a blessing to others and bring Him glory. Allow the perfecting that comes in the waiting place to have its perfect and complete work that you will be mature and lack nothing.

Perfecting of It

You would think after these experiences, I would have had no problem with waiting and not being in a hurry or making rash decisions. Forced or volunteered; the truth is, maturity in waiting right is perfected with every waiting encounter. In your waiting place, God is seeking – desiring to perfect and prepare you for what HE has for you and desires to release and give to you. So often, people break and run from their waiting place because they are tired of waiting, perhaps afraid of what may or may not happen. God's Word tells us in Isaiah 40, verse 29, that HE gives power to the weak, and to those who have no might HE increases strength. It is with this promise that Paul could say in 2 Corinthians 12, "*Concerning this thing* (that I wait on you to do Lord) *I pleaded with the Lord three times* (how many times have you asked and yet to receive His rescue, answer, release) *that it might depart from me. And HE said to me, "My grace is sufficient for you, for My strength is made perfect in weakness." Therefore, most gladly, I will rather boast in my infirmities (Really Paul? Lord help me – help us to grow to this) that the power of Christ may rest upon me. Therefore I take pleasure in infirmities, in reproaches, in needs, in persecutions, in distresses* (in the frustration of waiting and waiting on You), *for Christ's sake. For when I am weak, then I am strong."*

For most, waiting has been appointed to perfect us. Yes, to mature us. It is a necessary and unavoidable discipline that we must not only submit to, we must surrender to it. Submitting to the discipline of waiting and developing patience will make your process less difficult and shorten your waiting season. Even when we don't know what God is perfecting in us, HE knows. It is not only waiting that we do not like and do not want to submit to, but waiting with unanswered questions is even worse. And this too is necessary and good for us. Kind of like exercise. Most people do not like it or want to do it, but it is necessary and good for us to be and stay healthy. Much of the work is being done underneath the skin long before we see the results on the outside. Hebrews 12 tells us *"Do not make light of the Lord's discipline..., the Lord disciplines the one he loves, and HE chastens everyone HE accepts as His son. Endure hardship as discipline; God is treating you as His children... If you are not disciplined—and everyone undergoes discipline—then you are not legitimate, not true sons and daughters at all... God disciplines us for our good, in order that we may share in his holiness. No discipline seems pleasant at the time, but painful. Later on, however, it produces a harvest of righteousness and peace for those who have been trained by it."* (verses 5-11). When we abort or leave the waiting place where our perfecting has been set; we reject the discipline of the Father. Thus we miss out on the harvest of righteousness and peace because we could not or would not allow the discipline of waiting to train and perfect us.

Luke 15 gives us a very clear picture of the discipline of waiting instituted by God in the parable of the lost son that we refer to as the prodigal *(wasteful, impatience, unwise)* son (the younger son) who leaves his father's house after demanding his share. Historically, inheritances were given when the father passed away. So for him to demand his portion while the father was still alive was like him saying, "I don't want to wait for you to die to get mine. I want it now...Give me my third now." It was like wishing that person (was) dead. Now there are several other things wrong with this. One, the father was not dead. Two, the third he got now would probably have been more had he waited for his appointed time and his turn. And three, while his father was alive, he had access to everything his father owned and could use it as he pleased. For him to take "his portion" before time could have put his father and brother in a financial bind. Also, in this time; where parents were highly respected and revered, for a child to demand anything and certainly before its time was almost heresy. He took "his portion" and verse 14 showed his youthful, unperfected (immature) foolish behavior. The Word says, *"After he had spent everything,…he began to be in need. So he went and hired himself out to a citizen of that country, who sent him to his fields to feed pigs. He longed to fill his stomach…When he came to his senses, he said, "How many of my father's hired servants have food to spare, and here I am starving to death! I will set out and go back to my father and say to him: Father, I have sinned against heaven and against you."*

When we come to our senses and stop rejecting the discipline of waiting and let God use it to perfect the things that concern us and make us mature so we lack nothing; including wisdom, the process of waiting right will be perfected and mastered in us. Beloved, let Him, let patience have its perfect work in you. Be assured, God is in control of the circumstances of your life. HE is very much aware of where you are and what you need. Trust Him and lean on Him and not to your own understanding. HE has promised to direct your path, to order your steps, and your life and to go before you and with you. If you are a believer, HE is in you, your rear guard, and your battle-ax. God does not want His people to fail, lose, or be ashamed. HE planned and set us up for victory. Yes, it is a fixed fight. We were made and perfected; for HE needs us to be fully persuaded and convinced of not only what we believe about Him but that we believe Him. When we let Him, HE will be our keeper. It is here that your pain, your tears will turn to joy, and you can be used to help others. Jesus told His disciples that HE must need to go through Samaria. Waiting is one of the 'must-need-go-through' things that we must face.

Truth of It

The truth is waiting is for and about us. Yes, the testimony that will come from it and the witness as others see you come through will be a blessing to all. This may be a disturbing truth for some of us, the longer the wait the better. Waiting should, can, and will cause you to trust and lean on God even the more. Let me speak to this thing of looking at others to substantiate or validate our purpose, identity, and what you believe about yourself and why you are in a season or time of waiting. Because we look at what others have or are doing, we can start to think that our faith is not strong enough or God is mad at us or does not (love) want us to have something, but none of that is true. For what good father who knows how to give and does give good gifts would withhold from you - his child.

Maybe someone else's vision and dreams are coming to pass but yours seem far from view. Perhaps, the process to obtain and achieve seems or really is more of a challenge for you. Hear me beloved; God is not a respecter of person. HE is a rewarder of the diligent seeker. HE is the author and finisher of your faith and fate. Remember, HE is not only with you, HE is for you. HE still rewards with blessings when you pray, petition, and praise Him. I submit to you that those you believe seem to have everything or their plans seem to easily fall in place, doors open, invites come, they have the money, the spouse, the credit or the resources to do it, get it done or make it happen; may not be true. The measure of their faith and perseverance will come when God puts them where you are and pulls back resources and forces trust without all the amenities. Because we all have to wait, we will all struggle with and in our waiting seasons; short or long-term. The real test of endurance, trust, faith, and maturity comes when HE says, *"Lay it all down. Be still and know, and wait on Me. And do it with very little or nothing. Do it without all the externals."*

We certainly do not wish anyone to struggle or their way to be difficult. Yet, like waiting, the struggle sent and set by God is necessary and unavoidable. It carries with it purpose. It produces (greater) strength, anointing, trust in Him, and matures us and our faith. It is in the waiting place with adversity that the men and women are set apart from the boys and girls. Until you master waiting, waiting will master you. Grasping this principle will be instrumental in your making. Not doing so will prolong your breaking. Do not allow your challenges or adversity to cause you to flee your waiting place or season before God has perfected you, matured you, and made you meat for His use.

The true test of our trust in God and being confident in what we believe about ourselves and God comes in the waiting. It is important that you remain confident and believe in your vision, dream, and desire; even when everything around you says, "Not so, not you, not yet." Can you wait with joy still trusting and believing God for the promise of being a millionaire with only 34 cents in the bank? Can you wait at the bus stop with a vision of a Bentley in your view? Can you wait in peace in the checkout line at the grocery store with a food stamp card in your wallet while holding on to a dream, a vision or a desire of being a philanthropist? Can you continue to wait believing God for healing when the last visit to the doctor tells you your diagnosis is the same or it has taken a turn for the worse? Can you wait when God is leading you to be still and wait some more? Can you find joy in the wait when no one is calling or when who or what you (think you) want stands before you but God says, "No…Be still…Wait."

None of these are small things. They require a knowing that comes from a close – intimate relationship with God. For me that is through His Son my Savior, Jesus Christ and the truth of Him and His Word. How can you have peace and believe when you do not trust in the One who is peace? How can we have trust when you don't want to hear, receive, or do the will of God? The will of God is that we believe in His Son. In this world, if you are not in the Will, you have NO access to the Trust. When you believe, you are heirs of the promise and joint heirs with Christ. HE sent His Son so you could have access to the Trust and the funds as an heir and a joint heir. The test of what you believe and know about yourself and God as God (your God) and as Father (your Heavenly Father) will – should become (more) clear in the waiting place. Beloved, it is well in the wait. It is good to wait on the Lord. Good things still come to those who wait, believe, and trust. All things (*in life, in His Kingdom and the Word are yours and*) work together (*for those who love Him and are the called (heirs and joint heirs) according to His plan (will))* and service for (His) your purpose (*for your life – the Funds are available to those who are His – in the Will*).

You must know in your knower (heart and soul) what you believe. Keep a clear head and declare words that bring life into the waiting place. The most ideal words you that can speak over (into) your life is The Word of God. Psalm 116 says, "*I believed, therefore I spoke, I am...*" Speak words of truth. Speak life and words of love and encouragement that declare God in you and you in Him. Speak the Word of God. As you wait on the promises God has in-store for you; construct your new world from this place of waiting. Not to stay there but to come out with a vision and a plan for your life. And as you share it with those who read it, they will be able to run with it. Use your waiting wisely.

If (when) you let it and learn to wait right, your waiting place will change you. It will mature you. Patience will have its perfect work in you. Your confidence in God and His Word will be steadfast, unmovable, and you will be able to abound in the work of the Lord. I speak expressively with all confidence of the Holy Spirit and Truth; you will mature and lack nothing. It is here that the working out of salvation; which is sanctification can occur (Philippians 2). Our personalized waiting places and seasons come to set us apart, prepare, and equip us for the work of service HE has for us to do.

Timing of It

Waiting is a process fortified, sustained, and supported by time. Waiting is all about time…God's time and timing. We exist in time but God exist and controls both time and eternity. The issue we have with not wanting to wait on the Lord; the answer, or others, and getting in a hurry is most often related to our not learning or not being familiar with the timing or rhythm of God. As I previously stated; rhythm is a step beyond agreement. Two people can slow dance, but if one is out of step they both get out of rhythm and it is visible to those who see. They are dancing, but it is a difficult partnership. Being in and respecting the timing and rhythm of God is key. Ecclesiastes 3 speaks directly to the timing and time of God. Pay attention to how God moves in your life. It won't look like anyone else's way. Don't measure or compare your time or testing to anyone else. Get in step with the will of God for your life. This is learned through waiting, watching, and listening.

The purpose of your tests and trials will be fully revealed and accomplished in time – in His time. Dreams and visions take time to manifest. Use your waiting time to prepare. Write your vision and make it plain as Habakkuk 2 instructs so that when others read it they will be able to read it and run with it. Prepare for your due season. It will surely come. The time you spend in the waiting place preparing for your purpose and vision to come to pass will be well worth the wait. Just as a seed takes times to grow into what it was created to produce, so will it take time for your vision to come to pass and fully manifest. Like the seed of life from a father planted in the womb of a mother, waiting has a maturation period. Like a seed planted, your purpose and the plan for your life must go through the process of time. In time, you, your purpose, your faith, your gifts, talent, and abilities will be defined and made clear to you. Ask God to know His timing. Let Him perfect you for, in, and through for the journey.

Our waiting often takes much longer because we keep moving when God is telling us to stand still. We keeping getting in the way trying to do it our way – forgetting HE is The Way. We prolong the time trying to hurry the season (Chronos) that HE has set for us and miss our moment (Kairos); moments to grow, moments to learn, moments to mature. Being in a hurry, we miss the opportunity to learn, grow, and accept ourselves, God, and others. Waiting and certainly waiting upon the Lord cannot be produced and perfected in a microwave. Which in itself; produces through its own man-made mechanism of agitation from manufactured heat based on a man selected time. I mean really, how many of us have stood in the front of the microwave waiting for the "ding." Thinking "this is taking long time." Forgetting, we were the one who set the timer.

God uses the time in waiting to get out of us what will hinder or hurt us or others. For His perfect work to be done in us in our waiting place, it often requires a slow cook at an even temperature. We cannot rush God or the process. HE is not your Heavenly Concierge or bell-hop to jump to your every whim. Though HE created time, it is not for Him. It is a constraint that gives us restraint and boundaries. Because HE controls time, HE is not limited to it or by it. For us, it limits and is limited. Therefore, we must use it wisely. I implore you to learn to seek, appreciate, and wait on the timing of God. In the end what you are waiting on will speak and it will not lie and neither can or will God.

As I have stated; trust, patience, faith, etc., becomes more difficult the longer you are in the wait. His Spirit is your comfort and your rescue in the time of need. God's time, timing, and seasons supersede the natural. Didn't HE say a day is like a thousand and thousand days is like a day? HE has this and you. Time is important to our being proven, finished, and remaining on the other side of release and receiving what God has for us.

Allow the old things to pass away and what remains (that is good for you) to become new. It is in the times of perfecting that our character is developed and we are authenticated. Oh, beloved do not grow weary and give up in your wait. Not now, you are closer than ever.

WHAT I LEARNED

I had to face that waiting is necessary because it is for me but it is not about me. It is ultimately about His glory being revealed in and through me for others. HE cares so much for me that HE wants this time to be with me and get me ready for my debut. Waiting is more about 'why' God has me in the waiting place. It is for me to know and learn God and myself. In my waiting and seeking, I learn who my Daddy God is. I learned that HE was my Father before HE was my God. I had to make Him my God. I learned my struggles, my weaknesses, my strengths, and my true purpose. I had to face how many times I have gone against His will and did it my way and yet, HE still loves me and forgives and this make me love Him more and want to know Him more. Every experience with Him (good, bad, or indifferent) I learn Him in another way. It is here that God can work on and out of me what is unlike Him. When I wait in and on God, God perfects the things (including me) that concern me. And I concern me more than anything or anyone else in my life. My sins and struggles concern me. Tests failed concern me. Things lost and not yet recovered concern me. Life is a test of my waiting skills and abilities. Waiting will develop and build my patience, endurance, and add to my faith. If I wait and wait right, I will not get to a place where my gifts, talent, abilities, ambitions take me somewhere my character cannot keep me. My gifts and calling are given to me without God's repentance but my repentance is daily. God I want to use them right to honor and bring You glory. It is good to desire and seek Him for the development of Fruit of the Spirit more than the Gifts of the Spirit. The Gifts will get stronger and be more powerful and effective when Fruit is there.

I have learned that...

_____

_____

_____

_____

_____

Scripture or Statement for Meditation

_____

What waiting means to me...

_____

_____

_____

_____

_____

_____

_____

_____

FOUR

Issues with *It*

Hard to Wait

The Bible tells us in Psalm 27, *"Wait on the LORD; Be of good courage, And HE shall strengthen your heart; Wait, I say, on the LORD!"* This scripture supports the truth that waiting can be hard but God has given us a promise in the same passage. Why is it so hard to for us to wait? There are several issues that make waiting hard.

1   Issue of Done
2   Issue of Movement
3   Issue of Trust
4   Issue of How
5   Issue of Who
6   Issue of Time
7   Issue of Silence
8   Interruption of Suddenly
9   Issue of Mediating

For many reasons, waiting is hard. Uncertainties make waiting difficult. Though you may know what you are waiting for, you are not always sure what will happen, if it will happen, or when it will happen. Like a pregnant woman nearing her due date, it is uncomfortable. She knows it is coming but does not know exactly when or where she will be when it breaks forth (takes place). Where there is uncertainty; anxiousness and fear are produced and blocks the flow of peace and interrupts confidence. Pain is often used and necessary to get to grateful and for the outward demonstration of praise to come through. As difficult as it may be to hear, understand or receive, our pain; when sent or allowed by God has and is for purpose.

There is also a waiting that is rooted in the unknown. The unknown is full of questions; bringing with it restlessness, worry, fear, and anxiety. Philippians 4 reminds us to *"Be anxious for nothing, but in everything by prayer and supplication (definite, targeted, specific request), with thanksgiving, let your requests be made known to God; and the peace of God, which surpasses all understanding, will guard your hearts and minds through Christ Jesus."* Anxiousness is the mental tension, stress, and worry that is rooted in fear. It is the opposite of peace. Peace comes when we focus on the expected outcome and not on the problem. In verse 8 of Philippians 4, the writer goes on to tell us how to think – what to keep our minds on. This will help us not to be anxious or worry. Anxiety can be a burdensome habit to break. God's Word tells us to let worry, worry about itself (Matthew 6). Simply put, worry and anxiousness comes to grip and stop us. The foundation of these is fear. The foundation of most things that are anti-God is rooted in fear.

Fear produces many things: anxiety, worry, stress, doubt, etc. It is the foundation of everything that is the opposite of faith and God's love. Fear of the unknown, of failing, succeeding, not seeing the end, the promise of progress are all real. Fear of life, fear of death, fear of rejection, fear of love. Fear of being alone and fear of having no one. Fear of all kinds; of the obvious and the not-so obvious. Fear of disappointing God, others, and yourself. Fear will cause you to question good things – God things, and very obvious blessings that are yours. Fear is a tormenter and a separator. There is no fear in love. If you have not love and do not love, you cannot obey or trust. Therefore you will be ruled by, led by fear, and operate out of fear. The vicious circle of fear and all its cronies comes to block love and freedom. The torment of fear is real and torment hurts. God loves you and His love makes you perfect. If you are not careful and mindful in your waiting season and place, you can be snared, entangled, or entrapped by fear. Allow the perfect love of God for you to cast out fear (1 John 4) and all that comes with it.

Waiting can be unclear and foggy when you don't know what you are waiting for or on but you just know you need to wait or are being led to wait. In the waiting place, our faith can begin to spread thin and weaken. Waiting on God puts our faith and trust to the test. In James 1, it is written, *"My brethren, count it all joy when you fall into various trials, knowing that the testing of your faith produces patience. But let patience have its perfect work, that you may be perfect and complete, lacking nothing."* For patience to have its perfect work we must trust and believe by faith in ourselves and in The One we are waiting on or for. Depending on how long we have been in the waiting place; many questions can arise.

In our season of waiting, our questions are often: why me, why so long, and when? We begin to question our faith. We become challenged to trust and obey. We start to look at and can become critical of ourselves, our decisions (past, present, and future), and our character. Self-examination is good no matter the season or reason. However, depending on your state of mind and heart; an overly critical examination of self can border self-abuse. As you are waiting, you may start to question God as if HE does not know you are in a storm – a struggle – a battle. Not only does HE know exactly where you are and how long you have been there, HE also knows how much longer you will be there.

Often the natural course is to start thinking and maybe even looking for confessed and unconfessed sin that may still be in your life. We start to blame our waiting place or lack of progress on our struggle or ourselves. It is imperative that you not measure your life according to man's way of thinking. God is not a tit-for-tat kind of Father God. The cause of your waiting is not God's way of punishing you. Are we accountable for our choices and decisions, yes? Are their consequences for those plotted, schemed, and consciously done acts that are against God's will and way, yes? But, God does not need to keep us in a holding pattern of waiting to chastise us. Though HE may use it to get our attention and allow us to see ourselves and call out to Him to help us; it is not a tool of punishment. HE loves you and desires what is best for you. Your success or failure is not contingent upon you in your human frailty having the ability to never sin.

Our waiting being hard, stressful, or painful is often a self-inflicted pain based on our choices. How we approach and handle waiting will determine the income and outcome of it. A desire to please God, to do what is right, and to sin-less goes along way with Him. HE recognizes your times and seasons of faithfulness. I often say it is good that someone is still struggling with a sin, a habit, a challenge. Why? Because the struggle indicates they have not given themselves over to the sin or struggle and nor has God turned them over (Romans 1). They still have a desire to please God. God knows, understands, and forgives our struggles and our sin. Keep coming to Him with a sincere heart's desire to change and HE will move in at just the right time to save you...to deliver you from that which plagues you and seems to have control over you. HE is willing, able, and can do a quick work that is perfect and complete. In His perfect will and timing, you will look up and one day you will have control over that which once had control over you. Keep coming to God. Keep crying out. Don't grow weary in trying to do right.

Let Him teach and lead you to righteousness. Until then, keep saying you are the righteousness of God in and through Christ Jesus. HE sees, HE knows, and HE cares. His timing is perfect!

God told the Children of Israel, I will drive out those nations; your enemies (your issues, your struggles) little by little. Why? They would not be able to stand against or destroy them all at the same time. It would be too overwhelming for them. Not because HE would not be with them, but because the beasts of the field (the wild animals, the unmanageable, out of control, unknown things, challengers) would become too numerous for them (Deut 7:22). If everything was removed all at once, the stuff they did not know was there would be free and have easy access to come against them. Maybe, just maybe, your waiting is truly your protection from outside sources, forces, and yourself. If HE released our blessing or dealt with everything in our lives all at once; in or outside of our waiting place, things that we were never meant to deal or battle with would come in and with a vengeance.

Maybe that is what some of you are facing. The beast of the field have entered in because you left your waiting place too soon, or you didn't rest in it to receive all that HE had for you there. Or maybe like the Prodigal; you went about getting your blessing or what you thought was your blessing sooner than you should have received. Understanding the protection of God and His grace will help you to avoid Proverbs 6 verse 18 where God's Word says HE hates quick – swift feet that run into trouble or mischief.

I once read a story of a young lady who during a tornado took cover in a bathroom tub. The wind was described as howling like that of a ravaging wolf. Her husband joined her in the tub and covered her with his body to protect her. HE took every blow and hit of the wind and the falling debris. She lived but unfortunately, her husband died as a result of internal injuries from the outward blows he took on her behalf. She was quoted as saying, "On my worst day; even now years later, I know that in the storm I was (am) loved." I share this to encourage and tell you that on your worst day, in the most horrific, difficult, and trying storms and times, God is with you, covering, and protecting you. No matter how long the wait or the circumstance that brought on the wait, you are loved. God is not only with you HE is for you.

Sometime ago, I had these questions and others. "Why am I still here? What am I doing wrong? Why do things seem to not be happening for me like it is for others? Why have I not been able to consistently move forward?" I posed these questions to my Pastor. With great wisdom and patience he addressed my concerns. "Those are good questions...Have you gotten an answer..." 'No, sir'. "Ok, may I suggest that it may simply be that it is just not (your) time yet...?" Light bulbs exploding and tears flowing; I know...I am always crying about something, the reality hit me. Anytime God chooses to reveal or speak clearly to me, I am grateful. I stand it awe at His providence, sovereignty, and love. These divine encounters tell me that HE loves me; HE really does hear and know. I thirst for these moments and am always satisfied, encouraged, and strengthen when they occur. All of these experiences were not and are not wonderful starting out, but they always end with me standing in awe of Him.

I had been beating myself up; literally, for years over what was wrong with me, why not me yet, etc. And in this case, the answer lied in the timing of God. I continued in my prayers of asking God to make me whole. Give me clean hands and a pure heart, make me more like you. That day I added, "God give me peace and patience to trust You, and to know Your timing. Teach me to wait and to wait right." I can hear the Father even now saying, "Tuesday do you love ME – can you – are you willing to trust Me with your life – to wait on ME – My timing – do you believe that

I have a plan for You and I know what is best for you…" And again today I say, "Yes, Lord…I trust you."

As time went on in this waiting season, this internal dialogue continued. A challenging thought began to plague me. Did I truly, truly trust God: my Creator, my Father…Had I truly made Him LORD over my life - every part of my life? I had to be honest with myself concerning God…I did not completely trust God. I had not totally surrendered my life to Him. My mantra became, "Lord, teach me to trust you. Help me to trust you without question or hesitation. I command my soul and my innermost being to trust the LORD…I trust you LORD." With honesty and self reflection, in time I got pass my pity party. However, there were other questions that I began to talk to God about. These were self examining freeing questions. I pose these questions to you for your awareness, examination, and consideration. Some were hard questions, but they had to be considered. I had to tell myself the truth about how I really felt about where I was and why (I was there and if) God had me there. Overtime, being truthful with me and about me became an internal healing that brought peace. A rest came that I cannot explain. I would describe it as a purging and cleansing. Where I am in my life today, I can sincerely say, "I trust God with and believe Him for all things for my life." HE has shown Himself strong and mighty time and time again in my life. HE has proven Himself to be faithful and trustworthy. Even though there are things I am still waiting on and have yet to receive, I still trust and believe God.

There is something about moving beyond trusting in Him as Savior to trusting in Him as Lord. This or maybe the combination of both produced in me a peace and confidence that goes past understanding. So evident that people often acknowledge it. There have been times of such trust and peace in God that at times it made others uncomfortable or they have confused it with complacency. Somewhere – somehow the pain of waiting subsided.

Consider these questions. Pause, think about it, and answer each honestly and truthfully.

1   Why am I so restless – frustrated
2   Do I operate in pride, control, selfishness or fear
3   What am I waiting on – is it God or man
4   Who am I trying to please – myself, God or others
5   Am I waiting on God or is God waiting on me
6   Is there sin in my life (omission or co-mission) that is delaying my release – my blessing(s)
7   Am I ready - mature enough for my waiting to end to receive
8   Have I learned what I should have learned
9   Can my character sustain and maintain the blessings that God has in store for me on the other side of this
10 What do I need God to do that only HE can do
11 What can I – should I be doing while I am waiting on God
12 Have I delayed my release - my blessing
13 Have I interfered with God, while trying to do it my way
14 Am I still the master - lord and captain of my ship (life)
15 Why do I really want what I want - for man to admire or God's kingdom to advance
16 Am I submitted under someone's mature leadership
17 Am I accountable to mature spiritual leadership – am I truthful and honest with them

Job said in Chapter 14, no matter how long it takes or seems to take, I am going to wait until my change comes. To you I say, 'no matter how uncomfortable it may become – wait patiently, passionately, and expectantly on GOD'. No matter how tired you get, remember the Word of the LORD, and His promises concerning you and your life. HE has promised and HE will do. I know it seems like you have been waiting forever and you probably have, but wait on the Lord anyhow. Remembering that to Him a day is like a thousand and a thousand is like a day. Again, I say, and encourage you to wait. HE will come and strengthen your heart, and with Him will be your reward.

When surveying the focus group, 69% stated that there is something in their lives from physical, to financial, to emotional, or relational that they have been waiting on God to do. Some have waited for years for it to turn around or for change to come. The longer the wait, the more our hearts ache at the very thought of facing another day – another moment of waiting and being in this situation. The prayers and conversations with the Father becomes 'when Lord...when – get me out of this wilderness – this holding cell – this waiting place – I am tired'. Like you, I wondered if there would ever be a time when waiting would wander-off and I would never have to wait again. I searched for a hope. Is it possible to experience life without waiting? Where every desire is fulfilled and every need is met without having to wait? And guess what, I found it. It's called eternal life in heaven with God and our Savior. Until we leave this earth, we will experience waiting times and seasons. There is no escaping waiting, but you can escape the pain of it. Even though God may not bring you out when you want; resting and trusting in Him, reading and meditating on His Word, believing and receiving His love for you; waiting can become a good thing, a hiding place, a safe place, a way of escape.

Issue of Done

On the Cross Jesus said, "It is finished" and in Heaven God said, "It is done." Beloved, God does not want you half-baked. HE wants to you done. Even when you are at a restaurant with or without a reservation; if your table isn't ready or all the guests are not there, they will make you wait until the place is ready to receive you. Though you may be ready, the place where you are going or others that are to be a part may not be ready. One of the things that cause us to be undone and not whole is our lack of patience. Anxiousness and impatience weakens you and allows you to be tossed by every wind and doctrine. Waiting can make you unstable. Don't get imbalanced or unstable in your waiting place. Not only do we not know how to wait right; we do not want to wait. The truth is; in God we are finished and done. Yet, we are challenged to live in or from the finished place. We live half-done or undone. We have enough half-done – half-baked Christians. Choose to be one who has a testimony of being healed, done, and on your way to wholeness. God desires to perfect (make well, whole, mature) everything that concerns you; including you (Psalm 138:8). I'm sure you concern you the most. I'm sure you concern you the most.

So what is a half-done – half-baked Christians? They are those who waiver between opinions and are lukewarm for Christ. Half-baked Christians are too impatient to let God finish His work in them. They have quick feet and tongues that get them into trouble. They have one foot in the Kingdom (Church) and the other (or both) still in the world. Drinking, partying, cursing, lying, stealing, cheating, abusing, fornicating, homosexuality, fighting, hurting, mean spirited, never taking responsibility, blaming, offending, adultery and alike. This is not the occasional mistake, mishap, slip and fall, but a life of daily practicing sin without conviction, shame or a desire to change. Godly sorrow that brings about repent evades them. They have a form of godliness; denying the power that is in and or available to them. Their pursuit is more of the world's way of doing things than God's way and will. Often their drive is more for approval. Their goal is to be blessed than to be a blessing to others and the Kingdom. They want more money, opportunity, status for themselves to impress others or out do another. Hosea chapter 7, verse 8 says, *"Ephraim mixes with other nations. Ephraim, you are like a half-baked loaf of bread."* Half-baked because they rushed out of the processing of their waiting place and did not get rooted, authenticated, fully baked, finished, and done. They did not complete the process. Their patience was not perfected.

They were not interested in fulfilling the assignment or passing the trust and belief test. Half-baked – half-done Christians continuously murmur, complain, and worry in their waiting place. They rule in competition with God and often with man. What does that look or rather sound like: I want, I need, I will, I can't let them get ahead of me, etc. Sound familiar? They sing the song "I did (I will do) it my way." All the while, oblivious that they are delaying their process. They have not died to self yet. They still are the head of their life. Jesus is their Savior, but HE is not their Lord.

They often have a humble stance, look, and voice but, inside they are still all about themselves. They have not and do not seek The Power of God to change them. They may think they don't need to change. If change is needed, they foolishly and pridefully believe they can do it on their own. They see the issue; their issues as everyone else's problem. They are full of pride and tapering with arrogance. Only scratching the surface and never getting to the root of self. They still think themselves worthy to be compared. True humility or even the seeking of such is not deemed as necessary. Often they speak highly of themselves in pride spouting their excellence, aptitude, and ability. They will compromise for self gain and will pull others into their choices, lusts, and drama. They may even speak of their issues but expect others to just accept them as they are in the name of love, relationship, pity, a bad childhood, etc. The undone half-baked person has (created) their own life support systems. They do this just in-case God is wrong, taking too long, or miss the mark. They have not learned to wait, nor are they willing to wait. They run ahead of God and soon find trouble. Outwardly, in the presence of others; confidence is present in certain areas of their life, while fear is their inward struggle and blocker. Your waiting place is ideal for our perfecting and the finishing work. It is ideal for taking you from pride, selfishness, and fear to humility, surrender, and authentic love.

During extended periods of waiting, you may be tempted to bring other non-Jesus sources into your waiting place. Half-baked Christians mix the principles, doctrines, and the truths of God with concepts, confusion, and half-truths of the world. Trying to create a whole thought, view, relationship, world; they seek half-truths and concepts. They have forgotten or maybe never knew that truth and wholeness are found in Jesus Christ; the Savior of the whole world. Just a reminder: a half-truth or a partial truth is still a lie? For them there is not yet a true reverence of or surrender to the Almighty God. They are not convinced or sold on the fact that HE is their source and resource. They lean to their own or some other sources understanding. But let me help you, God doesn't need help from psychics, motivational speakers, higher power followers, wacky wavering talk show hosts, alternative religions, or half-baked religious leaders to state or present His truth for Him. He is the Creator of all things including them. I think His got it.

I know this might shock a few of you, but I don't like gumbo. Why you ask? See my mind cannot wrap its self around land (vegetables), sea (fish), air (birds), and the beast of the field (cow) all being in the same pot in a red juice. I am told it is a wonderful delicacy by those who love it, but I just can't mix all these foods together. I discovered that I pretty much take the same approach with both natural and spiritual things.

Confessions of a Prophet…I too at one time was half-baked. I was not a "babe" in Christ. I was a little further along than an "immature" Christian. I was no longer on water or milk. I was on the meat of the Word but still undone, half-baked, struggling, taking longer than "I thought" it should be chew, digest, and apply the Word. I learned a great deal about me. I believed in God, but I did not believe and trust God completely. I had not made Him Lord; trusting in, being confident of His love, His ability, and desire to do the perfecting work in and for me. HE was and is my Savior but I had not made Him Lord. I had not made or allowed Him to be my first and key source and resource of my life. HE was not the control of me. I was still under the influence of self – of me – of Tuesday. Romans 7 verses 7 through 24 was where I lived. It is where all half-baked, unfinished, prideful, struggling, self-consumed, knowing right, but not doing right Christians live. But thank God for verse 25 and Romans 8; the saving grace of truth for the half-baked.

I lived for months, years in Romans 7 and 8. I was desperate to be free from verses seven through twenty-four – to be healed and whole. No matter how much I wanted to be whole; without sin or struggles, it required that I let God, His Word, and the Holy Spirit work in and through me. I no longer had to be hard on me and beat myself up and neither do you. Revelation…You cannot change you…This is the work and responsibility of the Holy Spirit. Some of our stress is placed on us because we do not or understand that everything we are faced with or struggle with was carried to and kept on the Cross with Christ. When Jesus said, "It is Finished" and God said, "It is Done", they meant that. To walk in the truth and victory of your freedom and deliverance, you must make yourself available, seek Him in prayer, HIs Word, and counsel if desired or needed. There is no perfect (without fault) Christian. We are all works in progress. Daily; prayerfully, seeking and desiring to become more and more like Christ.

Our waiting place(s) and season(s) are constructed to push and thrust us to and into God. It provides a safe place for the finished and done to be produced. Though we all have, can, and quite possibly will find ourselves in Romans 7, the distinction between those settling for a Christian life of being half-done and that of a maturing believer; on their way to wholeness, is that they recognize their weaknesses, insecurities, fears, challenges, issues, strongholds, and inability to do it on their own. They take responsibility and turn to God to help them do the work of change. They seek Him with all due diligence to change them. As a Christian, a believer; our salvation and eternal life, comes in and through Jesus Christ. It is not about religion, it is about relationship; a point that many (Christians and non-Christians) miss.

A half-baked Christian is different than a new Christian or a babe in Christ. The new believer has not had time to grow, learn, or experience God for themselves. The half-done Christian has been in the fire and did not learn. They have loss after loss but can only see this mistakes and wrongs of the others. They have encountered numerous failures and saves but give mixed praise. They surmise that what happens to or for them that may be good is because they deserve it despite their bad, ungodly, unrepented actions and behavior. Their "thank you Jesus" is for show and not to bring or give glory to God. They secretly believe their skills, talents, abilities, and efforts have achieved for them what they have. The half-baked Christian mistreats, mishandles, disrespects, and dishonors the things, people of God and His Word. Their reasons are really excused disguised to gain pity and deflect responsibility. They mix God with good and call it a blessing. They might be found saying that good luck or good fortune from the universe (some unknown entity) has lined up to bring all "good" things to pass.

I heard a story of a very popular comedian celebrity who was raised in church. Starting out in his early twenties, his mother (a faithful believer) agreed to support him for a year. About six months in his mom had not sent the money for rent. He called several times over a couple of months and asked her if (when) she had sent the money. She would ask him if he had read his Bible. No mom was his answer. I believe one time he told her yes. She asked him what he got from what he read. He confessed he had not read it. She said when you sit down and open your Word call me. With an eviction notice on the door, he finally did what she asked…and six individual checks for the remainder of the year fell out. His mother told him, your answer or need is always found in the Word of God. The same truth I submit to you. Now as he said, he was not an "overly religious" person (not sure what that means when people say that), but may I submit the moral to the story…Our answer or need is always found in the Word of God.

HE alone is truth because HE is Truth. HE is the way, truth, and life. HE is wisdom. HE is peace. HE is love. HE is joy. It is the wisdom that comes by the perfecting of patience through the testing of our faith in the waiting seasons that causes us to reverence and appreciate God. It is through this process we can be made whole when we surrender to the already finished and done work of God in heaven before the foundations of the world and Jesus on Calvary. It is His truth that takes us from half-baked, undone to finished and done.

Though some who teach their philosophies may provide "good information" and enjoyment, if their foundation is not Christ and the Word of God uncompromised, the things they say may cause you; if you are not grounded in Christ and The Word, to waiver. You may find yourself starting to question the truth, purpose and existence of God and Jesus; as well as what you believe, and your faith in them. As a believer in Jesus Christ, in your waiting you must guard your heart and mind and know that God is God and Jesus is still Lord and your help, hope, and answers are still found in them. Learning to wait patiently is waiting right. It will mature and humble you. Hearing, "no, not yet, wait" will drive you to seek God. You will learn to persevere and endure. You will add to your faith and be made strong. Beloved, let patience have its' perfect work that you can be complete, mature, and lack nothing (James 1:4).

In your waiting seasons, if you are half-done or full-baked, watch out for entering into relationships (court-ships, business deals, friendships, partnership, and definitely marriage) with another half-done Christians. I guess that should be period. There is great danger of joining, partnering with or following a half-baked, half-done person or leader. Whether appointed, called, or titled, it doesn't matter – half-baked is not done – not ready to be served or given to others. It might be pretty and smell good, but it is not ready. When it is cut into or shaken, it will probably fall apart. Have you ever bit into or come into contact with something that looked done; pretty, fine, good or tasty on the outside, but it was not done on the inside…Nasty? The fire; the heat that is needed to cook it all the way through was somehow interrupted or was not enough to finish the process.

I have wondered if God is more challenged by the half-baked Christian who takes on position, title and authority, serving and leading with their prideful controlling selfish undone ways with a form of godliness or more challenged with the straight sinner who is not trying to pretend to be anything other than what they are or the unbeliever who comes with a sincere heart knowing they are undone and need help. As I consider this thought, I am reminded that "half baked" is like being lukewarm and HE has said, "HE will spit you out."

As an ex-half-baked Christian and still being perfected for His good work, I have been put back in or I put myself back in the heat of the fire on a few occasions. The joy comes when the timer goes off. Someone yells, "It is finished" or asked, "Is it done?" Yeah, eating the batter from the bowl or off the spoon is good, but that finished and done iced cake is what all the fuss and waiting was about. It has to sit and cool for consistency and to become solid. Though all needed components are there; if it has not come together or settled and you cut it too soon, it will fall apart. Then the icing is placed on it. After these last steps or "little something" are applied, it is declared done. For many, most, all of us, God is still doing a little something in us that will be evident to all when we are presented done. The Bible says we will be presented faultless before the Father.

That cake can be leaning over, uneven, not perfect but because you know who made it and their reputation for good cake making and it is ready to serve; we receive it anyhow and eat it happily. God not only wants us good on the inside and look good on the outside but taste good to others. It is the mixing, blending, beating, and pouring of all the right ingredients; some salty, some sweet, some without taste, some we do not always knowing the purpose of but they are all necessary for the final finished product to come together and later be declared done. HE wants to present you to others for His good pleasure. It is God who created you to do good works (Ephesians 1, Philippians 2). Like that cake, we must go through the process. How you act, react, relate, respond, and deal with yourself, God and others during your time of waiting will impact when, how, and if you receive your promise and your release from the waiting place on time or even early. An on time, set-time of deliverance is according to the will and plan of God, but it can be impacted and influenced by our decisions and ability to wait right and to wait patiently upon the Lord.

As you read and have read this; God may have begun to speak to you, do not resist His truth. His love for you extends past you being half-done. HE simply desires for you to recognize, request, and react by you doing your part, and rest in the internal and perfect work of the Holy Spirit. The Holy Spirit does not come to condemn and castrate, but to reveal, teach, convict, and conform our will to His. HE comes to lead us into all truth. Do not unnecessarily be hard on yourself. By all means, please take off the old man and put on the new. You are not that person anymore. Even though you still may have some of the old man tendencies, habits, struggles a as leader, member, Christian, a person in general; know that God still has a purpose and a plan for you. Yet, we are not to go on sinning so that God has to keep extending His grace. Get a hunger for His righteousness and HE will make it so. In God's eyes you are already finished and done. HE simply desires that you workout your salvation and let Him perfect you so you will be mature and lack nothing. No matter how long it takes, surrender to it. One day, you will look up and back and what you use to do – how you use to act, think, and be you will not do or be anymore.

Remember God is not confined to time. Though we wait here in the earth and the clock is ticking away, the truth is what we are waiting on is already done. Jesus said, "It is finished and God said it is done!" What part of that do we not get? This is why we do not have to grow weary in our well doing. Whether on this side of glory, in glory, or your generations receive it after you have gone on to glory, you are destined to reap and win. That may mean that what you believe, trust, and are waiting on God for has to die or you have to die to it for it to be resurrected and received. Sometimes we have to let go and truly surrender and submit to God's will to receive His promise(s). John 12 verse 24 reminds us that unless a seed falls to the ground (is planted) and dies, it will remain alone but if it dies it will produce much fruit. I know this is a hard pill to take-in let alone swallow, but a necessary revelation and truth for us to hear and accept. There is a dying to you, your will, your way, what you think, and your plans. Please know that you accepting and receiving His will and plan for you and your life will always produce more than yours ever can or will.

If you leave your waiting place incomplete - undone, you will not be ready to receive what HE has for you on the other side of your through. God wants to prepare you that HE may present you faultless; not perfect but mature, ready for your big reveal. Stand still to know and trust that God is God and HE knows what is best for you. HE is bringing your blessing – your answer "there" to that place. Stay put. Do not allow impatience to get you out of place. Stop being a moving target and stand still. You keep moving in your anxiousness, worry, fear, and frustration (impatience). Sit or stand still and watch the salvation and victory of the Lord. Do not delay or miss what God has for you. HE has a set time for your deliverance, breakthrough, your freedom – your promised blessing(s). Wait on the Lord and trust Him. You will not be put to shame.

My life journeys with God (pilgrimages) have taught me how to wait right in and upon Him and the process. No matter the state (or line, situation) I am in, I have learned to wait patiently and yet learning to be content. We must accept that impatience gets us nowhere; except maybe in a line that we find ourselves waiting again. This causes us to become even more annoyed and impatient. Choose to practice living a life of peace and waiting patiently. You will get closer to living in the rest of "It is finished – It is done."

Issue of Movement

In the waiting place; we wait often feeling stuck, because there is no actual forward movement. Taking steps, but we are not really going anywhere. It reminds me of why I do not like treadmills. You are walking, running, moving, but going nowhere. This type of movement challenges my creative existence. God is a progressive God. HE is forward moving. HE instructs us to go ye therefore. It was in one of my seasons of waiting place that a question came to me. Is it possible to be in a state of waiting while moving? The Holy Spirit responded with this answer, "Movement encompasses change. Change in position, location or status. Movement starts in your mind. You can move forward in your thinking while waiting and being in the same place and space." There is always something to gain or glean in and from waiting. I began to ask God to change my mind about my waiting place. For Him to make me – cause me to see and know what HE has for me in this place. I became hungry to understand why I was in this place and or why it was taking me so long to transition out of it. I soon understood the nagging truth; confirmed again that trusting God was my issue. Knowing His timing, accepting how I got there, and recognizing who was really waiting on whom was the key to my getting out what HE wanted me to learn and know and eventually my coming out. I still do not favor treadmills or stationary bikes for that matter. However, a good brisk walk around an indoor or outdoor track is always a good day in life and in the waiting place to help me clear my head, hear, and listen for and to God. Change your mind about waiting and you will experience movement and advancement.

Issue of Trust

Why is waiting so darn difficult? Let me help you. We make it difficult because we get in the way. Most often we are not waiting on God, HE is waiting on us. It is not just about the waiting, but how we wait. It is the condition of our heart and mind before we go into the waiting place and while we are in the wait that is key. It is the truth of our relationship and revelation of God that we have before we enter into our season of waiting that will help us in our waiting. Would God call you "good ground" prior to you entering your waiting place? Will you allow Him to make you good ground while you are in your waiting place? Ultimately, HE desires that you come out as good ground ready and able to produce good fruit? Again, depending on the state of your heart as you go in, while you are in, and once you come out will determine how long your waiting season and what awaits you on the other side of wait. We must be honest about the condition of our heart and allow the seed; the engrafted Word of God to heal us. When we truly understand and recognize who Jesus really is; the Word made flesh, the wait becomes less difficult. In David Timm's book "Scared Waiting" he states that, "Waiting has and will always involve and requires both presence and service. It is more of a state of the heart than activity. Waiting on God means adopting a posture of attentiveness to Him."

It is difficult because of the dichotomy I mentioned a few pages back: our trust of Him is limited and conditional. I once asked a friend, "Can you love someone you don't trust?" They said, "Sure, spouses and parents do it every day." Sad thought, but true. The thought continued with this follow-up question, "Is that love or tolerance?" I discovered that this is often how we approach trusting God. Sure, we love Him as long as HE doesn't fail us. Notice, I did not say, "HE doesn't fail", because it is impossible for Him to fail. As long HE does what we want, when, and how we want it, we trust Him and love Him more. We sing songs about Him. But where are the songs that say, 'I love you more today, even though I didn't get my way yesterday.' I'm sure they are out there somewhere. To live a life of complete radical trust of and in God should become desire.

Trusting is a challenge in the waiting place because it is hard when you cannot see a way out, or you do not know when release will come. Waiting and trusting becomes more difficult as time passes. Often alone in the wait, you are forced to face the reality of your situation daily and waiting on God becomes more difficult. Particularly, if your waiting has been a prolonged period of time.

It is when we come to a place of trust and understanding that waiting and waiting right becomes easier and you can be at rest.

When it is designed by God, waiting has a purpose God is not punishing you by making or causing you to wait. HE does not want us to grow weary in our well doing (of waiting). There is a due season that belongs to and shall come to you if you do not give up or give in. David said in Psalm 23, *"The Lord is my shepherd I shall not want (I shall not have any worry or unmet need or desire) – HE maketh me lie down (HE makes me to be still - to wait.)"* Beloved, there is a waiting on God and in Him that will give and bring Him glory. It is His good pleasure to bring you through and out of your waiting place. HE desires for you to see and receive your expected end and manifest His glory. There is a way to wait without the weights of waiting consuming you. Ecclesiastes 8 states, *"For there is a proper time and procedure for every matter, though a man's misery weighs heavily upon him."* HE gives us a clear understanding that HE knows there is a weight, a heaviness, a challenge for us to wait. Consider reading this as such, "Though a man's misery weighs heavily upon him, there is a proper time and procedure for every matter."

God has a perfect plan for our process that includes a set time for us to come out. We can come through changed without scars or stench. In time, by His Word and prayer; if we let it, rest and peace will come. When we are tempted to run from our waiting place, HE gives us a way of escape from physical, mental, emotional, and spiritual devastations. It is possible to be in, go through, and come out of the fire and not smell like smoke or not look like you were ever in it. Everyone may know you have been the midst of something; "in it" (whatever your "it" is), but because you went through it right, your testimony while in it and once out of it is one of victory. You can truly say, "God is a keeper, a sustainer, a protector in the waiting place." You become an epistle read by many.

Issue of How

It is important that you recognize how you got here, or even more important who placed you here. What are you to learn or what have you learned from this place and season of waiting? What is and or was the purpose of it? Was it God or you who put you on this internal and evident quest? Was it sin or your disobedience to do or not do what God has said? Has your trying to do it your way prolonged your stay? Have you chosen to live with your man made stronghold? Was it your stubbornness, pride or arrogance that has you on this rollercoaster of standing still? Are you perpetually causing or accepting your stuck – paralyzed place? Are you being kept – held by fear behind your man made wall? A wall (a barricade – a stronghold) of confusion and believed or perceived lies about yourself that houses strange comforts, and restless torment of frustration, confusion, fear, anger, loss, hurt, and pain.

Confusion and torment come when we are racking our brain on what, why, and how to do something...our way. Instead of waiting and trusting God to reveal things to us, we often choose to learn the hard way. When we fight against the process of how and what God has done or allowed, we are making our waiting difficult. I have learned through my own challenges with waiting, that confusion and torment comes when we are racking our brain on what, why, and how to do something. Though why is important, it is often not answered or realized until you come through. It is His loving grace that answers this or any of our questions while in or on the other side of waiting. Imagine all your thoughts regarding whatever you are concerned, confused, or uncertain about colliding and becoming entangled and fused. This produces frustration and fear sets in. Perhaps this is why your sleep and rest are interrupted. Sometimes, it is not the prolonged waiting that has caused your restless. It is your inability to bring yourself and your mind into submission to God and command your soul and body to rest in Him. It is all your questions. That when you really think about it, you have no absolutely control over. Be still to seek the Lord for His plan and His will for your situation and life.

You lack focus and direction because you are trying to figure out what, why, and how to do the plan that God has designed for you. May I free you…It is His plan that HE has for you. He not only knows the what, the when, and the why, He knows the how. I once heard it said that 'how God does it ain't none of our business.' Just trust Him. But if you absolutely need to know how or the answer to any of your question's, it would behoove you to ask and wait on Him. Be still to learn, hear and obey. Rest your brain and body. Cast your cares on Him and receive His rest. Though 'why' is important, it is often not answered or realized until you come through and by then why and how won't matter.

Issue of Who

In Genesis 3, God asked Adam, "Who told you, you were…" I submit this same question to you. Who told you what you now believe about God and yourself that has put you in this place? What has caused you to continually go around and around? Then come back or be brought back to this same place. I call this the "mulberry brush ministry." Perhaps you came to your waiting place because you came into agreement with the lies of man or those implanted by the enemy through negative self talk, unresolved hurts, and unmet needs. And now, you have built your well designed, well decorated mansion of a stronghold. Was it man who has boxed you in with their ideologies? Was or is it the views and opinions of people who brought oppression by way of tradition, threats, abuse, trauma, drama, or the tempting your faith…words of defeat or impossibility? Is it the learned unhealthy behavior of your childhood? Who told you you were that…that you cannot do that? Who placed you here? Who did this to you? Who told you, 'you do'n too much' because you are purposefully using all the gifts, talents, and abilities that God has given you? Who told you can't have it all? Maybe it was you being in God's way. Maybe you did rebel against His good work in you that was for you. Because it was painful, you ran from it. Because truth challenged you and your bad behavior, wrong way of thinking and doing, you sabotaged.

Often, the issue in our waiting place is us. Often God allowing us to come back to a thing or repeat at thing or fall or fail again is God trying to get our attention. Again, delayed obedience is still disobedience. Disobedience, stubbornness, pride, fear, etc., will bring you back to or keep you in and the waiting place much longer than you desire and God intended. When you finally obey God: His instruction, His correction, His Word, you will pass go and collect your blessing. So who is really waiting on whom? Be honest, are you really waiting on God, or is God waiting on you? I encourage you to sit down and be yourself still to hear Him about you. Sometimes it is not about the other people, the problems, or your past, it is about you. HE is trying to show you you. You are the 'who'. HE is trying to get a message to you about and for you.

You will continue to face these challenges until you take responsibility for you – for your part and take your focus off of everything and everybody else. No more blaming others. Trying to keep score of their wrong, their right, their good, their bad, what they said or did not say, their opinions are an annoyance to God and so is your complaining and blaming. Let God show them them and deal with them about their wrongs. You are focusing on them when HE is trying to reach you and get you to focus on you. You are the 'who' God needs you to see. Often we are our worse nemesis. I know people say, "What God has for me is for me..." Well, only sort of. Remember the servants with the talents who waited on their master to return in Matthew 25. The one who mishandled his one talent, gift, opportunity, and time had his gift taken. It was given to the one who already had ten and had done what the master expected. When we interfere and delay what HE is trying to do in and for us, HE will make, cause, even use those very things (people and situations) to get our attention and make us to lie down to hear Him. I once heard a pastor say, "God can take you and leave the problem, leave the problem and take you or take both of you." I remind you, you have influence over your waiting season. Use it wisely.

Who did or cause this? Only you and or God know the answer to that. No matter the answer, be mindful that you must keep your hands clean and your heart pure in this place, season, and life. Remain confident and assured that God is in control. Here are a few hard questions you must ask yourself... You ready...Brace yourself... "What is causing my delay of release? Why am I not going forward? Why am I still here...stuck, believing the lies, limiting myself, my life, and God!" Remember Elijah in 1 Kings Chapter 19, who ran to the cave and waited wrong; fearful of the threats – the words of a person, Jezebel. Instead of Jezebel finding him and dealing with him, God 'found' him, and dealt with him. "Oh God, deliver us - your children from people pleasing and people fears." Ultimately, if God has not placed you in this place of waiting, and it was not the words or deeds of man...It was you!

It is you who has you stuck. Even if it was the words, lies, or deeds of man or yours; you allowed it. These things became your truth and drove you to your waiting place (a stronghold); a waiting place of no benefit or purpose. Yet, God still has a plan. I declare no guilt, no shame or condemnation; only truth, love, resolution, peace, and purpose in your waiting place and seasons. If conviction comes great. It comes to produce godly sorrow that brings about repentance; a desire to change your mind and behavior and clear your name. It produces a righteous indignation that calls truth truth and a lie a lie and a thirst to be right and do the right thing. In the final analysis, in our humanness 'who' may not matter as much as you knowing God is the Great I AM. And all that I need; in possession or person is in Him. HE is with you and for me and I win.

In my survey, overwhelmingly 96% of those surveyed indicated that God was waiting on them. God said if you love me you will obey me. Beloved, your obedience to do what God said, to wait right, to continue to do good, and keep a right attitude in your waiting place is necessary and better than your sacrifice. To not wait right is to not wait by faith, and anything not done by faith is sin (Romans 14:23). To know to do good and what is right and not do it is a sin; forgivable but a sin none the less. If you know you are "the who" – the problem, do the right thing and do something about it.

Forgive the "who" folk in your life; including yourself. So you can think, believe, see, and know differently. Wash your mind and heart with the Word of God from the lies and negative words spoken. Repent for the role you played. By this you and your mind will be changed and transformed. Seek the truth of God. Do your best to keep the peace with others, but seek first the peace of and right standing with and of God. Keep your environment – your waiting place clear of negativity. Fight for, keep, and maintain your peace. In your waiting place, be confident that HE who began a good work in you is faithful and just to complete what HE started until the coming of Christ Jesus. Be honest with yourself about yourself and your roll. No more blaming yourself or others. No more believing the lies of man; including those of your family and those who said they loved you, but mistreated you and spoke all matter of negativity and ill to and about you. In your waiting season and in life, separate and free yourself of all those who are with you but not for you. Release yourself from your past and the internal battle of your mind placed there by the enemy because of hurts, disappointments, failures, and fears. Believe and hear God and what HE has to say about you, your greatness, your future – His plans for you. Seek, no, command peace with God, of God, and from God. Let no-thing and no-one steal or frustrate your peace or your joy.

When waiting is designed by God, it has a purpose and a time frame. How can I discern if and when my waiting place; any challenge, test, problem, suffering, loss, etc., is ordained by God? Great question! Anything opposite of these being produced in your soul, spirit or life; such as frustration, worry, anxiousness, fear, doubt, etc. is not God's doing. Here are some indicators that God brought you to this waiting place:

1   Peace (rest in your soul)
2   Focus (can think and hear clearly)
3   Hope (expectation with anticipation, and trust is established)

If HE placed you there, HE has a purpose for you being there. HE has promised you in Romans 8 that, *"all things work together for good to those who love God, to those who are the called according to His purpose."* Are you in Christ? Is Christ in you? Do you love God? Do you believe and know that HE has a purpose for you? If you can answer yes to these questions; trust with all confidence that all things will work together for your good. No matter 'who' who is, His purpose for you and in you will be fulfilled in due time and due season.

Issue of Time

In passing, I once heard a quote that went something like this, "Time is a killing system with meaning attached to it." Ever heard someone say, "I'm just killing time." Basically, they mean they are wasting time. Even waiting, you don't have time to waste. You can recover and get most things back, but time is not one of them. Though waiting is predicated on time, time is not ruled by waiting. Waiting is a "killing system" that has meaning and purpose. What you are waiting on may be time sensitive, but time is not affected by waiting. Though we may be able to interrupt time (natural course of things); we in our natural and finite humanness have no power or influence to change or stop time or the timing of God. Time cannot be moved, changed, or rushed by you. It is a constant change agent that God uses to affect and accomplish change. Time is a part of what makes waiting such a difficult discipline. God created time and set it in the universe. HE has dominion over time. HE alone is not bound by it. We saw this with Mary and Jesus at the wedding when HE said My time has not yet come but God intervened and allowed Jesus to turn the water into wine. We saw it with Joshua when he prayed and God intervened and interrupted the sun from going down. And we witnessed this with Hezekiah, when he petitioned God and God stayed death for him for 15 years.

Waiting does not exist outside of time. Prior to receiving, waiting occurs. Time is the foundation or nucleus of waiting. Though time exists and will always remain, it is independent of waiting. Waiting finds its meaning and existence in time. Often we feel like waiting is our punisher and nemesis. We must resolve that as long as we live, waiting like time; whether minuet or of great magnitudes, it will always be a part of the natural movement and progression of life. Genesis 8 verse 22 says as long as the earth remains there will be seedtime and harvest. Between the time of planting the seed and harvest, there is germination. It is the process of dying to live. Only after a period of time of dormancy, does the seed (we) break forth and a new, expected, and anticipated growth and product comes forth. Like a seed planted, our human waiting process is affected by both external (environment and God) and internal (self and the Spirit) elements. What is produced is a product after its own kind. What is to come from us out of us in and from out waiting seasons, is what God has ordained.

Ecclesiastes 3 tells us that *"To everything there is a season, a time for every purpose under heaven"* and then in chapter 8 it states, *"There is a proper time and procedure for every matter."* Between these two scriptures, there are two Greek words that speak to the season and appointed time: Chronos and Kairos. These two words speak to God's infinite influence, power, and control over time. They support our desperate need to know and be in the timing and flow of God. Chronos refers to the chronological, sequential order of time or a pattern such as a season. It aligns with the set time that we discussed previously. Chronos is the time that was at the beginning of time. It is the 60 seconds in a minute, the 60 minutes in an hour, the 24 hours in a day, the number of days in the month, months in a year, and the years of your life. It is quantitative and can be measured. Meaning, the time a season occurs is set. It is Chronos.

The Old Testaments speaks continuously about our days being fulfilled and numbered. Chronos is the existence of our life and the length of our days. How time flows, what is produced or done within that season or life span is Kairos. How long you stand in a line waiting is Chronos. What you do that is purposeful, ordained and or divinely caused by God while you wait is Kairos. Kairos moments are the key, pinpointed, specific, marked moments that can never be repeated. It is the appointed time. If you saw the movie "The Perfect Storm", it is that moment; that space in time where all things line-up. Where a once in a lifetime moment would allow them to make it through the space to get back to the other side and through the storm and home safely. In the movie, unfortunately things lined-up, but not in their favor. The storm prevailed.

Kairos is the importance and quality of life, how faith, and how we use the time we have been given. Remember the "One Minute" poem...'All I have is 1 minute.' It is on purpose, strategic living. It is God moving supernaturally in and orchestrating your life; even interfering if necessary to ensure that your purpose and destiny are fulfilled. It is the time when God acts or moves (Mark 1:15). It is the clear and evident favor in and on your life that comes from God and man. It assists us in fulfilling our purpose and achieving destiny. It is not the length or number of the days of our life, but what we do with the days of our life. It is a series of favorable divine even supernatural moments of events or revelation that can extend past chronological times, order or seasons. It can literally be a moment or a longer than usual season where favor, blessings, revelation, or prosperity (wisdom, peace, joy, etc.) are specifically yours. What is most important is that you recognize the moment, season, and time and that you take every advantage of what you hear, see and experience to learn, grow, achieve and advance. It is the suddenly, expeditious, expedited, perfect quick-work moments and miracles of God. Have you ever heard someone say, "Don't miss your moment." That is Kairos. It is our time of sweat-less victories. Say it with me, "Lord, don't let me miss my moment. Make me mindful of my time, my season, and my turn."

The timing of God is divine. His timing is where your time and your season meet and favor ignites on your life making it your time and your turn. It is your due season; your appointed time. It goes beyond just living and watching time (your life) pass or the clock tick away. It is living life (your number days and years) on purpose. According to John 10, this is why Christ came; not only so that we can have life (Chronos) but have it more abundantly (and live this life on purpose). Often when I read Psalm 85 verse 10, I am reminded of Kairos where the

Scripture says, *"Love (God) and faithfulness (Christ) meet together; righteousness (Jesus) and peace (Holy Spirit) kiss each other."* It is one of those Scriptures that make you take a pause to think about what that looks like and how does that happen and what does that divine moment create in the heavens and in the earth.

Kairos is the favored time of God. So ask for favor in the (your) time of favor and ask that it remain. Kairos is all God. It is Him ruling and reigning supreme over your life. It is the God moments where you see His sovereignty and providence enacted at the same time. It is the time; the unspecified time (within time) that the destined thing; ordained by God is set to happen to, for, or through you. It is the moment it is released. It quantifies your days, so you can live a quality life. You are highly favored and blessed to produce and be a blessing. Identify, know, capture, and take full advantage of your Kairos time; your season(s) of favor. Kairos would be you in the hallway of life with a pass key to every door that has already been opened for you. It is not careless living but wise and purposeful living. You don't just live for the moment; which is self pleasure, but you live in the moment which is purpose. It is not flying by the seat of your pants, but being sensitive and purposeful of the divine moments, movement, and opportunities of God.

Don't be afraid, resist, undermine, underestimate or run from it, and please no false humility. No longer allow time to be your issue or excuse. You are cleared to go. Don't miss this (your) moment. It is God's favor from Him directly and specifically to and for you. Seize it and go get all HE has for you. Didn't HE say HE would cause men - people to bless you? Recognizing your Kairos moments and seasons is to not only expecting God do something for you at any moment, but anticipating it. Unlike Chronos, Kairos cannot be stopped by man. It is controlled and appointed by God. HE controls its start and its stop. Even when it may not look like it to you; behind the scenes it is working in your favor. Don't waste time or miss your moment. Something great and grand awaits you. Wait on the Lord. Listen to hear and to know. Obey, do what HE says, how HE says, when HE says it without delay. Your blessings are pursuing you to overtake you. They are trying to catch (up with) you. Stand still and wait. Listen to hear and get His direction. Why are you over here when God told you to be over there? Your financial breakthrough is there. Your future spouse is there. Your job or career is tied to there. Your answer is in a place called there. Go ahead. Go for it. Get to there. Don't allow fear, those strongholds of lies, past failures, unresolved issues to stop or limit you. When God comes with your reward and your release; your Kairos moment will be in full affect. No longer allow time to be your issue or excuse. You are cleared to go. Don't miss this (your) moment.

Issue of Silence

Waiting takes on many schools of thought or names: silence, stillness, meditation, and even surrender. There is waiting on God that demands our being still and silent. For some, being still and silent is surrender and could be seen as a punishment or problem. Waiting in itself is a challenge to most, but waiting in silence or being silent for any length of time would feel like an exile for many. Silence speaks in and to our conscious. Many of us do not want to hear or face what our soul is saying to us about us, our lives, our past, our choices, or others. You know those people; it might be you, who can't be or sit still long enough to see God or themselves. They are always going, moving, doing something. Sometimes what they are doing is God stuff, purposeful movement, but most often it is busy work. If we let it, silence can be contrary. It can be a sure place of safety and healing while we wait.

Silence is the condition or quality of being or keeping still or quiet in our waiting. It is the state of our soul (mind (thoughts), will and emotions) in the wait. This suggests that the quality or condition of silence is or should be seen as attractive. You can be quiet and or still, but not silent. You can have all the outward appearances of being quiet (without words) or still (without movement) but your mind and emotions are all over the place - racing. Silence encompasses both being quiet and still. It is not pouting or giving someone the silent treatment. Though this carries with it qualities as well; immaturity and an unattractive bad attitude.

The Psalmist writes in 62 verse 1 that *"My soul, waits silently (quietly) for God alone, For my expectation is from Him."* It is as if he is talking to his soul. HE doesn't say, *"My soul waits, but My soul, waits silently for God alone."* HE is celebrating that his soul has learned to submit to the right way to wait…in silence. Our soul: mind (thoughts), will, and emotions must be trained on how to wait; through our participation, as directed and guided by the Holy Spirit. When our soul waits silently on God our help, our answer, our victory comes. In your waiting season of silence, the words you speak (back) into your soul and how you direct those words is vitally important. In your season and times of waiting, your soul's peace will be imperative to how you go through and come out. The state of your soul is just as important when you come out, as it is while you are in.

Psalm 62 continues in verse 5 telling us that our expectation (hope) comes from God so why not wait and wait silently. There is purpose is waiting silent. No matter the cause or reason, we most certainly need to learn how to be still and quiet in the presence of the Lord. We cannot hear if we are always speaking. We all have heard it said, 'we have one mouth to speak and two ears to hear'. Learn to listen (so to hear) more than we speak. It reminds of the scriptures in Revelation that continues to admonish us, "He who has an ear let him hear." Learn to quiet your mind; meditation can help with this. Ask God to put a guard over your mouth; while HE is at it, put one over your mind as well.

Silent waiting can be deafening. Maybe more easily stated, "Waiting in silence can be deafening." It is in the times of God's silence that we appreciate Him and learn that we need Him, His Spirit, and His Word. We recognize that His presence – His voice is a must for us to hold on. Silence makes us ask God, "where are you" and even more "what is going on." What am I to do? Surprisingly, often your answer can be found in silence. She will speak clearly. His silence will draw you closer to Him to hear, to know, to understand. It will make you be quiet and learn a greater quality of being still and silence. It is the silence of Zacharias in John Chapter 1 that brought revelation and understanding. A study conducted by Sylvia Gunter published on a website states that "Waiting on God was one of David's secrets of being a man after God's own heart." Your season of silence (yours and God's) may very well be your protection. Why? To ensure that you not say something to overt or delay your release and progress. There may be times when God will mandate that you keep-to-yourself. Not to shut people out but keep 'it'; the promise, the prophecy, what HE has told you, what HE is doing in, through, or for you to yourself. Believe it or not, it is in this silent waiting that you will see and experience the glory. His overwhelming presence, peace, clarity, and direction can be made available to you. A fresh and new encounter awaits you in the quiet place

You can come to a place that you desire to be quiet and still. Why, because, there is nothing more or left to be said. The only words or voice you want to hear is God; Daddy God, our Father. You make a choice to wait on God in silence. During this time, you may find yourself doing a great deal of soul searching, less talking, and for me journaling is added. Your voice, your words, and opinions about what you want and think become less important. You wait to hear God speak. You pray but your prayers seem to have fewer words. In your waiting place, pray; pray without ceasing. If you have your prayer language, pray in the Holy Spirit. Allow the Spirit of God to pray through you to Him. This is extremely beneficial and will encourage your soul. If you do not have a prayer language, ask God for it. HE who gives good gifts will give to you generously.

In the Message Bible, Jude 1 verse 20 says it like this, "*But you, dear friends, carefully build yourselves up in this most holy faith by praying in the Holy Spirit, staying right at the center of God's love, keeping your arms open and outstretched, ready for the mercy of our Master, Jesus Christ. This is the unending life, the real life!*" Sounds like waiting to me. In the end, when you wait by faith with expectation; praying and believing you will be encouraged and strengthen. This time of prayer and stillness before God in your waiting can be powerful and effective.

When you can't feel Him, trace Him, or hear Him, silence can be deafening. Can you trust Him when HE is silent? Before HE has to make you, command, or force you to be still and quiet, I encourage you to submit and surrender to it. Waiting silently is not just about you not complaining. It implies our need to be still, have faith, trust, believe, and know that HE is God. HE is saying, "I got this - I got you." HE not only has that situation under control HE has you. Though it can feel like a sentence or a punishment, may I submit a thought to you, "His silence is often a testing of your trust in Him." You very well may experience Him in a different and deeper way. His silence is a teacher and trainer of trust. When you trust you have confidence. When you have confidence, you have less need to always have something to say or add. Appreciate your seasons of silence. Soon you will have plenty to say when HE releases to share your experiences with Him. Your testimony will be grand.

Interruption of Suddenly

May I share some good news with you...After you have addressed all your issues with waiting being hard, not wanting to wait, frustrated at wait or even back at waiting; God has a blessing on reserve for you. When you come to peace with and in your waiting place, there is a blessing waiting for you called "suddenly". When HE will release it? I do not know. But what I do know, it will be at the appointed – Karios time. Though time was present; Scripture bears witness of the "suddenlies" where waiting seemed to not be in the equation. It is Genesis 8 of seedtime and harvest. Note this is not seed, time, and harvest. The time is already accounted for in the process of receiving the harvest. The seed knows when it is to break-forth and manifest its' self. Suddenly, declares "at that very moment." It is the timing of God personified. The work of the farmer is to prepare the soil, plant the seed, nurture or cultivate it and wait. *Suddenly* is His timing on steroids breaking forth to declare purpose and seal destiny. *Suddenly* is the space and place between the last prayer and manifestation. It is the page turning moments of our life. It is the "and then" statements found in scripture and in your life. Our suddenly moments encompass all that happens between the prep, the planning, and producing. It is not only the chapters in our lives but the verses. It is the moment of receipt that takes you by surprise, catches you off guard, and puts you in awe. For a moment you forget that you have been waiting, asking, and believing God for the very thing you now possess.

Be mindful that long before the suddenly occurs there are behind the scenes things going on. You have prayed, others have prayed with and for you and now is the time. Now faith has manifested and produced. Over time, circumstances, and situations occur and prayers and requests go up. You have decreed (wrote the vision), declared (spoke it), fasted, and it is here. Things have lined up. Then out of what seems to be nowhere; when we least expect it, suddenly happens and due season manifests. Because you have no idea of when your suddenly will appear; it is crucial that you remain faithful over your little. Don't grow weary in doing well and in doing the right thing. Endure your hardship as a good soldier. Be steadfast (devoted and unchangeable) and work your faith. God will not; HE cannot forget your labor of love and faithfulness.

I have used this word weary many times but have not defined it. According to the Merriam-Webster dictionary; it means to lose or lack strength, energy or freshness, due to lack of rest or sleep. It implies a sense of worry, restlessness, or anxiousness. It is one thing to be weary for a moment or time, but to grow weary draws a different picture. To grow weary is to have many or frequent sleepless night, times of pacing the floor, tossing and turning, and wring of hands. The enemy's plan is for you to plant yourself in worry through weariness unto exhaustion. You go from weary to worry to frustration to fear. It is a subtle progression of oppression sent to wear you down. Literally, it is worrying yourself "sick or to death." To grow weary is a sign of one's lack of trust and faith in the God. Hold on beloved. Help is on the way. Get up. Shake yourself free of weariness, worry, anxiousness, and fear. Prepare yourself for your due and suddenly season.

In 'suddenly' there is no delay. What was not is now. They are appointed times that are pre-determined by God. They happen to fulfill Gods' will. Whether we think we are ready or not, HE decides it is time. They are a testimony for us and others that God is in control of time, timing, favor, and release. "Suddenlies" can come in the form of a blessing or a consequence of negative actions. In the case of a blessing that arrives suddenly, they appear when we have the capacity to receive them and often come in the form of what we call a miracle or favor. Ever heard anyone say or you have said, "It came out of no-where." To us it appears that way, but it really was just waiting the appointed time as designated by God to come forth. Many of us who are the recipients of "suddenlies" react as if we are surprised that God did it. We say HE can, HE is willing and able, but when HE says now and does it, we stand amazed as in unbelief. Our waiting should be in expectation and anticipation. To wait right is to wait expecting and anticipating. It signifies that you are waiting believing and trusting by faith.

"Suddenlies" often leave us in awe of His power, providence, and sovereignty. Ask God to move you into a suddenly season. That when you speak His Word – His promises over your lives that blessings will soon follow. Ask God to blow your mind, to keep you in awe of Him. And while you make this request, ask Him to teach you to wait right until suddenly happens. Ask God to put a guard; a watch over your mouth so you won't say the wrong things or negative words against yourself, life, loved ones, etc. Ask Him to teach you how to guard your heart and mind so you won't weary yourself. Watching your thoughts, feelings, and words can become a matter of life and death in your waiting place; for out of the mouth life and death are spoken. This truth still remains that so you speak is what you think and that is who and what you will become and may already be because of your thoughts and words have helped to create your condition.

Since waiting is inevitable and often necessary, there is another question that I would like to pose you: "What could or should you be doing while you await?" Many things could be listed, but the consistent answer should be these: pray, prepare (anticipate), praise, expect, and wait. Here's another thought, just as we celebrate God and the manifestation of the "suddenly" and the positives, why do we not celebrate and thank God for our waiting place? As sure as a suddenly season is a blessing, so is waiting. As sure as God coming through in the nick of time is a blessing, so is God blocking situations in the nick of time a blessing. Believe, ask, declare, expect, and thank God for not only suddenly moments but seasons; for the good, bad, and ugly. You can have an expectation that when you ask God, declare, and believe by faith it will manifest suddenly. Ask Him to teach you to wait until suddenly occurs.

Issue of Meditating

One of the words listed for waiting that intrigued me the most was meditation. Yes, one of the definitions for meditation is waiting. For the believer, it is being still, silent to listen, to hear, and know what God is saying to you, for you, about you, and others. However, due to a lack of understanding; some in "Christendom" have given meditation a bad report. It is often seen as a something associated with only eastern religion practices. The purpose of meditation in the Kingdom of God has very little to do with eastern practices as a whole. Our meditation is on God and His Word. Meditation is led by the Holy Spirit. We meditate; think upon things that are true, pure, and good (Philippians 4:8). By this we will fulfill the instructions of the Lord to know the Word (Jesus) more intimately (personally), to hide it in our hearts, and apply it to our lives. We meditate to get the heart of God and the mind of Christ.

Meditation is the quoting aloud of a truth, a promise, a scripture. We do this to not only learn the Word but also to hide it in your heart, to know it personally and to grow you by adding to your faith. You will get to a place of not just saying the Word to say it, but you believe and know it as truth for yourself. It goes past memorization (though this is good) to realization. It is to think in your mind, murmur (not complain – repeatedly speak softly the same thing) it from your mouth, believe it your heart until you see it in your mind and it manifests in the earth. Meditation is dreaming out loud. It gives you hope for your vision and purpose. It can help you know them and see your future now. It causes you to agree with God. Philippians 4 tells us *"Finally, brethren, whatsoever things are true, whatsoever things are honest, whatsoever things are just, whatsoever things are pure, whatsoever things are lovely, whatsoever things are of good report; if there be any virtue, and if there be any praise, think on these things. Those things, which ye have both learned, and received, and heard, and seen in me, do: and the God of peace shall be with you (verse 8, 9)."* I submit to you that this thinking on these things is meditation. Through meditation you are encouraged and strengthen no matter what state you are in. If there is unbelief, that will be overshadowed. As you apply the Word to your life and see God move, your faith, trust, and belief in God and His Word will grow. Ultimately, through this practice you add to and will be strengthen in your faith and your confidence in God. You will grow in wisdom and understand of God.

Meditation is a type of prayer. It is words or a prayer repeatedly spoken or murmured. In Joshua 1, God commands him and now us to always keep the Book of the Law (The Word of God) in our mouths. God goes on to instruct him to meditate in (on) the Word day and night. Here again a blessing or reward is conferred upon those who hear and obey. HE says, if you do this, your way shall be prosperous, and you will have good success (verse 8). All this is available and given to us just for mediating on the Word of God? You got to love God. Meditation is a form of active and purposeful waiting. To others when you practice meditation, you could appear to not be doing anything, but to God, you are doing the most. To others it may look strange as it was in 1 Samuel 1 when Hannah was mediating upon the promise of God and Samuel thought she was intoxicated.

Like contentment and waiting, meditation is a learned and necessary discipline that is not easy for most; but can be perfected with practice. Richard Foster defines meditation as "The ability to hear God's voice and obey His Word." It is when you find yourself lying in or sitting on the side of the bed, waiting. Waiting on what; you may not know, but you have learned to be still and wait quietly to be silent to hear. That is the start of meditation. Think of a Word and softly say it repeatedly. Allow your heart and mind to feel and see it, and hear God if HE chooses to speak or simply bring you peace or comfort. Psalm 4 speaks directly to this *"Meditate within your heart on your bed, and be still."* Meditation is a discipline required on both sides of silence: when you are called to be silent and when God appears to be or HE really is silent.

Meditation Exercise

You will need a pad and a pen. Place yourself in a quiet space. A place without interruption or distraction. If possible, let this time be without children, spouse, TV or phone. It could be your car, bathroom, a park, a garage, etc. Take a moment to still yourself. You must be intentional about this time of quietness to meditate to hear. Now, think of a scripture from your memory or heart or just open your Bible to a Psalm. Read it to yourself silently first. Now read it aloud. Take a moment to think about the scripture. Say it aloud softly; again and again. Now quiet yourself again. Be still and quiet yourself to hear what the Lord is speaking to you. How does the scripture relate to you, your life (past, present or future), and your situation? What is HE saying to you? What is your heart feeling? Write down what you heard, felt, how it speaks to you. Whether good, great, a not so good truth or realization of you; agree (out loud) with what you believe you heard in your spirit by the Spirit. Give thanks for what you have heard and received. As you go throughout the day, meditate; think on these things you just heard, saw, and felt. Disclaimer: This can get good to you. It can become an addictive food and medicine for your soul and spirit. You may have to set a timer to make sure you are not late for and too everything. Why would I say this? This has been me.

Beloved, you have just meditated, prayed, visualized, and spoke into your future. You should feel encouraged and strengthen by the Word and what you heard internally. Throughout the day, purpose yourself to reflect on that Word and what you heard. Allow it to speak to your heart and encourage and strengthen you. Meditation will change and transform you as the Word renews and conforms your mind to the mind of Christ and your heart (character, nature) to the heart of God. It is a very efficient and powerfully effective exercise that makes us more and more like Christ. Starting out, you may only be able to do this for 5 or 10 minutes before your mind wanders but start somewhere and stick to it. It is said that it takes 40 consistent days/attempts doing a thing to produce a new habit (good or bad). Over time you will be able to increase your meditation length and do it almost anywhere.

Psalm 1 encourages us again in the reward of meditation *"Blessed is the one who does not walk in step with the wicked or stand in the way that sinners take or sit in the company of mockers, but whose delight is in the law of the LORD, and who meditates on his law day and night. That person is like a tree planted by streams of water, which yields its fruit in season and whose leaf does not wither—whatever they do prospers"* (verse 1-3). The blessings for the Children of God that comes simply through meditation and other acts of obedience are clear. I have discovered that the practice of being still, silent, and meditating on the Word brings an assurance. The answers to the what, where, how and sometime even why are found in our silence and meditation. Through the practice of meditating while waiting, we get instruction from the Lord. We get downloads. Earnest meditation can bring a peace that surpasses understanding no matter the situation. It will develop and mature you in your relationship with God the Father, Jesus as Savior and Lord, and the Holy Spirit. With clear instruction and direction, meditation will order you steps.

Manifestation of Meditation

I recall a season of actively waiting on God to hear and know what to do. I found myself after only two years into establishing my business as an independent consultant that I started to lose my passion. I chalked it up to the process of growing pass the excitement of the 5-month win of earning my car and becoming a director to now maintaining the run. Should I continue in this? Should I keep operating my own Mary Kay business where I had found such great success and pleasure in helping other women get their win? Am I to go back to working for someone else or focus on the ministry and vision God gave me?

The uncomfortable draw to step away became even more heighten as my team began to wean off. In a short time, the majority of them completely stopped working their business. And though my encouragement and training of my team remained at optimum and my personal sales and recruitment continued, I was unable to shake what I was feeling. It was a similar feeling I had in my transition from Corporate America. I loved the business, organization, the people I had met, my team, and the opportunity it gave women of all ages, races, and economic status. As a Christian based organization, it allowed me to do Jesus and offered an even playing field for all who entered. Why was a feeling this way? I had to move pass what people would think, who I would disappoint, where, and how I would get another car and income. Lord help. I needed to hear from God. I purposely set aside time daily for pray, to sit, be still, and to meditate. This went on for weeks. All the while, I continue to operate my business. My prayer became, "Lord what would you have for me to do, speak to me as if I was a child, make it clear to me, Your will be done, I trust You and believe You Lord, I know You will provide."

I did not want to receive what God was saying. It took about 3-months; probably more before I obeyed. Yet, it – HE was clear..."minimize your business, send the car back, and be still." No matter how much I wanted to keep it going, I could not. I obeyed and finally surrendered. I remember journaling one night hearing the Spirit of the Lord say, "No fear, your time is coming." Such a peace and joy came over me. Three months later, I began a temporary job. Within three months of starting, I applied to graduate school. It was the income from this job that allowed me to pay for school. I completed my Masters degree. Nine months into the job and three months into school, I was asked by the president of a local 40+ year old organization to join the company. It was through this assignment that I was able to pay for continued schooling and went on to earn my Doctorate degree. This is just one testimony of how meditation and waiting on the Lord brought me the answer and the peace I needed.

I believe that in some way, God by His Spirit is always speaking through people, His Word, signs, patterns, nature, gentle whispers, and nudges. But because of distractions, frustration, impatience, busyness, etc., we miss it and Him. Even His silence speaks. HE has given you a promise that is for now and eternity. You must know that you know that HE is God and HE will never leave or forsake you and HE has a plan for you. That plan will be fulfill... *"Even when I Am silent, I am still with you says the LORD."* Mediation will bring this confident assurance that we call faith.

WHAT I LEARNED

My issue is the how and all the stuff that follows how. God, how do I do this, how do I get it all done, what do I do, where do I go? The waiting to hear the how and waiting to hear the answer is a bit challenging. I know that God is ok with me asking questions. The issue is the motive behind my questions – I don't presume to know – so I ask my Creator and life manager – what's next – what would You have me to do – don't let me miss You or my moment(s). Make me more discerning, slow to speak and quick to listen – make me to know. Lord knows I don't want to be like the children of Israel wandering in a dry place for years when getting to my destiny that holds my purpose within the journey only had to take days.

I have learned that...

_____

_____

_____

_____

_____

_____

Scripture or Statement for Meditation

_____

My waiting issue...

_____

_____

_____

_____

_____

_____

FIVE

Waiting States

The states of waiting can hurt and bring a great deal of uncertainty and questions. Though I advocate inward and outward examination of self and our lives, do not allow your place of between to beat you up or down. Your hallway may have nothing to do with any of things that have come to try you and bring doubt. Prolonged waiting brings agony. It hurts. Waiting hurts because we are being broken to be humbled. Since we won't humble ourselves, HE will do it for us. HE will use whatever means and ways HE has to do it (Exodus10). The Bible tells us that even Christ learned obedience (humility) through (by) the things HE suffered. Yet, even God promises us great rewards when we have come through our suffering seasons. 1 Peter 5 in verse 10 says, *"...after you have suffered a little while, God himself will restore you and make you strong, firm (solid, certain, sure), and steadfast (devoted, unchanging)."*

It is the between place. Between old and new. Lost and found. A dream and manifestation. Possibility and reality. The beginning and the end. Now and when. There is a pain that can come from waiting on the promise and His glory to be revealed in your life situations. 2 Corinthians 4 verses 17, God again provided a promise of comfort in times of suffering in *"For our light and momentary troubles are achieving for us an eternal glory that far outweighs them all…"* Our pain and suffering is often tied to things we have tried to make happen ourselves, made decision or desire and have not yet seen come to pass. It is the hope deferred. Proverbs 13, puts it like this, *"Hope deferred makes the heart sick, But when the desire comes, it is a tree of life."* The World Book Dictionary defines "deferred" as to postpone or delay, suspend, withhold, until a certain time, put off, a future time, to exempt temporarily. The pain we experience in waiting is for His glory to be revealed in and through us. It is our Lazarus longings. It takes time and pressure for glory to come forth. The good news for the Believer is that the Hope of Glory (Christ) is already in you to help you manifest and live out His glory. Consider this, even when we are hurt, broken, or bleeding; we can be treated, bandaged, and still keep moving forward. His glory shall be reveal in you and through you. You shall have and be a great testimony of what HE can, is able, and willing to do. Now is not the time to run. Be still and be encouraged. Hold on. You are closer than you think. In your waiting place, keep moving forward purposefully. Don't lie down and drown or die in your pain, your hurt, your suffering, your disappointment or your loneliness. Avoid, turn from; no, run from anger, frustration, and unwise rash choices and counsel.

Langston Hughes, the Harlem Renaissance African American Poet wrote this often quoted poem, "A Dream Deferred",

What happens to a dream deferred?

Does it dry up
like a raisin in the sun?
Or fester like a sore--
And then run?
Does it stink like rotten meat?
Or crust and sugar over--
like a syrupy sweet?

Maybe it just sags
like a heavy load.

Or does it explode?

How timeless is this poem. Written over 100 years ago, it still speaks. No matter a person's walk of life, these words will ring true. It was penned for anyone who has found them self waiting and feeling their dream has been held-up or delay. Unrealized and unfulfilled dreams hurt. Waiting to hear, to see, to know can hurt. The things in our lives that have been deferred not only can hurt but break, frustrate, and humble us. The longer the wait, the more our faith is tested and hope escapes us. When life is delayed it can hurt. When loss comes in, from, or due to the wait; pain comes. The pregnancy that has been deferred hurts. A healing (seemingly) withheld hurts. Matrimony has come for your friends but not yet for you that hurts. The call for job, from the bank, for the bid, the date; all the thing we have waited on that never or have not yet come hurts.

I liken the stages of waiting to a pilgrimage; a holy God ordained journey. Though a journey may have a purpose, a pilgrimage is a process set and sent by God. Anything other than this for a believer is just a walk. On your pilgrimage, you may feel like everything is taking way to long. It is simply the stages you will (must) encounter and go through on your holy journey. Yet, I have learned that delayed gratification can be good. There is something encouraging about waiting, trusting, sensing that what is coming is bigger, better, greater, even more amazing than what you had, what you thought you wanted or needed, what you gave up or walked away from. I'm not saying it is easy, but there is a confidence, a trust, and an assurance that comes when you stop fighting your waiting place. Receive your peace. Meditating; thinking upon your future, His will, plan, and promises for your life, reading His Word, and believing what you prayer, declaring it though you don't have it yet, all these things bring hope. It becomes real to your soul and will manifest in time. It can put a smile on your face. It has been said, 'delay does not mean denied.' I agree! What HE has for you is worth the wait. Whatever you are waiting on will be more amazing than anything you could have asked for, thought, dreamed, or imagined. Believe that your waiting has a reward. Expect the great for your wait. Don't settle and don't stop living while you wait.

Place of Between

Life's delays are found in the place of "between." I call it the "hallways" of life. The waiting times found in the hallways of life can become hope deferred. Dreams and promises that wait on the future called "an appointed time." Visualize with me you in a hallway. You see it? Is your hallway short or long? The length of the hallway you stand and wait in is determined by God. I submit to you; the longer the hallway, the greater your purpose and vision. Being between can be a horrible feeling; between jobs, between checks, between life and death…and the list goes on. Have you ever been stuck on an elevator between floors? It is not only frustrating; it can be frightening. Hanging in mid-air by a string (a cable) between this and that is nerve racking. Being in the place of between can stink. The more you wait without clarity the worse it becomes. I mean really what can you really do in a hallway except check knobs, look at the pictures, and read any signs that may be there.

Yet, even in this place of between, God not only knows the plans and thoughts the HE has for you (Jeremiah 29:11), HE also knows and declares the end and the result of matters from the beginning (Isaiah 46:9,10). Our waiting place and places of between come to show us us or show us God and sometimes in a new way. Though the hallways of life can be lonely, it is a sure and safe place. Think about when you were in elementary school and there was a tornado drill. Where did we have to go…? The hallway and assume the position to wait for the storm to pass…*on your knees, head to the floor and hands over your head.* The hallway is not only a waiting place, but great place to assume the position of surrender, prayer, and wait on the storm; the issue that brought to this place to pass. It very well maybe where God sent you to wait on Him and find safety.

Your hallway has many different doors. Doors represent opportunities. Consistent in most hallways is that the doors are closed. Some with knobs some not. Some have peepholes some do not. Some with frosted glass some not. Some are locked and others are not. Pretty doors and some not so pretty, but none you can see through to know what is on the other side. Though there are many doors representing many options; all doors (like paths) do not lead to God; nor are they for you to go through or take. Just like every good thing is not a God thing, every God thing is not your thing. What is not God and what is not for you will never lead you to Him, His will, or His purpose for your life.

Our temptation is to approach every door and test (try) every knob. The struggle is, "Do I try this one or that one…which door is my way is out...which door will take me directly to my purpose…which door is for me." The doors that you are led to open will open and will open not just for you but to you. These are your dominion doors. When your door(s) or opportunity comes and you cross that threshold and enter in; go ahead, take dominion. Walk in the authority, humility, and the favor God has given you. Your sphere of influence will be great and so might (will) be your resistance. While you wait in the "between place" – in the hallways prepare. So when you come out, you will be ready and just walk right into what God has for you. What type of work place, job, staff, co-workers, spouse, marriage, children, fiancé, wealth, bank account, health, etc. do you desire for your life? Declare it. You don't have anything else to do in the hallway. Decree it. Write it out. Make the vision plan. Your words, your decree and declarations have the power to create expectation and anticipation in your soul. That hope that was deferred becomes a hope that is now alive.

It is in the hallway where the questions, impatience, anxiety, doubt, and even boredom can arise. Frustration comes because your vision, dreams, desires, and goals have been held up - delayed. You watch others enter and go out. They pass right by or through the hallway. For them, doors seem to swing open. They have the money, the credit, the resources, the help to go forward, but there you stand; in the hallway, waiting. Does God love them more? What am I not doing right or what am I doing wrong? Is their faith stronger than yours? Do they pray more or better? Have they fasted more…but then again who can fast, pray, and believe more than you? Being in between is challenging.

Prayerfully, you are not jealous or envious of those who seem to be or are prospering. You don't want to nor are you in competition with them and we hope they are not with you. You are not angry at them and hopeful you are not mad at God. You have your vision written out. You have made your plan plain. But where are the people to help you? Though HE knows, be honest with yourself and Him. You are tired of standing, waiting, watching others go before you when you were there first. You feel like God has brought you here and left you. Doubt filled with questions ensues. Did HE forget about me – His promise? Does HE not see my service – my commitment – my worship? Does HE not hear me? You believe Him and His Word; so much so you say it, pray it, and meditate on it but what gives. HE promised to never leave me or forget about me? HE says HE has a plan for me. HE said that I would prosper as my soul prospers, so what is going on? Why am I still here? I know HE sees everything. Buy why am I still between? Why am I still waiting?

What is HE waiting on? What am I doing wrong? The answer may be nothing or it may be you.

HE knows and has heard your cry and complaints. You are trying to live right and do the right thing; not out of ritual, but genuine relationship and love for God. You desire and seek to please Him. Your motive for release and receipt are for purpose and Kingdom. So what is the problem? You find yourself asking, "What more - what else in me needs to be perfected before God rewards me; before the windows of heaven open to me?" You are a tither, a giver, and a sower. You serve. You are faithful. Questions of what is wrong with me? How much longer will I be in this place? Am I not ready? Have I not prepared? Am I not qualified for the blessing that has my name of them? Is there sin in me, my household? Am I connected to those whose life is not pleasing to you? Are there relationships that I need to end? What door have I left open for the devil that he has access? Is it the church I am? Am I struggling because they are struggling? My leadership is integral, but still, maybe...Lord I don't know. Help me. I need answers. This has gone on too long. When? Oh, I understand. I can talk about it. I have been there and it is all too real and too much. I have had all the questions. The times of waiting between a little and much; between obscurity and the notoriety, between stuck and free, between when and how, a prayer and an answer...waiting to only wait some more. Can we say, 'very challenging.'

Though these questions may come; be mindful in the between to not let them linger and cause you to grow weary. If you remain in this state, a barrage of other questions will soon follow that border unsanctioned self-accusation and assassination, and defeat. When we let our minds nurture negativity, we dismiss the timing and the sovereignty of God. If you are not careful; trust and hope will escape you and fear in the between – in the hallway will settle in and on you. If this is you, right now, let's stop and take a minute to pull down every thought that has told or is telling you that God has forgotten you, HE doesn't care, things will not change, you missed God, it will not happen for you... Replace those thoughts with the truth God and the power of His Word. Say this, *"God loves me, HE is with me, HE watches over me and His Word to perform It over my life. HE is for me – I will not fail, run, give up, or walk away from me. God is able and will do what HE has said and promised. I will wait and wait right until my change and turn comes. I trust God and His timing for me and my life. His blessing and reward for me is great. I wait with great expectation. My confidence is in Him. It will surely come to pass."*

Let me help you. Sometimes, it is not you, sin, the work of the devil, anyone else's stuff that you have attached yourself to that has brought you to this place. As I have shared, it could be God who has brought you to this waiting place, your place of between for His purpose and ultimately, His glory. Psalm 66 says, *"For you, God, tested us; you refined us like silver. You brought us into prison and laid burdens on our backs. You let people ride over our heads; we went through fire and water..."* (verses 10-12a). Yes, God did it. Maybe God was the driving force behind your between place; your hallway experience. Remember, the Bible says in Luke chapter 4 Jesus being full of the Holy Spirit was led by the Spirit of God into the wilderness, where HE was tempted for forty days by the devil. God sent Jesus to His waiting place; a dry hot (cold at night) lonely place that was without comfort and satisfaction of life. Jesus took Himself to the Garden to seek and wait on God. HE went willingly to the Cross, but God sent Him. Maybe just maybe it was God who ushered you into our places and times of between; of separation and alone time. Maybe HE has delayed your blessing and reward. Maybe what you thought was a loss was God doing a boss move. There are times that we can confuse and accuse the havocs of our life with the works and efforts of devil; when all the while it is the handy work of God.

So how do you determine this? The answer is found in verses 8, 9 and 12b of Psalm 66. The writer says, *"Praise our God, all peoples, let the sound of His praise be heard; HE has preserved our lives and kept our feet from slipping…for you brought us to a place of abundance."* If your delay, disappointments, deferred desires, hallway experiences, and hurts were the work of the devil, you would have nothing to praise God about. HE would not only let your feet slip, he would push you down and over. With him, you would not even see a wealthy place in the horizon; let alone be brought into a place of abundance. Even if your place of between was brought on or caused by any of the things previously mentioned; if you stay with and connected to God, you will have the victory and a great testimony! Peace in the midst of pressure and uncomfortable places and positions is a sure indicator that God is at the helm or at least in it, and always in control.

How long before you stop complaining, comparing, compromising, and confronting God about what you want and what you think and what you thought? 1 John 5 verse 3 says that God's teaching and lessons are not burdensome. Until you let Him have His perfect perfecting way, will, and work in you; the hallway will be your exile. Your waiting place will become your prison exile. Find a chair. Take a seat. Be quiet. Hush it up and take a big girl or big boy pill, and chill. Recall and rehearse the things HE has done in your past. Be encouraged. Rebuild and set your hope on Him. The sooner you quiet yourself (mouth and mind of negativity) to hear, reflect, and get a glimpse of His will, purpose, plan, and direction; the sooner (your) door(s) will open that no man can shut or close. These will be doors that you can freely walk through and receive what God has for you. HE knows the plans HE has for you – to prosper you, to do you NO harm, to give you a hope, and a great future.

I have experienced many hallways seasons. My finances have been in the hallway. My desire for a good, healthy, happy, godly love and marriage is in the hallway. Career choices have been in the hallway. A prolonged healings is in the hallway. Waiting on God for my moment, my time, my season, for movement; to take me, my ministry, my business, my vision to the next level can be found in my hallway. Our hallway seasons can produce a sense of uncertainty. Often the longer we find ourselves waiting; the less confident we remain. In uncertainty, we may rush and make wrong decisions or become overly cautious; fearful to make a decision. This will result in our staying in the place of between longer than God intended. It is the story of the Children Israel. Their journey should only taken 11 days but because of the condition of the hearts (fear, disobedience, complaining, doubt) of those who had experienced God in great and mighty ways; they wandered in the desert 40 years (Deuteronomy 1:2). Those all made it to see it many did not enter in. Only those under the age of 20; the ignorant, immature or less immature were granted grace and allowed to enter. No matter what state we are in God is serious about our obedience; even in the place of between.

Beloved, the issue is not so much about you opening the wrong door. It is you opening doors on your own; going ahead of or without God. It is about you going in and through it and staying on the other side after knowing, "This ain't it...I am not suppose to be here." Even sadder is the person who becomes satisfied in their hallway. They have tried some knobs and doors with no good results, so they stop trying. Then there are those who appear to be ok with their temporary place and never try any door. They are afraid; afraid of making the wrong decision and moving forward. They are afraid of leaving what has become familiar though it is clearly beneath them and uncomfortable for them; no longer what fits or what they want. God has made their stay resistible but they stay anyway. Did you know it was possible to be afraid of success and achievement, having it all, getting everything that God has said you can have and has promised you?

Yes, it is possible to afraid; lodged at between because you are afraid to go forth and advance.

Though less than what they deserve, desire or are capable of; they settle and become complacently comfortable with what was meant to be a temporary place or refuge. They get stuck in or at between; caught between loss and gain. They stopped between a failure and a "come back." They spin their wheels, pacing; walking back and forth instead of obeying God and walking out when HE says go. They are afraid to take a chance by faith and do – try something. Certainly, one of those doors is their way out, but they stay in the hallway. I call forth the boldness of Peter for you to get out. Take a risk. No more fear. I really dislike fear. It is such a tormentor. It is an enemy of purpose and destiny.

You can come out of this. You can have "it" again. You can have it all. You can get everything you lost, gave up, gave back; you can have it all again and then some. When you know that God is with you, the Holy Spirit is leading you, and Jesus; the Word is your way, truth, and light, you going forth is never a risk. You should never get satisfied with "between"; being in stuck situations and limited living. Do not settle. Though life's hallways are waiting places; this is certain, they are only (intended to be) for a season. They are intended to be momentary light afflictions. Listen, there is not a hallway from here to heaven or hell (if you want to go there) that was created to be a permanent dwelling. Hallways are not destination. Don't be your delay, your own block or offense. Get out of there. And get out of God's way with your fifty million questions, fears, etc. As critical as it is that you not be or get in a hurry in your waiting place; it is just as vital that you not become complacent or satisfied there either.

My warning to you in the hallways of life; in your waiting place: when you are facing hurt, struggling with fear, confusion, disappointment, uncertainty, lack of focus, becoming impatient, lonely, and even bored do not try to be your own counsel. Seek out those who can speak life and encourage you. Watch out for the wandering, wondering, and worrying hearts in the hallway; in your times of between. The place of between is not a place of hiding. Though we still have to make decisions in our waiting place, do not make decisions and choices in your temporary place that could negatively affect and impact you for a lifetime. Seek God for His plan and wisdom. Be careful to not build a house or monument; things permanent that were meant to be temporary in your place of between.

Our wilderness and between places are for us to learn to listen, obey, submit, and trust Him. So we won't be lost and wondering. Deuteronomy 8 verse 2 says, *"And you shall remember that the Lord your God led you all the way these forty years in the wilderness, to humble you and test you, to know what was in your heart, whether you would keep His commandments or not"*...It can't get much plainer than that. I don't think there is a better depiction or truth than what is found here. Our waiting place, wilderness season, and (sometimes) wandering and wondering times can be (are) led and ordained by God and when they are they are always for a purpose. If we let it, our place of between can bring us to our place of abundance. When we do not, we will remain lost, wandering, and wondering. Don't get comfortable and settle with the temporary and the ok. We settle and limit ourselves because of fear. Temporary and ok are not cool when God is calling you to great. You will and should never be satisfied with ok, cool, what if, and maybe. When HE has permanent, forever, and amazing for you; temporary, compromise, unclear, and uncommitted will and should challenge and frustrate you. Do not allow your hurts, disappointments, fear, and pain to cause you to make choices and decisions that will set you up for settling and situational consequences and failures. By God's grace you are still here and covered. Yet, there are still consequences that exist when we act in disobedience and do it our way. Ask God for wisdom, to remove fear and the things that have hindered and blocked you from moving forward and having all that HE has for you. Choose to obey and trust God.

Be careful not to pick up habits in your waiting place of between. Habits are tendencies or practices that are hard to give up. They can be blanket, comforts or an escape from reality. We tend to pick them up along the way and more so while we are waiting. The longer the wait, the greater the opportunity to be tempted to start or to revisit a habit. Habits are things or behaviors we would probably not have done had we not been in this place. But once picked-up, it is difficult to put down. They become practices that if we are not careful, can become a spiritual stronghold or a physical or mental dependency on a thing or a person. Watch out for soul ties in your weaken state of waiting.

Often we do not have the luxury of experiencing complete healing before we have to continue on without the promise. A broken arm is treated, bandaged, casted, and you keep going with hope – a guarantee; anticipating your healing in a certain amount of time. Protected from outside forces, in time it heals. We do not always have that luxury of a guarantee in life issues and our waiting places of between. However, we can have hope and expectation. We can be confident that we do have the Great Physician. HE heals not only physical elements but emotional, spiritual, mental, and like. All healing power belongs to Him. What I have learned through my waiting season is that our waiting place can become or be used as a healing place. If allowed, it can be a place used to ready us, strengthen, and equip us for the next. You may still be bruised and hurting, and God will call you to serve anyway, HE knows what you can handle. You will not always have the privilege to wait to be made whole before you have to move on. I had to accept that there will be times in life that I will have to keep moving forward even when it hurts. Sometimes it is an 'as you go' type of work. Ultimately,

God wants us whole and certainly to made whole in and through our waiting place. It is all for His glory and your testimony. Just make sure it is His doing and not yours. We have the privilege to participate in our healing and our being made whole. I encourage you to use this time to start and participate in your processing.

Whether your struggle with and in your waiting place is emotional, psychological, or physical; while you wait to receive the promise, keep moving forward. Notice I said, forward. You and I have seen people; us included, who have movement, but they are not going anywhere or they are going backwards. Sometimes what they call forward is really wheels turning. They are stuck in between suffering from loss, stuck in the past, making excuses, blaming, hurting, hiding, and disappointing. Any issue left unresolved, you will repeat and relive. It will become a struggle and a blocker. When suppressed, it will bring self-inflicted suffering (torment). Take comfort in God's Word. HE has promised to draw near to the broken, confused, anxious, worried, and the hurting. His Word declares that those who sow in tears we will reap in joy (Psalm 126:5). Practice guarding and protecting your heart, your promises, and your purpose in the waiting place. In Psalm 42 verse 9-11, in David's dismay, disappointment, distress, he had to encourage himself and tell his soul to hope in and praise God. As hard as it may be, praise, celebrate, and enjoy your life...Yes, even in your place of waiting place of between. Have fun. Enjoy the journey. You may be there a while. Do your part, and let God, watch God do His perfect work in and for you.

It is here that I must speak to a truth that many do not want to address. Often we remain in the waiting place, in limbo, in the between because we have not forgiven others or ourselves or we are mad, angry with others and or God. Our mind still swirling with questions: why me, why them, why did this happen? Going on with life; still hurting, angry, wondering. We continue with life, in church, saying all the right things, doing the day-to-day functions. Yet in your quiet times; you find yourself in regret, remorse, and despair. We run our business, lead our ministries, raise our children, pastor our churches, provide for our families, love our spouse, start and end relationships; only to start and end more relationships. Starting many things and never finishing them. Not recognizing that we cannot bring things to resolution and conclusion because there are areas of our life left unresolved do to unforgiveness.

I have witnessed people literally waiting to live. They are between life and emotional healing from a loss, a break-up, or a sickness. I've watched them; including myself at one time, diligently doing, in motion, but going nowhere. There is no progression. Functioning but not producing. It looks like they are moving forward, but they are only moving, going nowhere. They are doing life but not living. Many are purposefully busy but there is no progress. They are stuck in the punishment of their past and in the fear of their future. They have forgotten how to dream pass their past, loss, hurt, and disappointment. They talk a good game and go about doing, but in their heart and mind they really wish change would hurry up and come or things could go back to the way it was; even if it was not good. They live a dissatisfied life; functioning, existing, but not living. They hide behind masks and fake forward advancement. I guess for some activity is between than nothing. But for me with my type D/C personality type, this is excruciating. It is like the treadmill tragedy.

If we let it, the place of between - our waiting place will help us to let go, move forward to heal, dream again, love again, and be right to live right again. It was in my waiting place that I recognized it would be good and wise for my soul and good mental health to seek outside Christian counsel in addition to that of my Pastor, the Word, and the Holy Spirit. Beloved, no matter what you have done who you are or how you have handled your waiting place, God is still for you. He is still calling you, has given you, and wants you to have a life; a life more abundant. When we accept and receive live the abundant life we are living the abundant life. Even in your waiting state, freedom, love, joy, and a more abundant life are available to and for you. Submit to what God wants to or is doing in you. Allow Him to perfect in you all that you have run from or suppressed. Allow Him to perfect the things that concern you; including you and all that pertains to you. HE has so much more for you. HE desires to bless you and bless you to be a blessing to others.

When you are pouring out and into that which does not have the capacity to pour back into you; even to half full, let alone to full you will feel like Jesus when HE said, "Virtue (power, strength, the essence of me) has left me." Let Him heal you and fill you. You cannot give away what you don't have. If you do, you will find yourself continuously depleted. Armed with this knowledge, oh, the places you will go, see, and experience. Oh, the doors that will open to you after your season; your season of waiting and waiting right has ended. Forgiveness, self-examination, along with a time or season by yourself and with yourself in your waiting place is critical to your release and advancement. This is important not only for your earthly relationships but your relationship with God and to have (access to) success in all areas of your life. The Word is clear, unforgiveness is torment and where there is torment (an unsettled soul and spirit), true success, and genuine peace will elude you. Encompassed in His love is His forgiveness. And HE can and will teach you how to forgive and let go and find satisfaction in Him.

As you go through what I call the "Stages of Waiting", you will experience many emotions. In the Book of Job, we see almost; if not all the stages. And like Job, we must have confidence in the LORD concerning our lives, our purpose and our destiny. There are many scriptures; really the entire Bible that encourage us to hold to our confidence in God. Here are just the few: Isaiah 32:17, 2 Corinthians 3:4, 2 Corinthians 5:5-8, Ephesians 3:12, Galatians 5:10, Philippians 1:6, Romans 8:28-39, Hebrews 4:16, Hebrews 10:19, Hebrew 13:17, 1 John 4:16, 17, 1 John 5:14,15. One of my favorites is Hebrews 10 verse 35 *"...do not throw away your confidence; it will be richly rewarded."* Be encouraged. Psalm 27:2,3 says, *"The fruit of that righteousness will be peace; its effect will be quietness and confidence forever."* I realized receiving the peace of God that surpasses all understanding came with benefits. A quietness in my soul came and dare I say in my body. This was a rest that brought not only a confidence in Him but His confidence. His peace brings His confidence. It is an unshakeable truth; a knowing that everything is working together for my good. Everything really will be alright and on the horizon is bigger better great more. Be confident in God's love for you, His plan and purpose for you, in your relationship with Him through His Son our Savior Jesus Christ. The Spirit of God will direct your heart to understand, recognize, appreciate, and receive the love of God our Father (2 Thessalonians chapter 3). Be confident; be persuaded that nothing can separate you from the love and purposes of God. Listen, if HE did it for me, HE can and will do it for you. Ask Him for it and you shall receive. HE can, is willing, and able; HE is waiting to anoint you, to grace you to wait and to wait right. Our waiting expectantly in God is our demonstrating our confidence in God.

The Waiting States

1   Hurry Up and Wait
2   Frustration
3   Loneliness and Doubt
4   Self-Examination and Assassination

Hurry Up and Wait

In your mind you know you have to wait, but you want the waiting time to speed up – to hurry up – to end. Many of us have been even foolish enough to think we have control over the time and commission of God. We have said things like, "I don't have time for this...I don't have time to wait." You cannot rush God. Be honest, is there a "hurry" in you; an impatience? Is what you display only a form of peace and joy? Is restlessness your true state?

You have mastered the outward masks. You wear the false and forced smiles. You serve, get in relationships, do business, and interact with others with and from an anxious, unsettled heart. You faithfully show-up to distract yourself from the burden of waiting and living with and being you. You are never; you can't be alone with you. Let alone wait alone. What an exhausting way to live. Yes, "fake it 'til you make it" works sometimes, but not all the time or forever. From the pulpit to the pew to the parking lot and back, you perform. You wear the masks of disappoint, hurt, pain, frustration, loneliness, worry, fear, insecurity; screaming panicking on the inside..."I AM TIRED of THIS. I am tired of waiting. I am getting or I am too old. Who will...I want out of this thankless job, this unfaithful and unfruitful marriage, this unyielding situation...Hurry up God...When...When is my turn!" From your home to your job back to your home; you hurry only to wait. On the inside you are raging and quietly looking for an escape from your waiting place. You are using the business lingo: great day, awesome, team player or the church lingo: blessed and highly favored, praise the Lord, God is good, but on the inside internally and sometimes outwardly; you are impatient, anxious saying, "Hurry-up already. How much longer Lord?" I certainly can appreciate your feelings and concerns. Please know, for you to feel this way is not strange or demonstrating a lack of faith. You are not alone, most of us have been there and many of us are there.

You are looking for a way out. Anyway out. Hoping for a sign; spiritual or otherwise to escape, and get out of waiting. When you make your "*hurried* escape"; you soon find yourself right back – waiting again. Except now, you are in a waiting place you created. Though I don't blame you for wanting to escape; I promise you, God has a plan. HE has not forgotten your faithfulness; your labor of love. It is hard, but there are times in our life processing that we "must need go through" what we are being challenged with. Let God have His perfect and perfecting work. Don't rush from your waiting state and cause yourself to return. Returning to wait is trying enough but to find yourself back at waiting because of our own decisions and or the choices of others can be overwhelming. But this I know, God has a purpose and a plan for you and will use all that you go through; self-inflicted or not for your good. Your end will be better than your beginning. In this and many of our states, we can be guilty of self-sabotage. In your times of impatience and hurry, settle yourself. Breathe, be still to hear and know. No rash decisions. Do not entertain what looks and sounds good. Be patient. Use wisdom in your times of hurry-up and wait.

I shared this testimony of my hurry up and wait state at church and was led to share it here with you.

Salvation in the Wait

As I readied myself on Sunday morning to head to Church and then to Michigan to my niece's graduation, I discovered my eye was red. Off to the emergency room I went. I went praying, God let me get in and out of here. That drive to Detroit is a bear.

I got in, was seen, and ready for what I thought was check out. I thought, that was pretty quick - about 45mins or less - cool. But then it happened - a stall - when it was over the stall was about another hour or more. So long was the stall that I watched those who had come into the waiting room being process out before me and I was still waiting At one point, I got up and walked around - yes, paced - annoyed and restless.

I had to laugh at myself, "ok author of Waiting - get it together...maybe I am waiting for a reason - maybe God was protecting me from something up or on the road...so chill..." Little did I know if was not up the road but right there in the waiting place...the waiting room.

After some more waiting, I asked about the delay. They discovered that my paper work had been (mistakenly) covered by a pile of papers. I took a deep breath and went back to my seat. Still waiting, watching those who came in after me leaving before me.

I had been surveyed after the doctor visit on how the service was - all 5's. Had they surveyed me now, they would have failed. As I waited to be released, the surveyor came to survey a young black man who sat kitty corner from me.

Conversation

Introductions...Surveyor: May I ask you a few questions. Man: yes, you can ask me some questions...my brother died here in 2008. (unsolicited comment brought an awkward silence for a brief moment) Surveyor: How did the nurse do - 1, How did the intern doctor do - 1, How well did they demonstrate that they cared about why you were here - 1...my brother died here in 2008, How well did they listen – 1 and on and on.

The surveyor left. I asked the young man his name - Robert. I was just released from jail (sagg'n, morning still on him). I'm on work release. Oh, ok. How old are you? – 21. Son, may I ask you a question? Yes Ma'am. "Was your experience today that bad..." "Well, no Ma'am". He goes on to say again, but my brother died here in 2008"... But was I that young lady – that nurse – intern who was here then? No, but..." I listened to him about his brother. It was still a deep hurt for him.

I explained to him this would probably go towards the interns grade - Man: "They will probably change my answers anyway - people do what they want" Me: they do but if they do wrong let God deal with them but what about you trying to do the right thing..."Yes Ma'am". I asked him, if he had ever had a job that served people, "Yes Ma'am" Me: and what if you did a pretty good job - to the best of your ability but because of their previous experience with a totally different people they evaluated you on that - would that be right, "No Ma'am...Me: how did she really do - "She was good" Me: so what score should you have given her - Man: 5's.

So what do you think about having the guy come back and redo it - "Welllll - he gonna think I'm stupid or something..." Well no, what about telling him - you answered based on your overall experience with the hospital or emergency room... "Ok but I'm only doing it for you...my brother died here in 2008." I can respect that but I ultimately want you to do it because it is the right thing to do and God would want you to do the right thing..."You right Ma'am - ok"

I went and found the surveyor. He told the guy what we said, and added, "I was scoring her like that because my brother died here but she was not here then - she did good..." He changed all the scores to 5.

Me: Robert, proud of you son and more importantly God is...Are you a believer in Jesus Christ - Man: "Yes, Ma'am, kinda, yeah..." Ok. May I ask you a question..."Yes,

Ma'am." If you died today where would you go..."Probably hell because I just got out of jail and now I'm in work release - I been in trouble a lot - lot of bad decisions..." Ok, before you leave here I want you to be sure of where you would go. Would that be ok with you..."Yes Ma'am." He smiled.

I took him through the plan of salvation (nothing deep – simply). ME: Do you believe that Jesus lived, died for your sins, was buried, rose and is coming back - waiting for him to answer each before I went on to the next. With every "Yes", his smile got bigger and bigger. That's it...You are saved. Never again do you have to question your salvation and where you will go have internal life. Robert, do you know who Jesus is coming back for - "No Ma'am" - YOU - because you believe in Him..."Really" Yes really. "Wow, that's it." Pretty much. Would you like to ask Him to forgive you for your sins and to help you make better decisions..."Yes Ma'am." So we did. He said, "Cool...Where you go to church..." Healing Streams Word and Worship Center, I told him where it was located... "My work release program is out east so I can't come there" - That's Ok. I gave him some choices of solid and sound teaching churches on the east side. Man: "I saw you early (when I was pacing), I thought you had left cause they was taking so long..." Me: I'm glad I didn't.

I had an opportunity to speak with the surveyor and suggested they listen more carefully to people. How he never acknowledges the young man's hurt. I shared with him that the young man was continuing trying to tell him that he blamed the hospital for the death of his brother so based on that his score was going to low.

Unbeknownst to me, all the time I was talking with Robert, there was a young Asian man sitting near. He came to me after and said, "That was amazing. I've never seen anybody take that type of time with someone to tell them about Christ not even my Priest and then to explain it so simply - that was good - thank you." Me: No, thank you.

The moral of this is story is that in our Waiting, there is ALWAYS a blessing - for you and others. God always has a greater purpose than what you think. Trust in the waiting room experience. Don't always be in hurry. Something great - a blessing for or to you or someone else awaits you.

Not only was a gender and generation affected, but a culture and a nation. I love me some Jesus. Gotta love God.

What an amazing experience and lesson. God took me from impatience to celebration in a flat few minutes.

You can get ahead of God in this hurry up and wait state and have to start over or get set or sent back to where you started. Patience must have its perfect work in the "hurry-up and wait" stage. This is what Sarai and Abram did in Genesis 16. They hurried up and did it their way and was brought back to have to start over to do it God's way. Fully knowing what they (Sarai) planned was not what God told them (him – Abram) to do, they still did it. Sounds a little bit like Adam and Even in Genesis Chapter 3. In Chapter 12, God promised Abram and His descendants that HE would give them the (promised) land. The only way to have a descendant is to have a child. God made Abram a promise and an incentive, but Abram chose to follow an idea, and not wait on Him. Their (her) desire superseded God's plan and process. Not consulting with God, resulted in a rushed and faulty decision. An idea produced a child (Ishmael) outside of the will and plan of God. The execution of their idea created problems between Sarai and Hagar, Sarai and Abram, Abram and Ishmael, and Ishmael and Isaac (The Promised Child). An emotional decision created an internal mess. God had a plan. Had they waited, this sibling rivalry that still exists today would not have occurred.

They had been waiting a long time already. Sarai was 65, and Abram was 75, but God had a plan. HE had made Abram a promise and given him charge over it. From the time the promise was spoken to Abram to the manifestation, there was a 25 year wait. But glory to God, it came to pass. Hear me beloved challenges and oppositions will come, but when we let them, they always make way for promotion and opportunity. This is a rule to live by: the greater the challenge and the longer the wait; the greater the reward, and more powerful the testimony and the anointing.

For your purpose, destiny, and the plan for your life to be fulfilled, the promises spoken to you must come to pass. Think about how much time we waste, delay, causing setbacks for ourselves, creating lifelong problems, and challenges all because we lose hope in the promise, stop checking in with God, and run because we do not want to wait or don't want to face ourselves, do the work or do it God's way. Yet, HE loves us and is so very patient with us. HE waits for us when we miss Him and set out on our own with our plan. My Lord, God waits on me...What a revelation! Like David, I stand in awe of God. That is too lofty for me. God waits for me...Thank God for Your grace and mercy...for Your patience and love for me. It very well may be that the purpose of what is to come out of your waiting is greater and bigger than what you can think or imagine.

You can do this. I know this is a microwave society, but some things taste better when they are slow cooked, particularly; naturally in its own juices, and all the ingredients (circumstances of life) get mixed in and cooked together evenly. You can wait on the Lord. You can be of good cheer. Remembering that nothing is impossible for you; include waiting, because you have God in and with you. As a believer in Jesus Christ, HE is with you, in you, and for you. HE is more interested in you succeeding, finishing strong, and moving forward than you are for yourself.

His return on His investment in you is more than you can calculate. HE needs you to deal with you; get and learn the lessons and get it together in your waiting place so we can keep it together outside of it and be used for His glory. John Ortberg states in his book "The Life You've Always Wanted", "We must find ways to deliberately choose waiting, ways that make hurry (up) impossible..." Since you know you cannot hurry or rush God, you might as well choose to wait verses being forced to wait.

Like me when I read this, you probably said, "Really...make waiting a choice." Though I see the logic in it because making it a choice should make the waiting easier, I am honest to admit that the decision to do so would be difficult for most. Today, I can say, I can do this, but in the beginning of this journey of seeking to master the unavoidable discipline of waiting, it was extremely difficult. I often got in a hurry. Yet, I have learned to choose. One of the most concrete and lasting times was when I made a decision over fifth-teen years ago to wait on God to send my husband to find me. My choice was abstinence. It was not forced on me, nor was it out of necessity or circumstance. It was and has been a choice that I confessed to God and by His grace HE has kept me.

Did I ever think my time of waiting would have been this long, no? But I trust and believe God. I wait and have waited patiently with expectation and anticipation on the Lord for what I believe and know will be a great, grand, amazing, and an awesome man of God and marriage. It is His promise and for His glory that I wait. I believe for my obedience to honor Him and His Word by faith my reward will be beyond what I can or have asked for thought or imagined. When you choose to wait out of commitment to God, HE will give you the grace to wait and will bless you with more. Just thinking about the soon to come testimony brings me excitement. I cannot wait to tell the world..."Look what the Lord has done. My blessing for waiting and waiting right." Yes, I have a grand expectation of the reward for my waiting and waiting right and so should you. Choose to wait. Trust and believe God in the process. Get excited about what is to come. For he or she who shall come will come and will not delay. Wait on the Lord and be of good courage. HE will strengthen your heart and grace you for the wait. Don't worry…Wait and be happy and of good cheer.

Frustration

Let me first clear something up. Frustration is not an issue of faith but an issue of trust. It is not so much spiritual as much as it is emotional. It is in this stage that we start to ask and will force the question of why? Why 'force', because frustration says, "I am anger…sacred. I am annoyed by or because my situation. I feel like or I am truly unable to change this. I have no control. My progress and success is being hindered. I don't know what to do. I am confused. I want but how." Yes, this is what frustration sounds and looks like. Whether your issues or challenges are real or perceived, the frustration and emotion of it are real. If anyone in Scripture was frustrated, certainly Job was; at his friends, his situation, and at times God. In Chapter 7 Job says, *"Why have You set me as Your target, So that I am a burden to myself?"* Let me be clear, God is not tripping on you asking why. Jesus asked God 'why' on the Cross, (Matthew 27) and the "if it's possible" question in the Garden (Matthew 26).

If Jesus can find Himself vacillating, uncertain of why, and asking 'if possible'; our experiencing frustration, hopelessness, anxiety, fear, and being challenged by our circumstance, certainly does not shock or throw God for a loop or cause Him to love us any less. God is not thrown off by our futile, fleshly, flawed thinking or questions. When you get tired of asking questions and tired of trying to figure it out and work it out by your own strength, then and only then will frustration subside and peace will come. It is here that you demonstrate your trust in God. Your release from the wait will not be by your power or your might, but it will be by a submitted heart and surrendered soul that trusts His will and plan for your life. A humbled soul and surrendered heart is led by and rests in His Spirit that comes to lead us into all truth.

You will find yourself going from "do I have to", to "why do I have to", to "where are You God?" The warning Jesus gave the disciples in Matthew 26, and gives to us today, *"Watch and pray, lest you enter into temptation. The spirit indeed is willing, but the flesh is weak."* Oppression may try to grip you in the hope of pulling you into depression. If we are not careful, in our frustration our mind and or our mouth can cause us to give up and walk away…Not only from God but from what God has for us that is often around the corner or even right in front of us. You must be careful of your words in this stage.

Frustration is often brought on because things are not (yet) the way you want it. Or a person is not behaving the way you think they should. Out of this place of dis-ease, discontent, and dissatisfaction words are spoken and they produce. Words spoken in frustration are NEVER positive and often deadly. They create and birth negativity and death. Death to hope. Death to relationships. Death to dreams. Their end is never good. They are lasting and damaging. Your words frame your present and shape your future. You want good, you must think and speak good. It has been said, "Junk in Junk out." While you wait on your change in you, your situation, and others be careful and mindful of what you think and say. I charge and encourage you to watch your mouth in your waiting season. Do not allow words birthed from frustration to imprison, block, stagnant, and lock you behind a stronghold; a wall of lies. It is out of frustration that a mean spirit and spiritedness is birthed. Anything that is not

God's Word – His truth concerning you, those around you, and the things HE has for you that are good is a lie. Do not allow (your) mind to create a thought pattern that lies to you. That says what is good and God is now bad and an offense.

Do not live in fantasyland. If truth comes that says you must deal with, work on or fix that thing in or about you; then do that and seek God to help you in the maturing and perfecting process. However, even in your repair phase, seasons, and times do not beat yourself up. Always remember that HE who began a good work in you shall continue working on you and I complete it (the work in us) until the very moment of Jesus' return. We are all continued works in progress and that is why we need the hospital called the Church. So do not be hard on or become frustrated with yourself or others in the time it takes to perfect. Where you see yourself and others working towards better celebrate them and praise God. Where you do not, make a choice. Guard you heart, your mind, and your mouth. You shall have what-so-ever you say. Do not delay your release with your words.

Would you say you are a person of purpose? I would say you are simply because you are reading this book. Purposed people must be and seek to be prepared. Purpose people are pregnant with (a) promise and possibility that is tied to their purpose. Your waiting place is to conceive, prepare, to birth, and receive your promise(s). Waiting on the vision to come to pass can be frustrating. Because greatness awaits you, frustration can be intense as you wait for manifestation. It is like a baby in the waiting state of the womb coming up on its time of delivery. You are sensing your due season and this too can produce frustration. In your frustration, do not allow your thoughts or your mouth and mind to paralyze you or your purpose. Do not let your temporary place trap and keep you longer than intended or planned.

The promises of God are not small matters. *"For no matter how many promises God has made, they are "Yes" in Christ. And through Him the "Amen" is spoken by us to the glory of God (2 Corinthians 1:20)."* Our promises are tied to our purpose, vision, and destiny. Though joyful blessings when our dreams and vision come to pass, they are often heavy to carry while you wait for them. They can be weighty because of the momentary affliction of waiting right. It will produce a glory that is yet to be revealed. Our promises require preparation and a readiness in the natural and in the spirit to receive. You must learn to wait on the weighted promise. God so loves us that while we are in the waiting place; HE gives us "the little" to be faithful over. HE will even give us glimpses of that glory. HE desires to make us rulers, good stewards, and masters over much. This includes the things that have (tried to) mastered and ruled over us like in the past: waiting wrong, impatience, frustration, depression, fear, lack, etc.

I can honestly say that I have discovered, experienced, and learned a great deal on this side of the wait. I discovered peace, joy, contentment, trust, and truth. I learned more about me, faced and accepted me. I grew to love, like, and appreciate me. I learned more about men, relationships, and myself in them; not just romantic but business and friendships. My wants, needs, desires, and deal breakers became crystal clear. I have grown to accept the call on my life and became real clear about purpose. Waiting will make you be real with yourself and tell God the truth. The truth; good or bad that HE already knows but just wants you to recognize, accept, declare, and deal with. Remember Psalm 51 that says, *"HE desires truth in our inwards parts."* Tell the truth about how you feel about your waiting place; your situation. Tell the truth about how you feel about the things you are and have been waiting on. Tell the truth about the things that cause you fear and frustration. Tell the truth you and watch frustration be dispelled. It still can and will set and make you free.

One of my many frustrating discussions with God was related to my many years of waiting right on my Holy Adam or Boaz, as some may refer to him. It went something like this: "God I am tired of being single. I don't want to be single. I not only want marriage desire to be married. I desire to be the wife to the man you that he desires and that You have for me that is ready to be a committed loving kind supportive giving truthful honest full of God husband. I only want who You have for me. I desire to do ministry with my husband. I believe you gave me this capacity to love, to be a helpmate. I don't believe You gave me this desire and it not be Your will and desire for me to have it to share it. I never thought I would still be single at 45, with no children. I am a good woman – a great woman. I have done the work on me and my relationship with You. I have waited in obedience by faith. What is the delay? Is it me Lord? Is it him? What do I still need to work on? Is it Your will for me to be single? To not have children? To not carry and birth my husband's legacy? This cannot be my end.

Ok, God...Ok...If it is, I say, Ok Lord. I will submit if this is Your will. But God...LORD...Ok Father, I will serve You Lord with gladness...I will serve You. If this is Your will for me...You must be with me. You gotta go with me. Make my way successful, fulfilled, and completed. Satisfy me Lord with You alone. Sanctify me – anoint me – ordain me for this call. Open divine doors of business and ministry to me. When will doors (re)open for me...?

Do you sense and hear the back and forth. If possible, this is what anxiousness, a long time waiting, frustration, and fear will do to even the mature and the elect. Doubt will also try to enter in to oppress and tempt you with hopeless. I know I am not the only women; a few men for that matter who have had these conversations with the Father. Maybe about this and or other things but we have all been there. Somewhere along the way, my complaints became compliance. In my surrender, I remember telling God that 'I do not believe it is Your will for me to be single or childless but I surrender. I will wait without complaint for You Father God to give me away in Holy Matrimony to the man of God You have for me…But never the less, not my will but Thy will be done. I trust Your will and plan for my life. Help me to wait right.' In that moment, I heard the Holy Spirit say, *"I have not left you childless…you have many children I have given to you in the earth that no you have not birthed but they are yours – a mother to many you have been and your reward shall be great. But a husband for you can and will only come from Me – He shall be birthed from Me for you and you for him…A mother you can be too many – A wife you will only be t one."* I tell you, in that moment the presence of God came to visit me in a mighty way. It was a time with Him that I will not forget. Periodically, I beckon His voice, His Spirit, His comfort on this matter. Faithful is HE to come and remind me!

It was about this time that I gained a revelation that there are other purposes for grace. Not only does HE withhold from us what we do deserve (mercy – wages of sin is death) and gives us what we don't deserve (grace – gift of God is eternal life); HE also gives us what we need (grace) to do His will. HE graces us to do the things that we may not be able to do, don't know how to do, and what we don't want to do – the hard things. It has been by His grace that I have been kept. HE has equipped me through the waiting to be kept in my time of singleness and season of stillness in ministry, money, business and life. None of it have I liked or wanted but they have been teaching tools in my waiting seasons. Through His grace of wisdom and discernment, HE kept me from marrying the wrong men three different times. HE kept from entering into relationships that was less than equal. HE kept me from future divorce and abuse. HE kept me from friendships, associations, and decisions that would have ended in a less than positive way. I cannot take any credit for these blocks. It was not by my power, intellect or smarts. It was by His grace that I was saved from them, situation and myself.

As years turned into a decade plus five, surrendering to His will became less difficult. Can't say it has become easy, only less difficult. Now hear me, surrendering to God's will does not mean giving up on your dreams and desires. Not now not yet, didn't, and doesn't mean never. Surrender is simply you putting all that you want, desire, and dream under His rule – His Lordship. Surrender is the safest place you can be. Throwing up your hands to release all your efforts and giving it all to Him brings a rest and a peace. In your frustration and fearful times, I encourage you to take up faith as a shield. Obedience is said to be the highest form of worship. I would say that surrendering to God's will is the greatness form of faith. The fact that you ask God to reveal and to do His will in your life demonstrates that you are (already) in His will. When we by faith, seek and are obedient; even when it hurt and like Jesus unto death (to our flesh and will), we are demonstrating a surrendered heart. I know, I hear you…"Unto death…" Yes, the death of it having to be your way, in your time, what you want, when you want it, and how you want it. You have a choice: either kill 'you' softly and slowly and submit your controlling selfish fearful demanding self and will or surrender quickly or you can continue to resist what God is trying to do in and for you and force His hand and patience. The outcome will be the same. The choice is yours.

Now, someone might say that asking God questions is being double-minded, or untrusting. To this, I say, "Not necessarily." It depends on the motive, mindset, and heart behind your question. God already knows your heart. Thus, there is no need to lie or say what you think sounds good to Him or others. Whether you say you are frustrated, hurt, angry, lonely, fearful, worried, etc. or not, HE already knows. HE knows your thoughts from a-far-off. Before we think them, HE knows them. So tell Him. It is good to tell God the truth; the whole truth, and nothing but the truth. Tell Him the truth in your frustrated state. HE already knows the secret things and desires of your heart. HE alone can give you the peace you so desperately need and the answers you are seeking. To others and even yourself, you may seem or sound a little "mental", confused or indecisive, but to God, you sound like His child who needs Him to make sense of it all. I promise you, HE will comfort you and bring you His peace.

Talk to The Father in your frustration. It was a part of my therapy. I talked and talked to Him constantly. In my car, shower, lying on my bed, washing dishes, doing laundry, in the store; wherever I am at if something is on my heart or mind, I tell Him. Ask Him the many questions. There is a difference between questioning someone in authority and asking someone in authority a question. The first is pride and arrogance. The second is to understand. HE told Cyrus to ask Him for a sign. David constantly asked God questions. Paul asked Him to remove the thorn (three times). And we can't forget Jesus who asked God to take the cup (three times) and why have You (God) forsaken Me.

Never again allow anyone tell you, you can't or shouldn't ask God a question or questions. Petition Him. Target, be specific, and clear about what you need, want, and desire from Him. HE is a strategic and specific God. HE is your Father, your Daddy. So why would HE not listen to you and hear you and answer your prayers and petitions. Be clear and specific with Him. We know we do not come to God telling Him or demanding anything from Him. Yes, we can put a demand on Heaven but not on Him. Here is an easy way to remember this in honoring God and His sovereignty, with God there is a "Do Ask but Don't Tell" policy.

When you consider a petition, it is written and has the support of many witnesses who believe what you believe. You have gone to them and either shared and convinced or shared and they immediately agreed because they already felt the same way. With prayers and petitions to God, follow the same approach. There is no need to get frustrated. God is already in agreement with you. HE has been waiting on you to agree with Him and ask specifically for what you want, need, and or desire. Remember, the women in Luke 18 who kept coming asking for justice from a wicked judge. Remember the pigs in Luke 8 who asked Jesus to send them into the water. Now surely, if pigs (the unholy thing) and wicked judge (an ungodly thing) can make a request of our Holy Savior, Jesus...surely, our questions and supplications will not be overlooked. I would go so far as to say, our questions are welcomed when presented in reverence by faith so that we know better to do better. Our Heavenly Father who knows how to give gifts will hear our prayers and petitions, and HE will answer (John 14 verses 13, 14, 1 John 3 verses 19-22a).

Though our faith is frustrated, our trust is tested, promises questioned, and confessions challenged, and we can still come through and out as pure gold. All this is for our perfecting and maturing. It is a part of the making process. When frustrated, the "why" question are certain to come. It is in this stage that you must choose to trust God more and add to your faith to combat your frustration. 1 Peter 1, tells us that *"we have been given exceedingly great and precious promises, that through these you may be partakers of the divine nature, having escaped the corruption that is in the world through lust. But also for this very reason, giving all diligence, add to your faith virtue, to virtue knowledge, to knowledge self-control, to self-control perseverance, to perseverance godliness, to godliness brotherly kindness, and to brotherly kindness love."* Beloved, your trust has the power trample on and conqueror your frustration. Now that you have trust locked down, activate it and use your faith! It has the power to overcome all things; seen and unseen, the temporary and the eternal.

From frustration comes anxiety. Anxiety is the feeling of nervousness that comes from the fear of what "might" happen and wanting to do but can't because you can't predict the outcome. I know many say fear is the opposite of faith but I submit to you that anxiety is the opposite of faith and fear is the opposite of love. The root of all emotional, mental, and spiritual challenges is fear. Anxiety or fear can physically bring an unsettling – a disturbance in your body that produces sickness, infirmity, and "dis"-ease. You feel it in the pit of your stomach; the place of seated or seeded desires. Just the thought of how long you have already waited, and how much longer you may be waiting before you see the promise come to pass can bring anxiety. It moves from your head trying to figure it out to your heart, your hope, and your soul being disappointed and dismayed by the thought. It takes practice but when we resolve in our heart, "Never-the-less, not my will but thy will be done"; frustration and anxiety will pass. I contend that it is better to be in the will of God in the waiting place than outside of it without Him. Ask Him to remove the frustration and the pain of fear, frustration, loneliness, and uncertainty. Ask Him to teach you to wait.

One of the blessings of this stage is that frustration is the quickest way to peace. If you seek you will find it. I wanted and desired that God's will be done. I didn't want to be led by my emotions and certainly not the emotions of frustration that carries with it impatience, anger, doubt, impatience, quick feet, and so much more. I became confident in the saying that "Good things still come to those who wait." Even more so for those who wait right and on God, and His reward. It is a good thing to wait on God. If we just learn to wait, we can avoid a lot of mishaps and mistakes. When you are willing to wait on God, it shows that you desire to be in His will. His 'will' is found in the waiting. And being in His will in the waiting place is a good place to be.

Consider yourself in a line. You are standing in it…waiting. And you hear the lady say, "The lady in front of you is my last customer…This lane is closed." What in the world? Frustration ensues. But just as she says that the register next to you opens and the cashier says, "I will take the next person in line." If you didn't just get excited, it is because you do not understand what God is saying. Closed and over does not mean done. It can mean next opportunity. When we are frustrated and confused it is often because we see LAST as a negative thing. Let me introduce you to a new perspective, start seeing last and first as the same things. When you are last that means no one is behind you and everyone who was in front of is gone. This gives a whole new meaning to the last shall be first and the first shall be last (Matthew 20). God can flip a line and make what was last first in a matter of seconds. Yes, HE saves the best for last. The page is about to turn. The script is about to be flipped. Stay in line. What was at the end (tail) is now at the beginning. There is a blessing in the waiting. There is a blessing to being at the end of a thing. I think that is called commencement. Where the end and the beginning are happening at the same time. You got next? So you might as well call it..."I got next."

Loneliness and Doubt

This stage brings the question of "how long." You find yourself moving quickly, from "why" to "how." Fear tries to paralyze you with thoughts of "Will I ever get out of this place – space of waiting? Will I ever receive what I have been waiting on?" Interestingly, this stage is often used to develop our character and perfect (test) our faith. "Why" is good for that. Better said, 'an unanswered 'why' is good for perfecting us.' It is a holy ordained journey you must go through and for most of it; you will go alone. Yes, people may pray for or with you, but ultimately in your waiting place; it will be you and God that gets you through to the other side. When we feel exiled or away from Him...When we cannot hear or feel God...When HE appears to be silence in your sentence...It becomes even more difficult to wait it out.

Addressing loneliness, an article on the web from the Christian Science Sentinel states, "Often helplessness or resignation sets in. The problems of the world can seem insurmountable or, at least, beyond the scope of one individual's ability to make a difference."

As Christians we are never alone because God; His presence, His Spirit is always with us. Yet, the reality is that you can feel alone when flesh and blood (someone, a person) is not in the struggle or on the pilgrimage with you to talk you through it, physically comfort you or be there as a companion, friend or lover. What you are feeling is loneliness. It is real. I have often said, as many others have, "It is one thing to feel lonely or have times of loneliness because you desire what I just mentioned, but do not stay there. Remember, lonely does not mean alone." Do not allow yourself to be drawn into despair or hopelessness. Do not lose hope. Do not give up. If or when we give up in the waiting place because things seem hopeless, we are telling God HE does not know what is best for us. We communicate our distrust of Him. Loneliness and doubt are bi-products of distrust and the root of all is fear. Your concern has moved from mind to heart. Now you are struggling in your thoughts and your emotions. To give into despair is to let the enemy win. Job said, I will wait til my change comes. Can you – are you willing to wait…to wait for God's timing and His best? It will come! I mean really, look at Job. For his waiting; mine you he didn't always waiting right, he receive double for everything he lost.

At one time, I remember thinking, "How did Jesus feel when HE called out to God in the Garden and waited on Him to respond to His question of 'why', but to no avail…" How did HE handle it? HE waited. HE continued to believe. HE waited with a submitted heart and spoke these words, *"Never the less…not My will but Thy will be done* (Luke 22:42)." In His waiting place, HE was alone and lonely, but HE made it through. HE took it and made it to a borrowed tomb and back to Heaven. HE waited; hanging on the cross HE bared for us. Yet, we do not what to bear a headache. Waiting on God, His promise, and our purpose to come to pass is the cross we must bear. Abraham gives us a great example of someone who did not seem to mine bearing his cross. He waited twenty-five years for the promise God told him would come...twenty-five years. There had to be time or two of questions and doubt, but we read of none of this. The Bible says in Romans 4 that against hope he believed in hope and did not weaken in his faith. Against his nature hope that includes doubt and questions, he believed in hop; Jesus "the hope of glory." He kept believing and doing what he knew to do and what was necessary to produce the promise. Sometimes you will get instructions and others times you will just (naturally) know what to do. Stop waiting and praying and waiting on God to tell you what to do...You already know. Now, just do it! You are not waiting on God...God is waiting on you!

Loneliness can be felt to the depths of your soul. The longer the wait the more weighty and intense loneliness grows. Your thoughts and your emotions are attacked. It feels as if you are on an elevator going to or maybe coming down from the 40th floor and every button has been pushed. You experience the ups and downs; highs and the lows. The stops and starts. People getting on and off that you don't know but they are going somewhere and you are feeling stuck. If you try to make sense of it all, you will be wearied and weaken. It is here in the place of doubt and 'why', you will desire to talk it out or through, to vent or to be heard. This can drive you to seek answers and words of comfort and understanding from others and sometimes not the right some bodies. Sometimes resulting in them only saying what you want to hear. Ultimately, the only word we need in our place of uncertainty is truth. Pacifying will never satisfy and reasoning may not work either. We must accept that in most cases of extreme intense long term waiting, a great number of people will not get your waiting, understand your pilgrimage or you. Why? They have not (yet) experienced what you are going through – *a true waiting on God.* Doubt, frustration, and loneliness will often partners and bid against you. They have some roadies that tag along like anger and despair. Again, all of it comes from fear.

You may experience the pulling away of friends and perhaps family. They question your obedience to God, your faith, your trust in God, and your decision to wait on the very person they are questioning you about. They want to see His direction, instruction, you moving in it and forward. They want you released. Often implying that it should not take all that or as long as it has. A lonely place waiting can be. In Job Chapter 7 verse 16, his expression of loneliness and hopelessness was *"I loathe my life; I would not live forever. Let me alone, for my days are but a breath."* Thank God for a better and more positive testimony of hope spoken of in Romans 4 that I shared earlier about Abraham. The Word says of Abraham *"he did not waver at the promise of God through unbelief, but was strengthened in faith, giving glory to God, being fully convinced that what HE (God) who had promised HE was also able to perform."* And therefore *"it was accounted (accredited) to him for righteousness."*

Seek to grow in your faith and to obey God. The blessing of doubt is that you, if/when you allow it, it can be led right into truth. How awesome it will be that your witness to others and your testimony before God is that you not only grew in your faith, but it and your obedience is accounted to you as righteousness. Continue to do what you know to do. In God's time and timing, you will reap if you do not faint or give up. Desire and seek to experience the fullness of your promised blessings. It is okay to hope again. I charge, encourage, and release you to hope again – to dream again. HE who shall come will come and will not delay. HE will come with your reward.

Self-Examination and Assassination

As I shared earlier, waiting often involves our dying to something. That something is often our will and our way. We must be willing to admit the role we have played in our waiting, our delay, and our overall situation. Though we have addressed this previously, I compel you to be brutally honest with yourself. If you need someone to hold you accountable; run and find them. Be honest with them and yourself. I had to do this and still try to practice it. It was me who had delayed (and will again if I am not mindful and careful) my release. I had to admit that there were waiting seasons that my own hand, mouth, mind, and will had caused. I repented and submitted myself under and became accountable to someone. Being honest with you is imperative. It is a scary and prideful day and soon filled with loss and destruction to live life without being accountable to someone. Have you delayed your promise; your exodus from our waiting place? Not being an island unto yourself and dying to you will assassinate fear, pride, selfishness, and control. Transparency with God (as if HE does not already know) must be a part of your freedom and renewed mind. The longer you try to hide behind you, your self-image, your vanity, titles, positions, education, bravado, what others will think or what you want them to think, what they will say; you will delay your time and your reward. If you are not careful, some of you will die there. At a minimum, you will leave your dreams, desires, vision, blessings, and possibly God's plan or purpose unfulfilled.

Your waiting place – holding pattern is a great place to examine 'you'. Psalm 139 verse 23 says, *"Search me, God, and know my heart; test me and know my anxious thoughts."* Yes, in the stillness of waiting, your waiting place is an ideal place to die to you and be resurrected to a new life. It is an ideal time and place to develop or receive a new way of thinking, being, and doing. In our waiting place, we can work out our soul salvation. As we surrender to Him, we work out of us what is not like Him.

HE puts in us what is of and like Him. We again become good ground ready to do greater works. This is why dying daily and repentance are key to our sanctification and freedom. HE will release us from the wait when we are ready to do what HE has purposed for us do (Philippians 2).

Stop prolonging your release. Allow God to solidify; authenticate and perfect (mature) your character. All will know that God's hand (favor and so much more comes with His hand) is on us. The promise of Isaiah 1 is that when we are willing and obedient we will enter in, receive (the blessing), and eat the fruit (what we have and the land has produced) of the land. Dying to our will to get His will can hurt. Yet, I encourage you to die to you, so you may live for Him and do His will and see His plan for your life come to pass. You sing the song "I Surrender All", but do you mean it? Well, that is ok. If you keep singing it, one day you will not only mean it, you will live it.

Examine yourself, so you can be aware and know what is in you that is not of Him. Ask God to show you 'you' before anyone else has to show you, you. With all due diligence, go after what HE reveals. By faith, through the Word, assassinate the "self" in and of you. Ask yourself, why do I want what I want? Why do I do what I do? Is it for prestige, acknowledgement of man, worldly gain, approval, and acceptance of others? Is it to cover, suppress or deny a hurt, a loss, or a disappointment? Is it to mask an unhealed hurt, unmet need, or an unresolved issue? Do you want what you want to one-up or show someone…"Look what I did (without you), what I got, or have?" Examine yourself to see and ensure that you are in the household of God (which is faith) or are you in the house of self (which is flesh, pride, and soon failure). Remember, whatever is not of faith, does not come from or by faith is sin (Romans 14).

If you played a role in the loss i.e., divorce; let God show you, you. Face it, deal with it. If you haven't asked God or your ex for forgiveness, do it. Let it go, and move on - no condemnation for those who are in Christ. If you abused, admit it..."I did it..." If you lied about that, to them, on them...deal with it..."I was deceptive"...I stole that...I cheated in that...I knew they were like that when I got with them but I ignored it...I was mean ugly hateful in my actions and words to the one I (said) love(d) and who loved me...I committed adultery on my spouse and against God...I know what I did – what I said hurt my child, family, spouse, my friend, my lover...I got myself in debt...I played a role in losing my job. I lost the house, the car...I was irresponsible...I was a bad steward with my money, my relationships, etc. I still struggles with...Help me Lord...This type of honesty will aid in your release and ultimately in your mental, emotional, psychological, and spiritual freedom. To get to this place of health and wholeness, we must first turn that scalpel on ourselves. After we have been honest with God; as HE leads you, tell the truth to others. Particularly, those you abuses, hurt, damaged, appreciate, love, value. Confessing your faults one to another and or to a trusted confidant is a remedy for good mental and spiritual health. This level of truth and transparency is more for you than for them. The question was ask, "Will thou be made whole...? If your answer is yes, then tell the truth to you and others (who are safe) about you. Honesty is still the best policy. And obedience is still better than sacrifice.

In examining, you may find yourself questioning God's love for you. If you are not careful, you will begin to question your love for Him and your salvation as well. Am I really saved? If HE loved me I would be...this would not be...how could this be? You start to question your purpose. His will for you and your commitment to Him. The blame game and "if I had only" thoughts will try to consume you. It could be sin that brought or is keeping you here, but even if it is; God does not need or want you to assist satan by abusing yourself or assisting him in destroying you or your self-worth. HE certainly does not want you to doubt Him, or your place in and with Him. Job experienced this in Job chapter 7 verse 20 as he tried to figure out his 'why', *"Have I sinned? What have I done to You (God), O watcher of men?"*

I continue to address this because so many people live in a place of self-hatred and punishment; feeling as if they do not deserve the love of God. Strangely wanting, asking for, and even demanding His blessings but not accepting His unconditional love. We think and see God as "we are" or our earthly father is and not as HE is. We approach Him as we would come to limited a parent; particularly our fathers. We see Him more in His authority and judgment as God and the disciplinarian as Father verses seeing Him as daddy; loving and kind. God is not like us. We are exceptionally flawed and incapable of loving; accepting, seeing ourselves and others as God does. Yet, HE desires that we grasp how wide, long, and deep His love is for us (Ephesians 3:18). His love houses His grace, His mercy, His forgiveness, His favor, His protection and His guidance. Everything that is Him is for us and located in and comes from His love for and towards us.

Believe it or not, sometimes it is not sin. Sometimes our waiting place is a holding place to prepare us for transition; from waiting to reward. Do not help the devil bring about your demise. There is still no guilt or condemnation for those who are in Christ (Romans 8). Do not lend or give your mouth, mind, or hands to the enemy to entrap you or invoke pain, frustration, or anguish upon yourself. Satan is more than capable of bringing you negativity. HE does not need your assistance. Yes, die to you. Put yourself; your will; your selfishness; your attitude; your frustration; your fear, your anger; your pride; your drive (self and selfish ambitions); your opinions; your greed; self-pity, vanity, your flesh and lusts all your ways and means on the altar. Draw near to Him and HE will draw near to you. Acknowledge your faults and HE will direct you.

The truth is God really doesn't want to expose us. I earnestly believe, what keeps us from public peril is our private petitions and pleas for God to deliver us, set us free, make us whole, to help us in our weakness. This too is a part of our self-examination. It is the person who does not recognize, admit their raggedness, and has not humbled themselves under God's mighty hand that causes Him to be exposed. It is our mistreatment of others, entitlement, indispensable thinking and living, pride, greed, selfishness, arrogance, etc. that sooner or later exposes us. HE gives us ample time to come to the truth of ourselves and Him. God is gracious, loving, kind, patient, and merciful. HE is the Fruit of the Spirit. HE wants known to perish in their foolishness or ignorance but come to the truth of Him and His son Jesus Christ. Long before HE removes His hand of grace from His children, HE gives us time and chance upon chance to change. HE withholds His righteous judgment giving us signs and time to get it together. Your waiting place can be your Garden of Eden or our Garden of Gethsemane; you choose.

Perhaps, this is why we have to be alone to some degree in this season. In God's loving compassion, HE desires that our deliverance and freedom from ourselves, vices, strongholds, hurts, and our past be private; without on-lookers opinions and judgment. We have to come to the Garden alone. In His infinite love and wisdom, Daddy God would rather we be perfected in the privacy of our waiting place than be exposed to the world and the church publically and possibly be ridiculed. Though they say what is done in sin city stays there. We know no sin stays secret for long and never from God. God does not need to or want to embarrass us to embrace us. Humble yourself. I am grateful for the private, undercover, behind the scenes work of God. I have had some close encounter with myself, my struggles, and temptations...BUT God who is rich and mercy saved me from the hands and the perils of the enemy and me. I often say, we are all just one truth away from being free. If need be pray about who and find someone you can trust with your truth about you and confess your faults one another and be healed, made whole, and restored.

Note

To the leader – *those in authority, the person that you find to confide in while in your waiting place – in life; this person should not be someone in your church, on our job, anyone who is under your tutelage, authority, or spiritual counsel, and definitely not a family member (outside of your spouse). In your waiting or not; particularly where waiting that has gone on a while and where (secret) struggles, sin or character issues exist, I highly encourage outside (Christian) Counseling or Therapy. You need a safe, confidential place where you can put down your name, your title, responsibilities and or your position and just be _____ (you). Not even brother or sister...nothing. You (we) need a place – a refuge where we can run and find safety and share your truth without being judged – still held accountable and provided tools to help us to change, develop, and grow. Godly counsel and good Christian therapy would a wise tool to add to your arsenal in maintaining good mental health in your waiting place and for your life. If you choose not to do outside therapy, make sure your wise counsel and listening ear is gender specific; man to man and woman to woman.*

Being convinced of the promised resurrection, Paul said in 1 Corinthians 15:31, *"I die daily."* Self assassination is not fun, but it is so very necessary for us to awaken to righteousness and taste the true brokenness of humility that comes as we see ourselves compared to our Holy and Righteous God and Savior. We die to live and go from faith to faith (Romans 1:17). As we die daily, we add to our faith and more faith is produced. I believe with each daily diet of death the more humility, power, and favor we receive. Self-assassination produces a gratefulness that cannot be compared. 2 Corinthians 3:18 describes the character development and transformation as process. It says that we *"Are being transformed into the same image (of Jesus Christ) from glory to glory by the Spirit of the Lord."* It is by His Spirit and His Word that we are changed. It is nothing that we; you or I can do within or by our self. We must surrender and submit ourselves under His mighty hand. Our waiting place gives us a place and room to do that.

Transformation comes when we change our mind and repent. We must come out of agreement with (renounce) what is not of God; no matter how good it is, feels or looks and no matter how long we have done it and gotten away with it or been allowed to behave that way. I encourage you to repent; change your mind and God will change your heart and soon your behavior and attitude will change. Be transformed by the renewing of your mind. Be intentional. A true desire to change comes with true self-examination. Do not measure yourself against others; their "successes", failures or wins. Only measure yourself with and according to God's Word, His way, and His will for your life. Everyone's success and or failure in and or out of the waiting place will be theirs and ours will be our own. You can and should desire to come out not smelling like smoke and being better than you were then when you went in.

In your state of self-examining while waiting, get out, enjoy life, have fun, laugh. Keep yourself physically, mentally, and emotionally healthy. It is important that you do not beat you or others up. With loneliness, doubt, fear, and all of the others still looming; it becomes easy to use yourself as the target of your own verbal abuse or allow yourself to be used by someone to deflect their issues on you. Do not be heavy handed with you. That is the enemy's job. There is no need to assist him or his works to add to your personal struggle or strongholds. Submission and humility are not synonymous to stupid. Do not allow the cares of life or the non-Biblical opinions of other people, their drama, and selfishness to overtake or overwhelm you.

Say this with me: *"No regrets – where I am at – no matter how I got here, God knows and HE is with me. HE has a plan for me - my past is the past and I make a choice to leave it there – no matter how good it was or bad it was – I will not resurrect the good or bad - I will not live in or with my past or in or with or by it or regret – I accept God's plan for my life – my future is bright and full of manifested miracles and possibilities. I expect bigger, better, greater, more. Lord, Holy Spirit help me to not go back to weak and miserable ways, situations, or relationships that brought or bring me confusion, drama, hurt, or pain. Make me to never get stuck again. Keep Your hand upon me that I might not sin against, myself or others. My past cannot tell me anything new so I let it go and advance to pursue my future. By faith - I trust and believe You God. I am released to dream, believe, expect, and hope again. I seek and desire to live for and submit to the leading of the Spirit. I move will forward."*

Transition in the Wait

1 Resolve
2 Resurrection
3 Satisfaction
4 Move

Resolve

The World Book Dictionary defines resolve as to "make up one's mind, to make a decision, to settle it in one's mind (heart)." It is when we come to or reach a firm conclusion about a matter. It is here that you start to believe again. Resolve is the learning to be content no matter what state or place you are in (Philippians 4). It is the peace that comes in the waiting. You TRULY come to the statement of truth and faith found in Matthew 26 that Jesus had, *"Never the less, not my will but thy will be done."* Resolve recalls, rehearses, and speaks what it believes. In this place, I was encouraged by 2 Corinthians 4:13-16a, *"And since we have the same spirit of faith, according to what is written, I believed and therefore I spoke," we also believe and therefore speak, knowing that HE who raised up the Lord Jesus will also raise us up with Jesus, and will present us with you. For all things are for your sakes, that grace, having spread through the many, may cause thanksgiving to abound to the glory of God. Therefore we do not lose heart."* Resolves says, "Come what may, in my favor or not, the way I want it or not, my soul still says, "Yes, Lord." I have prayed, and if it comes now, soon, later, or never, I still trust You God. Help me Lord not to lose faith or grow faint!"

Resolve is a place of maturity and confidence. Evident is the perfected work in us that has matured us to be at peace within ourselves, with ourselves, and others. It does not compare its self or state to others. It is in resolve that we have allowed patience to have its perfect work in us. It is when you realize you really know nothing and are nothing without God. You recognize it is God who brings you any success that you have, have had or will have in your life. Resolve recognized that all good things in your life come from and is because of Him. Resolve is to have learned to be content no matter what state you are in. Resolve anticipates the right action and responds accordingly. It sees and expects the best. Resolve still expects but it does not demand. Demand forces, accuses, and controls because of insecurity, frustration, and fear. Though in its' most earnest sincerity and simplicity, demand's frustration comes from a place of fear. A need – a cry that seeks to be heard and respected...honored. Demand is a soul in unrest. Whereas as resolve is a soul at peace. It is from this place that the ability to find contentment and or resolve becomes difficult to recognize, accept, confront, and deal with our inter-demons, struggles, and challenges. It is fear that produces a since of distrust, unbelief (in), and lack of confidence in ourselves, the process, others, and God. Fear makes it very difficult to resolve, receive or reciprocate God's love and be at peace with ourselves or others.

Resolve is a confident and rested place and position of expectation. To have true resolve, you must know in whom and what you believe. It rests on who their resolve is in. For the believer that resolve is in God and His Word. It rests on the Word. It becomes a part of your character; your nature. It demonstrates that your mind is made up and your heart is fixed. It is not double minded. It believes and trusts God. It agrees with God. Housed in resolve are trust, faith, belief, confidence, security, agreement, and acceptance. Resolve is grasped through His Word and each experience with Him. Paul said in Philippians 4, *"For my determined purpose is that I may know Him - that I may progressively become more deeply and intimately acquainted with Him, perceiving and recognizing and understanding the wonders of His Person more strongly and more clearly, and that I may in that same way come to know the power out flowing from His resurrection which it exerts over believers, and that I may so share His sufferings as to be continually transformed by and in spirit into His likeness even to His death, in the hope that if possible I may attain to the spiritual and moral resurrection that lifts me out from among the dead even while (yet, still) in the (this) body."*

Abraham had resolve. Job, David, and Joshua had resolve. Paul and Esther had resolve. Resolve is Abraham's statement that nothing is impossible with God. Resolve is what Noah had when he obeyed God and built the ark. Though he had never seen or experienced rain, he still believed God and obeyed. It is Esther's declaration of if I perish, I perish. It is Job's proclamation that though HE slay me, yet will I trust Him. It is Paul saying after an extensive list of oppressive possibilities that nothing will separate him from the love of God. Resolve is Moses saying if Your Presence does not go with me, do not send me. It is Isaiah saying I will go, send me. Resolve is what the prophets had when the Word said they died in faith, not having received the promises they prophesied about. Yet, having seen them afar off, they were assured of them, embraced, and confessed them. Chapter 11 of Hebrews testifies of their resolve while they waited. Some received on this side of glory what they believed God to do and some did not, but generations after them did receive the promise. Of course, resolve was what Jesus operated in that allowed Him to say send Me, when HE went to the Garden, His response in the Garden, and on the Cross. Jesus lived a life of resolve.

Like surrender and contentment, resolve does not suggest that you are giving up, but that by faith, you have submitted your will to His will. It is patiently waiting and waiting right. It is trusting Him and choosing peace over pressure and the cares of life. You have come under the one who has ALL the power, knowledge, and resources to change you and your situation. A humble and confident knowing that we are not anything, cannot do or be anything without Him. It is not negative or complacent. It is not hopelessness, helplessness, or throwing your hands up in frustration because of impossibility. It is the lifting of your hands and heart to God in trust. A person of resolve knows that they need God. It is the confession of that need. They believe and have decided and declared by a formal resolution (faith) that if God doesn't do it won't happen. It is the resolve of the three Hebrew young men in Daniel 3. Resolve says, despite what it looks, feels, sounds, or seems like, I know HE can, is willing, and able. Resolve believes and knows that no matter what is before them and happens, nothing is impossible with God and everything is possible with him. Resolve speaks faith and calls things that are not as though they are. Resolve trusts and believes that HE who promises is faithful to perform. Resolve is confident that God knows what is best for me. HE cares for and about me. He is with me and for me. Resolves knows that win every time. Resolve waits gladly, joyfully, patiently on the Lord.

For a few reasons, I am sure this talk of surrender, submitting, and resolve may be a bit discouraging or challenging for some. Fear, insecurity, a need to control or be in-charge of others and the life you think is yours, etc. are the primary reason. What I know is this is most often a challenge for those who think it is all about them. It is their way or the highway. Their way is right. It is challenging to those who find it difficult to receive correction or character improvement suggestion. They will find it difficult to take responsibility and be accountable. They may even think they know more God; The Creator…Well, beloved let me help you…That is pride and arrogance; two things that must die and what HE hates. Whether we surrender to the death of pride before, in or outside of the waiting place, it must go. We can choose to surrender by choice or be forced, it is up to us. God hates it and those who experience yours hate it and when continued will grow to dislike you. Pride is a feeling or a deep pleasure or satisfaction with one's self. It is the root of selfishness, control, and a demanding nature or spirit. Haughtiness is a spirit that presents its' self and desires to be seen as superior, better, smart, greater, more than others; even if and or when others are equal to or "better" than them. Haughtiness is birthed from a place of insecurity; whereas pride is birthed from a place of rejection. Both are rooted in fear and both are very unbecoming. By this we can understand why God says in Proverbs 16 that before destruction, devastation, disaster, or lose comes; pride (not dealt with) has long been present. And a haughty arrogant spirit precedes a fall, embarrassment, and eventually ruin.

I have a question. How do you handle not getting what you want? Whether it is from a spouse, a parent, in a courtship, a friend, a manager, at work, at church, from your pastor, sibling or in a rare case from your staff, employees or parishioners? How do you handle delay or the forbidden and irritating word, 'NO?' I think it is good to tell your children 'no' sometimes even when you can and it is feasible and possible. If you grow up never hearing no in a loving way, without any restraint, without responsibility and accountable (they are different); you don't know how to accept, receive, and handle 'no' in a healthy way when you get older. Resolve can handle the "no"; receiving it and giving it.

What have you asked God to do or have waited on God to do and HE has not done it? What if what you have believed God for you never see it come to pass? What if you have already waited and HE is requiring you to wait again or some more? What if what you have prayed for, fasted for, declared, have had faith for...does not come to pass? Resolve can and will steady amidst the "what if's." In the face of your enemy, people thinking you are crazy, with all your questions, and uncertainties; can you settle in your mind and heart, what you know about God and who HE is to and for you? Resolve does not run in fear or in times of need or hurt. Resolve remains. Resolve is a team player. Resolve stays and stands to see the salvation and victory of the Lord. It waits like Job did for and until change comes.

I charge you to resolve to hold on and do not give up on yourself or God. Keep coming in faith putting Him in remembrance of His Word. Keep coming with your petitions and requests. Keep doing the will of God from your heart. This is why guarding your heart in life and relationship is so important. Out of it flows the issues of life. Trust Jeremiah 29 that God knows and wants what is best for you. His thoughts and plans for you are of peace and not of evil, to give you a future and a hope. Do not give up or surrender to helplessness and hopelessness. You shall receive your reward if you do not faint. Why HE answers in some circumstances and situations and not others, I don't know. Why HE comes quicker to answer in one area than in others, not sure. Why in one instance HE does exactly what we have asked, prayed, and waited for but in another there is a no show. I cannot tell you the answer to this. Why they get their prayers answered and you have not (yet). I will not try to presume. David said, some things are too lofty for me to obtain (understand).

What I do believe and this I am sure, God loves you and me. His ways are higher than and above ours. HE has a plan and purpose for each of us. Sooner or later it will work together (in the end) for our good. It really is already done. We are just waiting on the manifestation and timing of God. Matthew 7 reminds us that if your natural son asks for bread would you give him a stone? If our earthly father who is not good by nature knows how to give good gifts to his children, how much more will your Heavenly Father who is love and loves us; why would HE not give good things to us, His children when (if) we ask Him…Even when we do not ask, HE still gives us good gifts; breathe, life, love, forgiveness, mercy, etc. The Bible says HE loads us up daily with benefits. When God is not speaking to you or you do not hear Him, HE is still speaking. His silence speaks and very well may be His response and your answer…And that answer is 'wait'. Be still to hear and know that I Am here and still God. If you take a minute and consider and be honest with yourself; you know exactly what HE has told you…Yes, even in His silence HE has spoken. Your resolve will bring you peace even when God is or appears to be silent.

Similar with our children when we are silent, there is an answer that can be found in God's silence. Remember Jesus' question in Matthew 26 in the garden, *"O My Father, if it is possible, let this cup pass from Me; nevertheless, not as I will, but as You will."* That semi-colon was what God did not say, but Jesus knew and resolved..."*Not my will but Thy will be done.*" Consider Joshua's question of the Man (Angel of the Lord) who stood before him in Joshua 5; when he asked, "*Are you for us or for our adversaries?*" The Man did not answer him. HE simply affirms His assignment for being there. God's plans for you are specific to and only for you. We must learn to wait, be still, listen to hear and trust in the transition times of God. Resolve trusts in the pauses: the colons, semi-colons, commas, periods, and dashes we encounter with God. We must get a resolve and trust the silent moments and messages from God. I do not believe that God is ever in a hurry. HE may put urgency in us to act and to do but HE in His nature is not hurried. HE is peace. HE is time. HE is waiting personified. HE is providence. HE is sovereignty. HE is resolve. Because HE knows the end from the beginning, HE is always in a confident state of rest and peace. HE has no cause to be in a hurry. So to you I say, rest in God. Get a resolve to be and to live always in the confidence and peace of and from God.

God is sovereign. HE is supreme excellence. HE has all power, and freedom from external control, pressures or influences. HE is the controlling influence over all things. HE knows what you and I don't know and knows what we need. HE knows why it; what we want and desire cannot be now, why it is not for yet, or why it will not cannot be ever at all ever or just not the way you want it. When you resolve, your wait will become easier to deal with. You will be able to face life's issues and challenges with hope, expectation, and dare I say joy. Yes, joy. Joy is possible in your waiting place. Let His providence keep your thoughts in knowing that HE has the sustaining knowledge and power to guide your human existence and order your days and life. Resolve that whatever my cause and reason for being in this waiting state, I will get out of it from it what God has for me to gain and know. I will learn and apply it as wisdom. I will never pass this way again.

Resurrection

What was lost in battle. What was taken unlawful. Whatever you gave away in ignorance or loss due to sin. Whatever the enemy or your actions have held up; God has promised to restore. What you (think) have lost in the wait, be it God's will you will get back. And it will be better and greater. It is in the resurrection stage of waiting that your miracles, dreams, and visions are revived and rebirthed. Resolve has increased your faith and you begin to speak faith and possibility. Despair has left and hope and confidence are restored. Dead, dry bones of dreams, hopes, and visions receive the breath of life through the words and a changed mind and heart. For out of that changed heart your mouth speaks hope, possibility, and life. Things come alive again. Life is breathed into every part of your life allowing you to flow.

The promise of life and life more abundantly comes alive in the resurrection. It comes with power to help us walk by faith and do our part to manifest the promise. It comes with peace and wisdom. Go ahead, start now. Choose today; this very moment to dream and plan. In your waiting place, you can experience and see the miracles of the Lord. Your expectation in the waiting is a seed to seeing your miracles come to pass. Everything you need to manifest your breakthrough, your miracle, your dreams come to pass is already in you. Like Abraham, our hope, future, and prosperity are in us. We just need to do what is necessary and plant the seed; the vision and connect with the right person or people to help us carry it and birth. In the transition from resolve to resurrection, God will give you a testimony. It is found in your imagination, mediation of dreams, thinking, believing, and speaking.

You must learn and practice the art of speaking from your place of waiting into your promise(s) and purpose. Speak and write what you desire and believe God to do for and through you. *"Write the vision and make it plain on tablets, that he may run who reads it. For the vision is yet for an appointed time; but at the end it will speak, and it will not lie. Though it tarries, wait for it; because it will surely come, it will not tarry"* (Habakkuk 2:2,3). This is such a powerful Scripture that speaks to waiting on God in our transition times and season. I found this word tarry to be intricate in waiting on the timing; the appointed time of God. We know that the primary definition of "tarry" means to delay or take long. Interestingly, the first use of this word in this scripture has a slightly different meaning then the second time it is used. With the first use of the word the secondary definition of "tarry" means to wait and wait expectantly. Now, this blows me away. If we rewrote this, it would read something like this, *"Though it (vision, promise) waits expectantly (an appointed time, a set time, an anticipated date for manifestation) wait for it...it will not delay."* I had shared earlier that "waiting" by definition seemed to have a character; a personality. Now here we find in Habakkuk that waiting has to wait. Wow, God wow. Waiting waits for whom – for what? Waiting waits on the one who has authority to release it. Waiting waits to be released. Waiting waits for its' time; its' turn to be released and manifest. This reminds me of when Jesus spoke to peace and told it to be still in the storm.

Because time and timing and everything in between in creation belongs to God; we can be confident and trust that His plan, purpose, vision for our life is sure...It will come to pass. If waiting waits its' turn in assurance why can't or don't we? So I ask you, is your purpose worth waiting on God? Is the vision HE has given you worth waiting on Him to show you the way, to order your steps? Are the plans; the thoughts He has of you worth waiting on and trusting Him for them to come to pass in His time? If so, I charge and encourage you to learn and practice waiting patiently, expectantly on the Lord; His time and His timing. Though it tarries; seems to delay or take long, wait for it. It will surely come to pass. Hold on. Do not grow weary in your well doing of waiting and waiting right. The time between the promise and the manifestation may seem or be long, but it will come forth. Remember a thousand days to Him; in Him is like a day. It shall (absolutely will) come to pass.

Satisfaction

God's seasons supersede natural seasons. The seasons of God in the waiting place are not aligned with the seasons of nature but the supernatural. Your due season will come according to His timing for your life. I know that may not be comforting but if you let it; if you resolve, surrender, and trust the process it can. Though you may not know when due season is God knows. The process or timing of release and freedom does not have to take long. Remember suddenly. I believe we can play a role in how long our season or time in waiting lasts. Certainly, God has a purpose and appointed-time for us, but the extended stay is often related to the choices and decisions we make. To be satisfied with and in God alone is the epitome of success in and with God. This is the unseen seen success that comes from being satisfied with yourself, your life, and with and in God. It is the internal peace that meets our external expression. This internal peace is one of the outward manifestations of our faith. It is when we can say, "No matter what state I am in, I will thank and bless the Lord my God." You can be satisfied even when you have yet to receive the desires of our heart.

There is a place in transition where time and season collide. It reminds me of the scripture in Psalm 85:10 that say, *"Mercy* (God) *and truth* (Jesus) *have met and righteousness* (Holy Spirit, The Teacher of Righteousness) *and peace* (Jesus) *have kissed."* Can you see God and Jesus meeting on your behalf and Jesus and the Holy Spirit kissing in agreement about you? How awesome and exciting! This is the timing and favor of God. It is my due season dispatched. In my Holy imagination and belief, my assigned angels are sent to bring, protect or defend my promise. Daniel 10 supports this truth that resides in my spirit. My appointed time has come. There will be nothing that man or outside forces can do to thwart it. It will be as if the windows of Heaven open and you are walking under an open Heaven. Favor follows, pursues, and over takes you.

Because you have learned surrender, resolve, and satisfaction in God, your obedience is being made complete through the things you suffered; yet, you rose from these. Not only have your dreams and vision been resurrected but so have you. You are the phoenix of your testimony that God can, will, and is able to do just what HE has said and promised. Your faith has increased and satisfaction in God has come. The motto on money is now your slogan, "In God I Trust." Let the peace and satisfaction of and in God guard your heart and mind in Christ Jesus as you wait on Him. If Christ had to learn through suffering why do we think we do not have to and would not have to learn in a similar (or same) way? There is always a reward – blessing for obedience and yours reward is on the way.

To become satisfied with God and God alone, you must trust, know, and believe that God has so much (more) stored up for you. Scriptures about His purpose, plan, and love for you can aid in this. I often tell singles; particularly women, "You need to be so in love with God and so intimate with Him that when God sends your spouse they are almost jealous of the Him as other man; the other lover in your life." Even within a relationship between believers, your coming together in covenant should not be to steal or take the person from God, but to include Him in. Jesus and the Holy Spirit are the only two entities that God is not jealous of. I encourage you to welcome them as the center and foundation of into your relationships, business dealings, and fellowships. This is the only time a threesome should ever be allowed. Jacob said in Genesis 29 that because of his love for Rachel working for her father for seven years to receive her as a bride seemed like only a few days. Now that is satisfaction when our work for what we believe God has for us is not laborious or a burden.

This shows me that satisfaction; being at peace with whatever state we are in and having to do whatever it takes to receive God's blessing (promise) is a choice. Like contentment, we have to work at it. Just ensure that whatever you do, with who or what you are in relationship or fellowship with, be sure to not snuffed God out. Do not forget about Him or leave Him out or behind or pushed Him aside or away. Your satisfaction in God has the power to release or draw to you the things that God has in-store for you. Your reward will be more than material things. With (from) a surrendered, satisfied, and obedient heart; ask for and expect a supernatural encounter and collusion with God and what HE has for you. Who knows, maybe God and Jesus are having a discussion about you as we speak and the Holy Spirit and Jesus are coming in agreement about you to release your angel(s). Who knows, this may be your 'such a time as this' moment. It could very well be your time and your turn. Armed with this hope, can you walk out your salvation and sanctify yourself in being satisfied with the sacrifice and love of your Savior Jesus Christ.

To get to this place of surrender and satisfaction, you must be willing to give up control and not only trust in Him, but trust Him with your life and destiny. In any relationship trust and peace are necessary. And so it is true in our relationship with God. We must trust and know that HE is in control and wants, knows, and has (in store for us) what is best for us. HE is your creator, designer, builder, and manufacturer. HE really does know what is ideal for us. We are His workmanship, created in Christ Jesus for (His) good works, which God prepared beforehand that we should walk in them (Ephesians 2:10). We live and walk it out of His place but it is His plan for our life. If you are not sure what it is, use your waiting place to ask and learn of it and Him.

If you owned a Mercedes would you go and find a Chevy manual to get instructions on how to maintain it or how it functions or operates. Of course not, but we do this every day in our relationship with God. We go to psychics, horoscopes, our friends; saved and unsaved, wise and foolish, our family, mentors, speakers, conferences, etc. And certainly, when it is wisdom and of God and His truth it is good. But there will and must come a time when your first stop is the Father. To know His truth about you and get His plan, direction, and understanding, we must go to Him. The Creator of all things; including you. Anything else will be insufficient; a delay and a distraction to your purpose, and quite possibly, detrimental. Friends, family, pastors, ministers, and mentors will all mean well. Their counsel will prayerfully be wise, but God is there for you to go to Him directly and ask. I often counsel the mature Christian that before you go to others make sure you have sought the Father first. This way you come with a thought or something that you have heard the Holy Spirit say to you in your spirit or through the Word.

Our pastors are here to instruct and teach us, help us believe, and watch over our souls. Yet, your relationship with God must be and is personal. You are responsible for working and walking out your salvation and growing in our relationship and satisfaction with God. We do this primarily through hearing, receiving, and applying the teachings, studying and praying His Word on our own and through corporate fellowship. In your waiting place, HE is waiting on you to call on Him. HE will incline His ear to you and HE will answer (Psalm 116:2). We can influence and impact our destiny but we are not in control of it. HE has the blue print of your existence, the diagram, and map for your life. HE is Lord. HE is Elohim your Creator. HE created you thus HE has all knowledge of you. HE wrote the owners' manual of you and is concerned about every matter of your life. Remember, HE is the owner. So, you may want to talk with Him and get insight about you, your purpose, and His plan for you from Him. Then make a choice to be satisfied with His response.

Move

Do Something

Moving forward is subliminally imbedded within change, growth, development, and hope. I hear you…how do I move in the waiting place – in between? How do I move forward? How? Your prayers are movement. Remember we are talking about transitioning in the waiting states. You must us this time to plan, prepare, declare, praise, serve, fellowship, do something new, have fun, and dream right where you are. All of these are aspects of moving forward. If you don't or can't find your way to do these things on this side of through what will do on the other side. Use your time wisely. Our waiting place is practice. To practice our dance. To practice our praise. To put into practice your change in character. We all have heard it said, "You gotta praise Him in advance." In Luke chapter 1 verse 46, Mary starts to praise God for the promised blessed she carried and was soon to manifest in a few months. Her praise was on this side of the promised blessing. It was on the faith side of the blessing (the substance) hoped for but not yet seen.

Over committing or extending yourself, becoming a work-a-holic or another kind of holic, doing many good things but not the God assigned purposeful things, never sitting still to reflect to feel to heal or making time for what is good and healthy for you are not forms of forward movement. These are busy works that hinder us in our waiting place. They are often the way we use to hide in the house and conceal hurts behind our work, accomplishments, and busy schedules. Resulting in our being and staying stuck; often without knowing it. They are existing (functioning) in life but not living. No, they are not the walking dead but a dead man (woman) walking. It is not active waiting or forward movement. It is movement, but not forward movement, which implies better.

Forward movement is going from ok or mediocre, to good, too great, to excellent to outstanding. It is progressive. It is active waiting. It is productive and positive. I am frequently heard saying, "I am not busy, I am purposed. Being busy is a stronghold and is a form of being under satan's yoke...busy. A life of consistent busyness is often of sign of unfulfilment, dissatisfaction, and restless. Consistent busyness that causes loss, conflict, guilt, strife, stress, sickness is never good or obviously unhealthy. This level of busyness is a form of avoidance. Avoiding what you ask? Truth that brings and internal or external conflict! Whether the truth is about us, someone else or a situation, it is easier or less painful to avoid than to deal with and confront the pain or issue. The root of avoidance is fear; fear of failure or fear of success. Either way, we can be guilty of avoiding and never seeing, tasting, experiencing or having the entire promise that God has for us.

When HE breathed life into us and we accepted His Son as Savior and Lord. HE did not give us the spirit of fear, but a spirit; His Spirit (a new nature) of power (God the Holy Spirit), love (God the Father), and a sound mind (God the Son). Because the same power is in us, HE now charges us to do something. To walk by faith and not by sight. To do greater works. To be a son of God. To be the righteousness of God in and through Christ Jesus. To live victorious. To accept Him, His love, and all His promises. To live holy (set a part for a purpose). To be and live godly in our character. To move forward. If you have not discerned by now, if we let it; our waiting place can be and is essential to our healing and being made whole. It can be our launching pad to bigger, better, greater, more.

To find your motivation to wait and participate in forward movement, you must find your 'why.' Not asking God why, but why you want to be free. Why you want to need to desire to be or have better. It is a cleansing question that helps to find your conviction and will often solidify your purpose. Use your time of waiting to discover your 'why.' Why do I want what I want? Why do I do what I do? Why do I think the way I think and approach life the way that I do? Sometimes these questions can cause us to go to places within ourselves that we have not visited in a long time or never have touched. As you pursue this, I invite you to welcome in wise counsel as you search to find your 'why'. Why will get you up in the morning without an alarm clock. It will cause you to plan your days in advance. Your 'why' will keep you going when you want to give up. It will awaken you to dreams and visions that you had laid down. It will get you early and keep you up late. It will drive you with excitement and joy towards purpose and fulfillment. It will keep you moving forward with balance. Find your 'why' and you will locate and unwrap your motivation to wait and wait right on, in and with God.

WHAT I LEARNED

Resolve is not negative. It is my faith in action. I must resolve – trust that God is in control and HE always wants what is best for me. HE will always cause me to triumphant. His silence does not mean no. It may mean not yet. HE knows what is up the road and what all is tied to my request – to what I think I want or need. I must trust Him to make the best and right decision for me and submit to His way and will. Resolving is a choice and though it can be scary because it is the sold out place in God – God or nothing – if HE doesn't do it - it won't be done. In God I resolve myself to trust Him. Resolve and satisfaction are a choice. I accept that my waiting place can be my healing place. I must fight and be intentional for my freedom and purpose. Finding and keeping my motivation is as simply as finding my 'why'. I know this to be true. My why has kept me moving forward because answering it really has solidified my purpose.

I have learned that...

_____

_____

_____

_____

_____

Scripture or Statement for Meditation

_____

My waiting issue...

_____

_____

_____

_____

_____

_____

SIX

Everybody Waits

Even the Elite

The Bible gives us many lessons on waiting:

- Adam waited in God as he slept to make his help mate and received a wife
- Abraham waited 25 years to receive his promised heir and was called a friend
- Moses waited on God for direction and got a glimpse of His glory
- Joseph waited on God and it was 13 years from His dream to manifestation and his blessing was to oversee the financial mountain of a nation
- Job waited for his appointed time of restoration and received double
- Elijah waited for miracle provision and received more than enough and produced miracles even in his death
- Paul and Silas waited on God in jail and was supernaturally released
- The Children of Israel waited 70 years for their restoration
- Paul waited blind, shipwrecked, in jail, and the list goes on

- The earth – all creation waits with eager expectation for the revealing of the sons of God
- 120 waited in the Upper Room for the promise of the Holy Spirit
- Jesus waited to go and see about Lazarus and truth be told, Lazarus was waiting on Him to come
- Lazarus and his sisters waited for Jesus to come see about him and HE was raised from the dead and he was the 1st resurrection from the dead
- From the time that Anna became a widow, she waited 84 years (fasting and praying in the temple) on the coming of Jesus and the redemption of her and her people
- Mary waited for the expectation of the miracle child that came without the assistance of man to manifest in & from her womb – a miracle worth waiting on
- Jesus waited at the well for disciples to return with food and HE gave living water to the women and her entire household was saved
- All the believers everywhere (dead and alive) wait on the return of Jesus Christ

Waiting to be healed

- The ruler had to wait on Jesus to come to heal his daughter while HE healed the women with the issue of blood
- Who had waited 12 years going from doctor to doctor
- For 38 years, the man waited at the pool of Bethesda
- The man waited at Gate Beautiful

We could really discuss Paul's waiting seasons all day. HE waited to be rescued, to be delivered from man and himself, to be set free, to receive his sight back, and the list goes on. He waited on his thorn to be removed, prayed three times but it remained. Everyone, men, women, children, old young, black, white, brown, and all others have and will wait. John the Baptist needed reassurance when he asked in Luke 7, *"Is it you or shall I look for another."* He waited on a response to his question to know if Jesus was the One and never received it. Before the Disciples fell asleep, they waited with and on Jesus in the Garden. They were invited to wait; to watch and pray. They were unable to wait and complete their assignment. They waited less than an hour before they fell asleep but others have days, weeks, months, and years on the Lord. God has certainly waited on us; His children. In the Old Testament, His waiting included sending Judges, and Prophets to help in the wait. Isaiah sums it up in chapter 30 verse 18 saying, *"The LORD will wait, that HE may be gracious to you."* 2 Peter 3 tells us that *"The Lord is not slow in keeping his promise, as some understand slowness. Instead HE is patient with you, not wanting anyone to perish, but everyone to come to repentance – the truth and knowledge of Him."*

I have often heard people say after they have received a questionable report from their doctor that the wait is the worse. That was probably true for Jesus when HE waited on God the Father to answer or respond to His prayer of supplication and petition in the Garden. HE prayed (pleaded) with God. Three times HE; Jesus, The Beloved, Our Savior, Our King, Our Lord asked and was regulated to waiting. HE agonized with what HE had to do and pleaded with God to take the assignment from Him. Yes, the Redeemer, the Keeper, and Sustainer waited and pleaded. The one who had and has all power, said "Send me" waited and cried out to God, The Father. HE waited. With no response from God, HE resolved…Never the less not My will but Thy will be done. All creation had to wait on God (the Trinity) to create man in His image, so that they could be named and have a purpose. Still today, creation waits on us to know who we are in Christ and for the glory of God to be revealed in and through us. If creation, Jesus, and God the Father has waited so patiently for us, what makes us think we will not and should not have to wait them or others.

Most people; if not all of us, are waiting for, or on something or someone. If you are not currently, waiting, you just came out of the waiting place or are about go into it. We have all wasted time, life, space, and purpose waiting on stuff. Sometimes we seem to be waiting on the wrong things, people or persons. May I pose to you this question, "What or who are YOU waiting for?" "Who or what are you waiting on? Is it God or man or is God waiting on you?" There are several purposes for why God may have you waiting. God either desires for you to:

1 learn obedience – submission and surrender
2 know His will so you can do His will
3 know His voice so you will hear and follow His leading and direction
4 humble ourselves
5 trust Him no matter the season, challenge, trial or length of time
6 die to self - change
7 see ourselves – good, bad and ugly
8 be delivered – heal and made whole
9 grow in the knowledge, truth and love of Him

Yes, everyone will be made to wait. We even saw that the earth is waiting. Angels in heaven wait to be sent to our aid. The farmer waits patiently for the rain and the land to yield its harvest (James 5:7). God waits. HE waits on His enemies to be made His footstool. There is a set and appointed time for even that. HE waits for us to change our mind, know we need a Savior, and ask for forgiveness and receive Him as Savior and Lord. Jesus is waiting to be released to come back and receive those who have died in Him and the living who are believers in Him that we can return with Him to heaven.

Everyone! Everyone will experience waiting for a season or a time. Everyone will have a cause to, be forced to, or place themselves in a place of waiting. Why, you ask? Throughout this book you have read, reflected, and rehearsed all the many reasons and benefits to waiting, waiting right, and waiting on God. All of our waiting places, states, and seasons can be summed up in a few words: faith that includes trust and believing in ourselves, Him and our future; love that holds His forgiveness, grace, mercy, favor, our freedom, and purpose; and our growing in Him by being healed, made whole, and forgiving others. Whether the wait comes to grow, develop, or transform us; ultimately its purpose is to make us more like Christ and trust Him in the process; in the waiting place, seasons, and states. Waiting is a teacher. Teaching us to listen, hear, trust, and obey. We learn the timing and the seasons of God. Through the waiting times, I have experienced and learned God in many different and new ways. I have learned to seek and appreciate Him. I have learned to value my time with Him, to wait in Him and on Him all at the same time. My trust in Him has been elevated to words like fully, solely, forever, always, completely, and sold out. It is in the wait that you learn who you really are, what you earnestly believe, and what you are truly made of. Waiting is a processor. Through the process, we are authenticated; particularly, in the silence and unanswered wait state. Since everyone has to wait, you might as well learned and get what has been ordained for you in your waiting place.

I understand. Waiting can make you feel unheard, forgotten, but God has promised to never leave you or forsake (forget about) you. HE is not slack concerning His promise toward you. The time we have to wait is according to God's wisdom and standard. It is directly related to our need, our purpose, and the perfected work of God. However, how long it takes us to get it – to change – to mature or grow is up to us. The love, grace, and mercy of

God will not allow Him to leave you in an unperfected state. His desire for us is that we lack nothing; including wisdom and that we and our soul prospers, and are (or live) in good health. HE desires for us to be ready, mature enough to receive and handle the blessings HE has stored up for us. HE desires that we be able to stand up under, and overcome the challenges that will come (along with) because of the blessings. HE desires His Kingdom on earth and in the earth of you to come and be made manifest. HE knows what HE is doing. All those who wait and wait right will come forth beholding His glory. The glory; His glory, a greater anointing comes forth from, out of, and because of our perfecting and learned waiting season(s). Great gain can be ours.

I remind you that the Trinity waited and stills waits (patiently) for all to come to the knowledge and truth of Jesus. Satan had to wait and get permission to mess with Job, Peter, you, and me. And as many times as he may ask for me and you, God doesn't answer him either. Jesus had to wait on God to send him, anoint Him, and call Him from the tomb. HE had to wait on the Cross for the His appointed time. The people in the Upper Room had to wait on Jesus to come and for the Holy Spirit to be sent. Everyone...Absolutely everyone has to wait. If and where and when possible I make a choice to wait right and let waiting be my teacher and perfecter.

WHAT I LEARNED

Everybody has or will have to wait. What a reminder that creation is waiting on me – on believers in Jesus Christ. In order to wait on something you have a trust and have an expectation see, hear, encounter something. A pregnant mother has to wait til the baby is ready to enter the world. No matter how much she pushes, if it ain't time and the baby ain't ready – it is not coming down or out. Most of the time, I (we) am not waiting on God – HE is waiting on me. What (all) is God waiting on me to do? Selah – pause and think (meditate) on this…be honest and answer.

I have learned that...

_____

_____

_____

_____

_____

Scripture or Statement for Meditation

_____

My waiting issue...

_____

_____

_____

_____

_____

SEVEN

Waiting Right

I have talked or rather taught a great deal on waiting right. I thought it wise to dedicate some time to focus on what that looks like. Our greatest challenge before God is not that we are waiting, but how we wait while we wait. Waiting in its self is a difficult discipline and quite possibly the most difficult discipline you will face. And even armed with that I still tell you, you must need learn and master waiting right. Waiting right is a waiting that lives and acts by faith, *"For whatever is not from (done by) faith is sin"* (Romans 14:23). Waiting is a choice but to wait right is a sacrifice. It is a surrender of all of your emotions, your will, your thoughts, your way, your plans, etc. You may now be saying, "I don't want this if I have to give up me...I can't see any benefit or purpose in this for me." Or you are asking, "How do I learn to wait right?" "What does waiting right look like and how do I do it?" "Can some really master waiting?" Here is your answer. We learn to wait and to wait right by waiting. We must do it and practice it to become perfected in it and master it.

I submit to you that since you are going to have to wait at many and varying point(s) in your life...why not learn to wait right and alleviate the challenges that come from waiting out of order. Andrew Murray says, "Waiting on God is the highest salvation. We must resolve at once that it shall be the one characteristic of our life and worship: a continual, humbling, truthful waiting upon God."

So, what does waiting right look like? Glad you asked. You must wait by faith; trusting and believing God, with the right perspective, with expectation, without worry, without fear, with patience, peace, and with praise. For a Believer in Jesus Christ, it is impossible to wait on God without prayer, the Word of God (which is Jesus Himself), and in some cases there may be a time of fasting. A greater level of sacrifice of self - the flesh used to conquer fear, feelings of inadequacies, anger, unforgiveness, to hear from God, to get direction and clarity in the wait; fasting will be a saving grace. Waiting right is using your waiting time wisely to deal with you, to grow and better you, and in your relationship and fellowship with God. The Word of God will become your guide and your peace. In your waiting place, it will truly become the lamp unto your feet and the light upon your path. I contend that you cannot and will not survive in your waiting without the Word and without Him. His presence, His Holy Spirit will be your invisible visible truth. For those who are not a believer in Jesus Christ, I submit to you that you will and do need something to encourage and strengthen in your seasons of waiting. I implore you to identify what that source of unchanging, never failing truth and love is for you that brings you strength, hope, comfort, and direction.

As I consider those who waited; Lazarus experienced a waiting that was him waiting for himself to be called out and come forth. His very life and existence would be the waiting right witness to all. He was the very miracle he was waiting on. Talk about the earth groaning. He had a "waiting place" like none other. He was called out of a grave. Through the story of Lazarus, we can learn to appreciate the waiting place and the blessings that come in the wait. Here are a few of those:

1   Jesus will show up personally – you will have an encounter with your Savior and friend – John 11:4-7
2   Call on Him – speak things that are not as they are – speak – declare God's truth – His Word – John 11:11
3   You will see – experience a miracle – supernatural intervention that last – John 11:14
4   Be encouraged – John 11:23, 26
5   You become a witness to and of your own breakthrough and deliverance – John 11:40-44
6   Jesus will command others to get involved in your coming out – John 11:38, 44
7   You can be - will be loosed from your bondage – if you just wait – nothing not even death can't hold you any longer – John 11:44
8   Grow to know and appreciate His love for you - His blessing you will draw others – John 11:53, 54
9   When you wait right, you will be talked about (good and bad) and remembered – John 12:9, 11
10 End will better than your beginning – you will be better when you come out than when you went in

As we make waiting on God our lifestyle, it becomes a fountain of change that brings love and peace flowing through every part of our lives. The greatest obstacle we will face with spiritual discipline of waiting on God is our inexperience with waiting. In Darryl Harris' book, "When God Says Wait," he suggests that "We are just not equipped to wait." We do not know how to wait. In this hurried and culture of microwaves, Easy Mac, fast food restaurants, food delivery, instant coffee, instant marriage, instant fame, instant divorce, instant riches, etc., waiting is a lost art. Things that use to take time to prepare, process, develop, and serve can now be served and delivered within a short amount of time. Depending on what it is that could be good, bad, or just ok but may not be the best.

Time is important to the proving, finishing, and remaining process. Reflect on the last time you had to wait in a line, on the mail, or on someone. How well do you do? Yes, we wait, but do we wait right. Do we finish the process? Do we wait by faith; trusting, with the right perspective, with expectation, without worry, without fear, with patience, and praise. Can you say you wait right on the Lord? Have you learned to be content (not complacent); at peace, waiting on the Lord. When we learn to wait and wait right for the promise(s) of God over our life, we become even more confident that whatever our "it" is, it shall come to pass. Wait on God and you will receive it!

By Faith

"By faith", what a mouth full? Hebrews 11 lists the hall of faith of those who obtained a good report, a witness, pleased God, were heir of the righteousness, and received strength to conceive seed, and was delivered simply because they operated in and was led by their faith in God and what HE could do. Like those in Hebrews 11, all that we do must be done by faith; including, waiting. To wait and most certainly to wait right requires faith. In this same chapter, it tells us that without faith we cannot please God. I submit to you that it is a waste of time to just wait and not make every attempt to practice waiting right. We must have faith to believe that we shall receive not only while we are in the waiting place but definitely on the other side. Great shall our reward be for actively waiting; doing our part and waiting right. What awaits us will be better and greater than what we could every thought or imagined.

Trust and Believe

We spent a great deal of time earlier dealing with the trust issue. However, to define for you the necessity of trust in waiting right, it is worth briefly addressing again. My definition of 'trust' is to have an assured confidence at rest. When we fight against God's waiting place, we are telling Him, "I don't trust your way(s) and your plan(s) for me for my life." We must all face this truth that we may not fully or completely always trust God…At least; we must admit it becomes even more difficult in the in the long-term - extended parking of waiting. You may find yourself trusting less the longer you are in the holding pattern of your waiting place. Perhaps there is a partial trust in Him. We trust Him with this but not with that. It is the part of your house you would never want anyone to see: your closet, under bed, your attic, your bathtub, your cabinets or around the bottom of your toilet. Love Him yes, but do you really - always – in all things trust Him. For some time, I too struggled with this thought. It was after several circumstances and situations that God showed me I had a trust issue. My trust issue of God stemmed from my relationship with my earthy father. Not to go into detail in this book (that another book) but I believe a piece of this God wants me to touch on now.

My inability to trust God was indirectly related to my inability to trust my earthly father. In pure ignorance, good or bad, we all at some point have been guilty (consciously or subconsciously) of measuring or comparing God's ability and integrity to that of our earthly father. Though he (your father) may have been (or is) a great dad, he is not God. Your earthly father may have failed you but God will never fail you. The excellence of God as Father cannot be compared. Our natural father will leave us in death or in life, but God The Father will never leave or forsake you. HE can be trusted. You can depend on Him. You can wait on Him and be of good cheer. Long before I saw God as Father; I received and accepted Him as Daddy, Abba. What? Ok, let me explain. I saw the Daddy side of God as loving, nurturing, kind, accepting, giving, without motive, approachable, gentle, patient, encouraging, supportive, a safe place, forgiving, patient. Unfortunately, I did not know my earthly father as daddy. He did not know how to be that for his children. He was certainly a father; disciplinarian, set and expected order, protector, provider, the authority, etc. It was with this truth of God as Daddy that I began to see Him a whole new way and found the relationship with God was looking for and needed to start on my journey of healing and wholeness. Though God has never lost His place as God in my life but in time, HE transitioned from being my Daddy to my Father.

What you believe about God, who HE is, what HE can do and is willing to do for you becomes the evidence of what is not yet seen. How you see Him is based on what you know about Him and have experienced through your relationship and fellowship with Him. If you fear Him or see Him as an unforgiving, unloving, punishing, and a judgment only God, your wait will be very difficult. It may take some time but I encourage you to take the journey from seeing God only as your God to Him as Father and being your Daddy God. We come into this world with Him as our Father because HE is the creator of all things but we have to choose to make Him our God and prayerfully His Son our Savior and Lord. Then there is another level of appreciation and love when see and experience Him as Daddy God.

God as my God is Him having control over all things. HE is the ruler of all and has control over all. God is the Omni of all. The Father nature and side of God; provides, protects, covers, and instructs us. In my waiting and my struggles, it was me growing up in to and experiencing God as Father and as Daddy that kept me and brought me through. I progressed from approaching God only as God to Him as Father. But the day, I ran across "Abba"; which means Daddy and my world turned. The Dad of God is His loving, patient, evident forgiveness, encouraging, listening, and compassionate side of Him. At least this was how I grew to experience and know Him because this is what I needed. Typing this even now, His love still draws tears when I think about what all HE has done and brought me through. My God, I love Him. That day, that revelation and still today, my eyes were opened and heart softened to a new and more loving relationship with my Holy Father God. It was and is this love that teaches me how to love others. My earthly father was my father but unfortunately, he didn't know how to be a daddy. I needed a daddy and I found it in God.

Over time, with each experience trust grows. It built upon and added to through relationships that have mutual respect, honor, and proven track records. Consider this. We love our children but do we, can we, should we, would we trust them to take our new $100,000 Mercedes Benz on a joy ride or even the prom. We love our spouse, but where there is an issue of an unhealed hurt, an unmet need, or an unresolved issue, it is difficult to trust and sometimes to forgive and let go. This is proven by the very statistics of divorce founded on "irreconcilable differences." *Side note:* I never understood how Christians could divorce with this as the cause when God has given us the ministry (service) of reconciliation.

Trust is a valuable asset. It requires that you measure each relationship, encounter, and experience independently. You cannot measure or even subconsciously compare your earthly relationships to each other. Each one holding its' own experiences and depth of importance and value. So why try to compare our supernatural one with God to that of anyone in this earth. In earthly relationships, trust is one of those things that if (when) it is gained, it brings great comfort and peace. Yet, if it is lost, it is a greater challenge to regain and even more difficult to reestablish and continue on. I'm not sure what goes first; peace or trust but without trust there is not peace and where there is not peace, I can almost guarantee that trust has been shaken. Trust built, give or restored requires an ex-change of honesty, truth, and transparency from both sides and most certainly the side that caused it to be lost. Once trust is built and established, confidence is built and peace comes. Confidence (trust) is strengthened through communication, consistency, and common interests. This is the same process in our relationship with God The Father.

How do we grow to trust God? Before I address this, may I pose a question to you? Can God trust you? Can HE trust you with His Word, with His people, with His blessings (material, people, opportunity), with His church? Can God trust us do the right thing in His name? Can HE trust you to love the one you are with solely and wholly? To honor, care, respect the (spiritual and human) gift and gifts HE has given you? Can HE trust you with where HE is taking you and with what HE desires to give you? Remember Peter and the question Jesus asked Him in John Chapter 21. *"So when they had eaten breakfast, Jesus said to Simon Peter, "Simon, son of Jonah, do you love Me more than these?" He said to Him, "Yes, Lord; You know that I love You."He said to him, "Feed My lambs."He said to him again a second time, "Simon, son of Jonah, do you love Me?" He said to Him, "Yes, Lord; You know that I love You."He said to him, "Tend My sheep."He said to him the third time, "Simon, son of Jonah, do you love Me?" Peter was grieved because He said to him the third time, "Do you love Me?" And he said to Him, "Lord, You know all things; You know that I love You."Jesus said to him, "Feed My sheep."*

The question and its purpose intensified each time Jesus asked Peter and he responded. It advanced in responsibility as He went from: Feed (provide – give nourishment, substance to sustain) my Lambs (children, innocent), to Tend to (care for and about) My sheep (older, mature believers) to Feed My sheep. Jesus caused Peter to examine his heart and go beyond surface love to a deep, abiding, and trusting love. The way God and Jesus showed Their love for us is how HE desires and was telling Peter (us) to show his love for them. How we love and care for others, demonstrates our love relationship with and for God. Here is another question for you to ponder, "Is it possible for us to love Them (God The Father, God the Son, and God the Holy Spirit) as much as or how They love us?" I do not believe it is. The closest we can get is to obey, trust, believe, and have and love our faith. Similar is the love a parent has for their child. These attributes please Him and screams out loud of our love and commitment for Them.

Christ knew what Peter would do. HE is all knowing. HE gave Peter a great opportunity to validate his love and their relationship. I do not believe that God expects us to love to this degree. Yet, to truly know the depth, the height, the expanse, and the length that HE would go and did go because HE so loved us is unfathomable. This is why Paul said in Ephesians 3 that it was his hope that we may be able to comprehend God's love. In Chapter 1 he says that he hoped that the eyes of our understanding be opened. What I discovered was that this is not possible without God who is love and the demonstration of love from His Son; The Savior of the world. No more evident of His love was the clear display of it on Calvary, in the Garden and that HE came. As we grow in our understanding of His love and earnestly love one another, HE will increase our influence and responsibility in His Kingdom and make known to us more of His plan. Love, God's love is such a rare commodity. So, when HE finds someone who seeks to know it and operate it in, HE cannot help but bless it and them.

In conclusion, our inability to wait on God shows we do not trust Him fully. Your first step to building your trust and belief in God is to admit that you struggle with trusting God. I would even suggest that if you have a challenge with trusting God, you probably have a distrust of people. You will struggle with fully giving of yourself and withhold. This is not an ingredient for a healthy loving relationship. I once heard it said that a person that trusts no one is a person that should not be trusted by anyone. I am not sure if I agree with that but I get the premise. Where you struggle with trusting ask God to help you. John 6 tells us that it is the will (work – effort – act) of God that we believe. So if there is unbelief in God or yourself, HE will help you in this as well (Mark 9:24). HE has more than proven Himself throughout your life. Choose to trust Him in and with every area of your life.

His plans for you are great..."*They are plans for peace and not disaster plans to give you a future filled with hope. Then you will call to me. You will come and pray to me, and I will hear you. When you look for me, you will find me. When you wholeheartedly seek me, I will let you find me, declares the LORD. I will bring you back from (out of) captivity (your waiting place). ... I will bring you back from the place where you are being held captive*" (Jeremiah 29:11). You must trust Him with the plans that HE has for you. It is His desire and will for you to advance, progress, and prosper in all things and be in health, even as your soul (mind (thoughts), will and emotions) prospers (3 John 1:2). Speak what you believe about God and His will for your life. Speak the Word and watch the Word of God go out from you and accomplish that which it was sent (spoken and believed) to do. It cannot and will not return void. Speak over your life and wait patiently on the Word to come pass. The Word still and always works, if and when you work (speak and live) it.

Patience

Psalm 40:1 says, "*I waited patiently for the LORD. HE turned to me and heard my cry for help.*" That is exciting to know. God – our God – our Father in Heaven will respond when we wait. Let me be more specific, HE will respond and turn to us when we wait patiently on Him. Patience is a part of waiting right.

Patience is your soul being at rest. It is when your soul: your mind (thoughts), your will (heart), and your emotions (feelings) are all in agreement. It is a Fruit of the Spirit that is also called longsuffering. I remember not wanting to use that word to describe patience. It sounded so unyielding and never ending. Strong's Hebrew and Greek Dictionaries describes longsuffering as to bear long, suffer long, to patiently endure.

The patiently enduring definition is the definition I could most easily digest. I was able to even point that my impatience was more with me than with others. I would say patience is probably one of the most challenging manifestations of the Fruit of the Spirit that most people face. This is why the Spiritual Discipline of waiting is so difficult to walk out and master. We must come to terms (resolve) accepting that waiting in unavoidable. Therefore, in order to wait right we must adapt ourselves to applying patience to our life and relationships. Patience is letting the peace of Christ rule in your heart. It is allowing the Word of God to dwell richly in you with all wisdom (Colossians 3:15). Yes, patience is a virtue but not one that most of us do well in. It is a quality that should be desired, sought after, and must be perfected and put into practice.

Let me use me as an example of what patience does not – should not look like. I really deplore waiting in lines. I am much better than I use to be, but in the past, me waiting in a line was not a pretty sight. It did not matter if it was long or short (both are relative depending on my state of mind at that moment); I tried to avoid them. I did not do well with them at all. Today, I have learned (am learning) to stand there but in the past, I would rock back and forth, murmur, complain, ask can another line be opened, and sigh…sometimes loudly. All the while looking – hoping for the next line to open or a shorter line to move. Of course if one opened, I would move to the shorter line. Inevitably, you know what would happen. I would move and that line would start to move slower. I would look over at the line I just left and see that the person who was behind me is now ahead of me. Frustrated, I would think, "I should have stayed where I was at." I know I am not the only person who has that experience. And do not let us be in a "hurry" needing to be or get somewhere else. But really, what can you do but wait? And now learn to wait right.

In the midst of exploring waiting, I recognized that my issue was not the line, it was waiting. I deplored waiting. Like lines, waiting is an unavoidable inconvenience. Even the self serve lines would test my patience. Stacie R. Stoelting a columnist for The Christian Broadcast Network wrote an article titled, "Hate to Wait for God." In it she states, "I hate to wait… In fact, my entire generation hates to wait." Though I get what she is saying because I recall saying the same thing. It is the title I cannot get with. Even those I survey agreed with an overwhelming 76% that most do not find their challenge with waiting on God, but waiting on people and things. We must never discount, overlook, or forget that our waiting maybe caused or allowed by God. So, to hate to wait on Him is to openly confess we do not trust Him or what HE is doing in our life.

I have observed that when we ask God to expedite our time in the waiting place – we are also asking Him to speed up our process(ing) because we don't want to or like to wait. It is our impatience. Proverbs 6 says that there are six things LORD God hates. One of them is quick (impatient, unwise) feet because they rush into trouble or evil. It is our impatience, frustration, and all the other emotions that arise within us, because HE has (does) not responded to our request quick enough that causes us to move too quickly or before our time. This delays and prolongs the process. It is the food we take out of the oven, microwave, out the fire or off the stove too soon. And after you have set the table, got everything and everybody ready to receive the 1st cut or 1st bite you or someone else realizes it is not done. It needs to cook some more. It has to go back in oven, back in the center of the fire. Who wants an undone cake or under-cooked turkey? You have waited this long. Hold on a little while longer. Do not give up now. Finish the process. You have sweat equity in this thing. Do not jump in or out too quickly. Let all parts get done.

The Word instructs us is James 5 verse 7 to be patient as we wait on the coming of the Lord. We are to be like the farmer who waits for the land to yield its valuable crop and patiently waits for what each season brings. The farmer does not plant without knowing they have to wait. Nor do they plant without expectation. With joy, they expect and anticipate the rain, the sun, and the harvest. They can because they did the pre-work. They did their part they were assigned to do; now they can wait patiently and expectantly with a confident, strong, established heart. We do not see them going out pulling up the seed or the immature crop. Let the patience and expectant attitude of the farmer be a teacher to us. Like the farmer waits patiently and expectantly for their reward of their work, we must wait patiently on the most precious promise of all – The return of our Savior. We can't rush Him or His coming. I believe waiting on the return of Jesus is less difficult than waiting on a very present man and on earthly stuff. With His coming, we have a sure promise of the blessings and rewards that come with Him. With people, we have no guarantee of them or that what comes with them is a blessing.

Beloved, as you wait patiently on God stay in line, stay in your place. Things will turn around for you and they will turn in your favor. Trust and believe God and in yourself. Your impatience and moving too soon to do and have it your way will delay the process and your processing. Impatience is an internal struggle; a warring within that comes to disturb peace and negate God's purpose. Just as waiting and patience are learned and practiced behaviors, so is impatience. You must practice patience to overcome impatience. To learn and apply patience is to wait right. Take a moment to ask God to help you wait on the glorious promise that HE has spoken to you through His Word, by His Spirit and or through Holy men and women of God: "Lord help to me wait on the promise that You have spoken to me, strengthen, and grace me to wait on You and on those You have commanded to bless me – I trust You Lord."

As a single woman waiting, at 45, I never thought I would still be unmarried without children. Fall of 1996, at 29 years old, I had a conversation with Daddy God. I pray this encourages you. My talk with Him went something like this, "Help me and keep me for and until (You send him) my husband comes to find me. I do not want to be with another man until my honeymoon night – send him to find me..." As I write this, I am nearing at 18 years waiting and 16 of waiting right...It was a choice I made not out of despair, fear or hopelessness but in obedience to His Word. I put my trust in Him. HE has promised that I would not be put me to shame. By His grace; I am and have been a "kept women". Has it been easy? No. But, I have learned to wait on the Lord for my special order and trust Him for my great, grand, and fine reward. I learned to wait patiently and wait right.

I know there are many who are waiting; some by choice, others it has been forced upon them, others because of circumstance, and still others out of fear and hurt. There are also those who are not waiting but have given up. Let me encourage you; you can do this. You can wait on the Lord and wait right. Your blessing is too great to give in to a form of godliness, short term, temporary satisfaction or non-committed love. Seek to not do the things that you believe or know will place you outside of His will. Though waiting is not easy, I invite you to choose to wait. If need be, find someone to help you be accountable. Tell the truth. Ask God to help and keep you. HE will turn to you and hear your cry for help. In Romans chapter 8 verse 18 Paul says with great resolve and conviction that, *"I know with certainty that the sufferings of this present time (today, in the season of my life) are not worthy to be compared with the coming glory which shall be manifested (revealed, shown, given to) in us."*

As I have said before "He (she) who shall come will come; the desires of your heart and the needs you have will happen and will not delay…Though it seems to be taking a long time, wait for and wait on it. It will surely come to pass." Ensure that what you are asking for in and outside of your waiting place is His will. Seek to know and do His will and not our own. You can receive and have it all. Just wait for it.

I recently attended a singles event where Bishop Joseph Walker, Senior Pastor of Mount Zion Baptist Church, Nashville, TN was the speaker. They asked us to submit anonymous questions. In all honesty, I really did not want to go but a co-worker was unwavering in her invitation for me to go. I earnestly felt like and still do that I have mastered this single thing. I mean really, I teach and speak at singles conferences across the country. I am at sixteen years. I believe, teach, and speak what I have put my confidence in that God is able to keep you from falling and present you faultless. To God be the glory, the struggle of most singles is not my challenge. I could not image what could be said to help me in my current state of singleness. Reluctantly, I went.

I sat through the first night session. It was good. As I was leaving my friend asked if I had submitted my question. Challenged, I sat for some time and thought about what I would ask. I wanted my question to be something that could help and encourage the others singles but I could think of nothing. So I wrote a question that was clearly about and for me. I never thought it would be pulled and certainly not read. My going and being led to write a question was one of the most amazing encounters with God I have experienced. My question was, "What would you say or recommend to the person who desires to be married and has been waiting right and waiting right for a long time – 15 years to be exact?" I returned the next day, and can you believe, my question was pulled and read? It was one of three questions pulled, read, and answered that night.

Before I share what he said, let me say to those who are waiting on your Holy Adam, Boaz, or Rebecca; this will bless, encourage, and strengthen you while you wait. To a few, it may be insignificant but it touched me to my core. As a single, it changed how I thought about waiting for God to send my husband to find me. It impacted me so much that when it came time to write this book, I contacted Bishop Walker to do the foreword. Periodically, I go back and recall the event. He starts walking and talking – sharing a story about a ordering a meal at a fast food restaurant. A story designed for me...

"One day I decided I wanted some McDonald's. I pull in. There was a long line. People were in front of me and people behind me. I watched those ahead of me order, pull ahead, pay for their order, and receive their order. Before some of them left the line; they are already tasting, eating, being satisfied by what they ordered. Now, it is my turn, I ordered my meal and noticed how many people were behind me...seems like everyone wanted McDonalds today...I didn't have to take a lot of time to order because I knew exactly what I wanted – I pull to the window to pay and there greeting me was a member of my church...I'm feel'n good...other Christians – I'm in the right place. I paid for my food and was expecting to receive my order...I was excited that my need was going to be met and satisfied because I waited my turn, told them what I wanted, did what I was supposed to do and paid for it – I waited some more and was ready to receive but the next words out of the young ladies mouth – a Christian brought me dissatisfaction and disappointment, "Pastor, could you please pull over there...we will bring your order to you..."

Challenged with my desire still not met - I pull over – confused. I did everything I was supposed to do and now I have to wait again - some more. I know many of you are already with me and being comforted and encouraged. Now, those who were behind me in line have gone ahead of me and have gotten their order. And like the ones who went ahead of me - they are now enjoying their order. Finally, though it seemed like forever though it was only minutes, they come to my car and what they said made my wait worthwhile, "Sir we apologize for the wait, but what you ordered was special…so it took longer to prepare…"

By now, I am in the full manifestation of His glory with tears of peace and joy flowing down my face over my lips. I recall I was sitting on the second row. He is now standing directly in front of me. Tears that once tasted salty from wondering when, if, why, still rapidly flowed down my face. They now seemed sweet, full of peace, joy, hope, understanding, and great expectation. Pastor is now standing in front of me and dare I say; though the question was submitted anonymously, he is looking directly at me – at least that is how I saw it through my tear filled eyes…He continues,

"Then she (the employee) said, "Because you had to wait, we put an apple pie in there for you".

Bishop: It has taken God so long because what HE has for you is special and it is more than you have even asked for – thought or imagined."

Needless to say, I grabbed hold of this and have held on to it and will until my special order comes. Today, I still and will continue to wait on the promise of my special order. What God has for me – for you is too magnanimous and too precious to limit Him to what and how we think it should come or what it will be.

Beloved, this is a testimony of waiting right as a single. However, no matter what it is that you are waiting on God to do; I charge and encourage you to wait on the Lord and be of good cheer. Just like HE did for me that day, HE will strengthen your heart. Believe and trust God. Declare in agreement with God according to His Word and the desire (HE has placed) of your heart, "My special order – what I desire from God is on the way." Expect, believe, and anticipate God!

I absolutely believe, trust, and know (confidently trust and believe) that nothing bad can come to those who choose to wait on the Lord and to wait right. Good things still come to those who wait. For the Lord our God has promised in Psalm 84 verse 11 that HE is our sun and shield. HE bestows (gives, places on you) favor and honor and no good thing (health, healing, marriage, spouse, children, debt freedom, wealth, and the list goes on) does (will) HE withhold from those whose walk is up rightly (purposely seek to do the right thing, safe, secure, in truth). HE has promised that daily HE will load us up with benefits (Psalm 68:19). Psalms tells us time and time again in scriptures declaring the writers desire to, *"I wait for the LORD, my soul waits, with hope I wait."* Our confession must be to thank and praise Him for the promise of His Word; even those that have not yet come to pass. Are you His Child? If your answer is yes, you are His beneficiary…Act like it! Every benefit that is yours as a Child of God; claim it (Psalms 103:2, 116:12). No good thing will He withhold from you! HE desires to bless you and rises to show compassion to you.

In Peace

Like patience, peace is also a Fruit of the Spirit of God. Patience is the positive manifestation of waiting. It is an internal peace. Waiting patiently is resting in peace on this side of Heaven – on this side of your promise. Living in or being at peace is also a learned behavior that must be practiced to be perfected. When we are actively practicing patience, peace will come and rest in and on you. Peace and patience are both weapons against the enemy. I submit to you that you cannot have true peace (an internal rest of oneness of the soul with and in the presence of God and Him in you) without His clear existence and presence in your life and His Holy Spirit in you. Romans 15:13 says *"May the God of hope fill you with all joy and peace in believing, that you may abound in hope and peace by the power of the Holy Spirit."* Remember Philippians 4:7 says that the peace of God (Jehovah Shalom) will guard our heart and mind through Christ Jesus. One of Jesus' descriptive names that highlight His character and existence is the Prince of Peace (Isaiah 9:6). 2 Thessalonians 3:16 confirms this truth that Jesus is the Lord of peace and able to grant you peace at all time in every way. HE has all power and ability to keep you in perfect uninterrupted full peace and to sanctify you through and through (Isaiah 26:3, 1 Thessalonians 5:23) when we keep our minds on Him. Peace, your state of mind is critical. You must fight and contend with those that come to disturb your peace. Even in the midst of confusion, uncertainty, and challenges, you must maintain your peace in your heart, soul, home, in every environment and as must as possible in situation.

What you keep your mind, thoughts, and emotions on will occupy, influence, and impact your focus and time. Interruptions of your peace come to distract and control you. Confusion, frustration, and worry are not representative of peace. The only reason we need peace is because these attributes are present trying to distract us and take us off course. John 14:27 brings comfort with Jesus speaking of Himself saying, *"Peace I leave with you, My peace I give to you; not as the world gives but my Peace. So let not your heart be troubled, neither let it be afraid."* The peace of God is not only obtainable it is accessible because Christ is in the believer. Peace is in us. The believer has the power and ability to have an internal rest within their soul and live in and manifest peace daily; even in the midst of caucus. During and after your release from your waiting place, peace will be the positive manifestation, demonstration, disposition, and attitude of you waiting patiently.

You must choose peace. Where there is strife, tension, and confusion; there is the absence of peace. It was for our peace that Jesus; every human created by God that the Savior of the World was punished (Isaiah 53). Yet, only the believer (those in Christ) whom Jesus is their Savior and Lord have full access to Him as The Prince of Peace and receive His peace. Again I remind you, peace lives in us. You have the power and authority to do what Jesus did on the boat in the storm. When peace had been disturbed and HE and the disciples peace was being confronted, HE spoke to the source of their trouble; the storm and commanded peace. Command Peace to do what it was created to do...to bring stillness...for Peace to be at peace.

Expectation

As with trust, we had a great study and discussion of expectation in an early writing. Here I would like to guide you in how to build and nurture your expectation. Expectation requires faith, belief, and trust. Expectation is a knowing that you know that what you have prayed for, asked for, fasted for, spoke of, and been told shall come to pass. As you see there is a common thread that flows throughout understanding and effectively waiting. I heard it said that expectation is the breeding ground for miracles. To see miracles manifested, your soul must expect and your spirit must anticipate. It is a trust and belief that God can and will do what HE said! There is no unbelief or doubt in expectation or anticipation. Command your soul to bless the Lord, to wait expecting and anticipating! It is here that I started to say, "Any way you want to bless me Lord, I receive...Any day now, Lord, come, show Yourself strong. Make Yourself known and real to me."

Another way I like to describe expectation is that it is an internal confident hope of the manifestation of promised, declared, decreed, and spoken blessings. Those who lose hope have no expectation. In His Word, we must hope and trust. Three times in Psalm 25, the Word decrees that if we hope and trust in Him will not be put to shame. Though he had to wait 25 years, Abraham expected God to do what HE said and he received the promise (Romans 4). His expectation came by faith.

Psalm 130 puts it this way, *"My soul waits for the Lord. More than those who watch (the anticipation) for the morning (of a new day) —Yes, more than those who watch for the morning."* Those with an expectation are not procrastinators. People who have an expectation get involved in their breakthrough, their future, and their success. Their soul (mind (thoughts)), will (wants and desires) waits for the Lord. They actively wait and put action to their expectation. How do you do that? Simply by moving from just thinking about it and hoping for it to anticipation through preparation. Readying yourself for the promised blessing. Do something in anticipation by faith of the manifestation of the expected promise. Remember Abraham, he and Sara had to go beyond hoping for a child. Against hope, he believed and acted (Romans 4:18). They had to do what was necessary to conceive, see, and receive their promise; their gift, their blessing. It is the bib the young wife purchases by faith believing they will soon conceive.

Consider Noah who built an ark in obedience to God and then waited; expecting something he had never seen before – rain. He and his family boarded the boat with two animals of every kind at that time. And for 40-days they waited inside the closed in, sealed tight boat that had only one window. After 40-days the rain stops. In Genesis 8 verses 10 through 14, we read of Noah's waiting experience. With expectation, he sends out a raven and then a dove to judge the readiness of the land. He waits for the return of the dove. Two more times he sends the dove out. Waiting a total of 14 more days to see if it the ground and earth were dry. After the dove did not return from the 3rd flight, Noah waited another month and 27-days before they exited the boat.

These waiting times were of Noah's choosing. He chose to actively wait. In his wisdom he participated in producing, ensuring, and validating his promise. Nowhere in scripture do we read that God spoke to Noah during the 40 days on the boat, the 2-weeks, or the month and 27-days. I share this to help us understand that waiting can be a personal choice. Perhaps you need to gain information or insight, or you need to investigate before you move forward. This is ok. Sometimes we just need to be still to listen, to hear, to know, and to obey and this is ok. However, be careful to not over think or over anticipate God. There may be a delay between God's instructions to you. Be confident in yourself when you believe you are to wait and when you are to move forward. Let a confident peace be your guide. Sometimes you will know that you know that it is not time. You know the answer is not yet, be still, hold up. This is what we often call intuition. As believers we know this is the Holy Spirit. And sometimes it is just plain old common sense. Even when it is our personal choice to wait and not be in a hurry, to wait patiently, our waiting should remain in a place of peace, patience, and expectation with anticipation. Living in a place of expectation and anticipation is exciting. It is a careful and submitted walk to do and be in the will of God. When we do, we operate in wisdom allowing peace to reign.

Right Perspective

Waiting right requires that we change our mind about waiting. This will mean changing your perception of your reality. It means changing your philosophy and attitude about waiting. In your waiting place, the longer the wait, the enemy wants to fill your mind and mouth with lies and negativity and stop you from speaking and declaring truth. His plan is to use your words and thoughts to entrap you and build you your personal stronghold. You are what you think and believe about you and your state. This is a part of changing your perspective. In you is the power to change your circumstances. Take authority over your situation. You are not the victim or prisoner of waiting.

We must get a different, better, and right perspective about waiting. Waiting is not a punishment or prison. The right perspective focuses on God, His Word, His promise(s), and His purpose for you. The way to know is to ask Him. His promises are still yes and Amen. The right perspective seeks God's will and His way. You cannot have the right perspective without hope, the Word of God, and a positive mindset and attitude. You cannot have the right perspective unless you believe. Like Peter in Matthew 14; we ask God for something (spoken in silence or aloud), HE bids us to come, gives us what we want and need, let's us go forward, and brings us closer to Him, but we get scared, and start looking around, worrying, not believing, being concerned about others and their opinions and many of us stop or turn back (verse 30, 31). We take our eyes off God.

Often our asking and crying out for help is because we do not believe HE really cares and knows. We cry out in despair, hopelessness and fear. Not from a place of faith, trust, and belief. We do not trust or believe in Him or ourselves. We often see ourselves as deficient, without or lacking to do what HE has released and called us to do in, for, and through us. So it was for the spies in Numbers 13 who went into Canaan where there were giants and fear and lack of confidence allow them to see themselves in their own eyes as grasshopper.

God is waiting on you to do what HE told you to do (the last time) and or finish what you started. HE would not tell you to come, to go, or to do, if HE did not know you were capable of doing it. It is His intent and plan to be with you and see you through to (the other side) completion. To do anything less than what God has told us, ordained us, anointed us, commissioned us, and graced us to do is our operating out of unbelief (in Him and or ourselves). It is disobedience. HE knows your flaws, your insecurities, your inadequacies, and your struggles. Yet, HE still called and chose you. HE desires to use you, have fellowship with you, and send you. Did you forget HE formed, created, and made you…And let's be clear…Made in His likeness and image? HE has and knows His plans for you. You must change your perspective about how you see you and God. Consider this: HE seeks to advance is Kingdom via the greatness HE has placed in you. Until you change your mind, seek, believe, and obey; something in this world is going left undone and someone is not being positively impacted because you are out of place and purpose.

Did you forget that His gifts and calling are without His repentance? When HE called you, chose you HE meant you. HE did not misread your make-up. HE knew you before the foundations of the world. When you learn to believe Him and in yourself and not doubt, you will trust Him and soon peace and a true revelation of you and your purpose will come. Jesus said to Peter *"You of little faith…why did you doubt?"* His Word tells us if we believe and not doubt, it will be done (Mark 11:23). HE describes the doubter as a person who is like a wave of the sea, blown, and tossed by the wind (James 1:6). They have the wrong perspective because their soul (mind, will, and emotions) is unstable. An unstable wavering heart and soul makes you, your character, walk, and life liquid, inconsistent, and uncertain.

I remember having a talk with my Pastor and Spiritual father (A. Thomas Hill) about not wanting the call of ministry. At that time, I felt it was too heavy to carry. My insecurities, struggles, challenges, personality, and feeling of inadequacies plagued me. At some point during our conversation, he said to me; in his most fatherly and pastoral voice, "Too late." It is funny now but back then I thought, "Dang that was cold. Where is the love and comfort in that...Can a sista get an out?" But no, he continued by saying, "The call and the gift isn't for you, it is for the people HE will send you to."

Sometime later, I had a talk with God about why HE called and chose me. The question was full of fear that brought with it those same insecurities, inadequacies, doubts, and uncertainties. My talk with God was absent of faith, belief, and trust. If my Pastor was not going to free me, certainly God will confirm that I miss read Him. God would clear this up...I just did not hear Him correctly. Teach Sunday School and the teens but not minister the Gospel to the World. Because surely, I would not be feeling this way if it was God and I was in His will...Surely not. My conversation with Him went something like this, "God why me – why do I struggle with this, I keep messing up...if you would just take the sin – the struggle away – the temptations away – the flaws of my past and personality...I could serve you better – if you give me clean hands and pure heart and I could and would teach others – more people your ways – I would reach many, many more (Psalm 51)."

The Father's answer was full of everything but what I wanted to hear. I had to accept what God said and says about me and to me. I had to change my perspective of Him. I had to trust that HE really does know me because HE created me. That HE really is my Father Creator and has a plan for me. HE really does have a purpose for me and wants what is best for me. Renewing of my mind brought transformation in me. Not only did my thoughts change, my words changed, my actions and interactions changed. My prayers changed. How I studied and approached God and the things HE has called me to do were impacted. I started seeing myself through His eyes, from His perspective, and what His Word says. I could no longer see myself through my own eyes and my words or satan words that would sneak into and settle in my thoughts. Negative thoughts will only produce and feed fear and ultimately produce negative actions. An unrenewed mind because a stronghold will hold us back from pursuit and purpose. As sure as I am crying and typing this now I recall the Holy Spirit saying *"If I took the struggle away, you would have no cause to come to Me. You would be sinless and have no need for a Savior. Your purpose would be fulfilled and you would be with or on way to Me. You would be headed to glory and no need to remain to let your life transformation and service give me glory. My grace is sufficient to keep you...from falling. Do you trust Me - My love and grace for you?"* That day and many since then all I can say is that my Daddy God loved on me.

It was that day that I understood struggle. Struggle, whatever the struggle that is not the sin. The struggle is our internal battle. It is the warring within ourselves. God counts our faithfulness to stand and say 'no' to sin, even when we are tempted or want to give in to sin in or have fallen temporarily and gotten up and repented. HE honors your time – season of remission.. Struggle is the stuff we do not want to do but find ourselves doing (Romans 7). The struggle is no better represented than with Paul in Romans 7 when he said starting in verse 15 *"I do not understand what I do. For what I want to do I do not do, but what I hate I do. And if I do what I do not want to do, I agree that the law is good. As it is, it is no longer I myself who do it, but it is sin living in me. For I know that good itself does not dwell in me, that is, in my sinful nature.[c] For I have the desire to do what is good, but I cannot carry it out. For I do not do the good I want to do, but the evil I do not want to do—this I keep on doing. Now if I do what I do not want to do, it is no longer I who do it, but it is sin living in me that does it. So I find this law at work: Although I want to do good, evil is right there with me. For in my inner being I delight in God's law; but I see another law at work in me, waging war against the law of my mind and making me a prisoner of the law of sin at work within me. What a wretched man I am! Who will rescue me from this body that is subject to death? Thanks be to God, who delivers me through Jesus Christ our Lord!"*

I felt it important that I scribe all 11 verses here so those of you who read this who have your own struggles will be encouraged. The struggle and the temptation to give in to the sin is real. You like Paul and I; must resolve (change your perspective and attitude and acknowledge it) that the only thing or rather person that can save you, keep you, help you is Jesus Christ. HE is your Anointed Savior, Brother, Advocate, Lord, Defense, and Friend. By His grace, His Word, and the Holy Spirit; we are and can be changed. You can and will be transformed by His Word and Spirit. A new perspective and appreciation of Him and self is yours to grasp. As you go low in humility and truth about self and die to you; HE will exalt you. Let Him raise you up and take you higher in Him. It is time for seeing things from a new vantage point. Sounds like Isaiah 40 references to soaring on wings of eagles. Even if you are still struggling with or dealing with old things, you must see them as gone (passed away) and yourself as done. Declare your end from the beginning that old things have passed away. You must see yourself as new in Christ Jesus. I must admit there were parts of my inquisition of the Father that HE did not respond to but I had to keep trusting Him and moving forward in what HE called me to do and be. My perspective changed and so can yours.

You do not have to live in fear, intimidation, or condemnation because you have issues or a sin struggle. Whether it is character or flesh, get with and give it to God. Be intentional, deliberate, and committed to being free and liberated. Denounce and renounce what and where you were. This process of freedom and transformation should start (unless God orders differently) privately with someone you trust and once delivered it can be public. Declare; celebrate the work and glory of God in and over your life. Rest in Jesus. HE is the leader of the Angel Armies – Jehovah Sabaoth. HE will fight our battles, including our internal ones. HE is Christ the Anointed One in us. HE is the Hope of Glory (Colossians 1:27). Who would not serve and love a God who comes with all that and is all like that. Our testimony in waiting is the witness that we have not given ourselves over to the sin. Our struggles will be our victory testimony that we overcome the enemy.

It is not about you simply changing your habits, but asking God to change your heart and renew your mind and give you a right spirit (nature). It is not about you never missing it or being perfect as we think of perfect. It is all about being perfected; being matured in and by the truth with every experience. Whether you passed the test with flying colors or failed what matters is your heart. A heart of conviction that produces Godly sorrow and brings about repentance to want to and seeks God to do and be better and change is what HE desires. If we are not deliberate about asking and seeking God to change our heart and our doing our part, the challenge or struggle and the sin will remain and eventually have rule over us. The 'want to stop, do better' and the 'don't want to do or be' may go away for a while. It will lay dormant or you may be able to suppress your problem, struggle, or sin for a time; years even, but without a heart change it will surface when you least expect. If you focus only on the habit or struggle and not the root of it; the reason you do what you do, you will only manage it and have only a "temporary deliverance" or "momentary breakthrough".

Like satan said to The Savior, I will return at a more opportune time. You may have times and seasons that you feel you have victory over it and from it. You may feel and believe you are free and delivered but it will only be temporary without a true and genuine heart change and repentance. You must change your mind about it and separating yourself from it and your heart will follow. You may have a time that you might have to struggle with it before you walk in total freedom from it; which is deliverance. Yet, I declare as you change your perspective your ability to overcome and walkout your deliverance will become easier. Struggle no more. Live. Don't wait to live free and be happy receive the love of God and His heart.

A heart change requires a mind change and encompasses hating what God hates, loving what HE loves; including you and repenting for our part in the sin(s) you have done. Yes, even the sins of unbelief, self-hate, rejecting Him, His love and forgiveness. The song says, free your mind and the rest will follow. I agree. Scripture tells us in Proverbs 23, so you think in your heart you are and it is out of that heart you speak. Through dedicated and consistent time with Him reading His Word, studying, meditation on God Word and promises, prayer, declaration of your good life, repentance (includes both renouncing and denouncing), and applying the Word there will be heart change. That is worshipping Him in Spirit and Truth. A new heart and renewed mind can only happen by and through the Word of God and His Spirit. As we consistently delight ourselves in Him, growing in our relationship with Him, in serving Him, and in knowing Him by His Word our mind will be renewed and overtime we will see the struggle pass away. We will be transformed. His Word and His Spirit will snuff them out. It will be suffocated because you are no longer giving it life or breath. Without Jesus we can do nothing but with Him you can do anything and everything (Matthew 19:26).

Without a heart transplant (change) and continuously renewing our mind with the Word; we will put down one habit and pick up another. We must love God more than the sin you enjoy. Meaning, focus on God and His love more than you focus on your flaws and failures. Ask for forgiveness, repent (change your mind about God and the sin), get a new perspective or way of thinking, focus on God and His Word, and keep it moving. God seeks to change your perspective and transform you in the waiting place. It is a process that will continue as long as we are believers, in these bodies, in the land of the living – on this side of Glory. Even now, just ask God to forgive you, "Lord forgive me for the things I have done…thoughts I have had concerning You and others…forgive me for my sins…those I knew better to not do and those I foolishly walked into or was deceived into."

Beloved, believe God. Believe in Him and in yourself. Trust His timing for your life. We say thing like, "HE is always right on time" but do we believe it? Find out who HE is and resolve who HE is to you. Please note, HE nor who HE is never changes. It is you, us who change and get shaken about Him. When we return to our right way of thinking, we often know Him in a new way. It is new to us, but HE is the same loving all knowing perfect God and Savior. HE is very much aware of who you are, what you have done, and what you are capable of doing (again). Yes, hate what HE hates and love what HE loves. HE loves us but hates our sin. Trust and accept God's grace, love, and forgiveness. Continue to come to Him. Take your burden, sin, struggles to Him, and leave it with Him. Keep earnestly asking Him to give you clean hands and a pure heart. Keep asking Him to make you over. The very fact that you are seeking Him and asking Him is an indicator that you are in His will. The very fact that you are struggling with a sin is good. Why good you ask? Because that means you have not given yourself over to it and HE has not turned you over to it. So, keep crying out. Repent for your old way of thinking and doing and seek Him for a new heart and changed mind. Let the Word wash and renew you. Celebrate your good days, repent for your bad ones, and praise Him that HE still loves you despite it all. As Paul charged Timothy in chapter 1, *"Fight the good fight of the faith. Take hold of the eternal life to which you were called when you made your good confession (of faith and belief in Jesus) in the presence of many witnesses."*

It was during one of my many visitations or encounters with God in my waiting place that I changed my perspective. I changed my mind not only about sin and struggle but about who I am and who I am in Him. One time when I was praying and telling God about my struggles and sins; I said something like, "Lord I know I am sinner..." You know how the church says, "We are sinner saved by grace." That day while waiting in the presence of the Lord, The Spirit of God led me to read several scriptures in Romans (1, 3 and 10) and 2 Corinthians 5:21. Studying and meditating on these a new thought and truth was revealed to me. My mind (perspective) was renewed and changed (transformed). I heard the Lord say, "Are you the righteous of Me, My Son, your Savior or are you a sinner...You can't be both?" Woe and Wow. This was truly a new perspective.

Yes, we were all sinners and probably did it really well, but if you believed and confessed Jesus Christ as Savior and Lord and received God's love, His Son, His grace, and forgiveness by faith; you are the righteousness of God. Is Christ your personal Savior? Is HE your Lord? Do you believe you are forgiven? Do you know that you are loved – accepted in the beloved? Do you believe in Jesus and God? Do you believe Christ was the perfect sacrifice for your sins and His life and blood was enough? Do you believe through and by our confession and belief you will go with Him when HE returns and live internally with Him and God in Heaven? If your answer is 'Yes, Lord I do believe', then you are no longer a sinner. You are the righteousness of God in and through Christ Jesus. Not of you or man but of God. His blood and God's love has cleansed and covers you. His grace is more than sufficient. Today, change your perspective, "I was a sinner but because I believe and have confessed, I am the righteousness of God."

That day I stopped referring to myself a sinner (saved by grace). A sinner is a person who practices sin or has a life style of sin. That would not be me. That would prayerfully not be most believers. It may be a struggle that you continue to take to God but it is not a life style of sin. We are children of the Most High God. The Scripture says that "you might be called" because you have to choose to be called. You have to choose to accept, be called, and walk in your righteousness. You must get the right perspective and a fresh revelation (truth revealed) of who God is and who you are in and to Him. It is a must. What better time than now to do it now. Your fresh or new revelation from the Holy Spirit will keep you and your mind in perfect peace in your waiting place. If you do not have the right perspective, you will sink like Peter and drown in the midst of your waiting, fears, and wrong thinking. Thank God for Jesus who reached out and grabbed Peter before he went all the way under in his sin of unbelief and fear. The right perspective requires that you take your thoughts and eyes off of you and others (comparing ourselves to them) and put them solely on God. HE is the author and finisher of our faith (and fate) (Hebrews 12:2).

Continue to believe expecting to receive. God told Joshua and the Children of Israel in Joshua 3; since you have never been this way before, when you see the Ark of the Covenant of the LORD your God, move out, and follow it. Then you will know which way to go. The Presence of God went ahead of them. God is telling us the same thing today. You have never been this way. You have never been instructed on how to wait and that waiting is a blessing and can be mastered. You must understand and operate in the principle of actively waiting by faith. Wake up from thinking God will do it all. Yes, HE can do all…all of His part but faith without your work of faith is dead. You have to do your part. Yes, pray. Write the vision HE gives you but give it to Him. Cast every care on Him. Stay focused on Him. When you finish praying, listening to hear, and receiving instructions, get up and do something. Do what and how HE tells you. Obey. Keep all things; you, your soul, your flesh, and your situation(s) in the right perspective.

Do not allow your waiting place and states that you experience and the tests you face to cause you to get and stay stuck and give up. *Isaiah 43 verse 19* says, *"Behold, I will do a new thing; now it shall spring forth; shall know it."* A new thing. A new perspective. It is good to wait and to wait on the Lord. Have you ever heard the saying, "A closed mouth won't get fed?" It is your mouth and your need. Open it and say something. Ask, seek, and knock. They are your feet, move them. It is your mind, think, explore, consider - use it. Think, see, and dream. Dream bigger. They are your hands, create and build. What HE has in store for you is great. No, eye has seen nor ear heard the things God has in store for those who love Him.

I had to learn His love for me and change my mind about it. I prayed, "Lord teach me how to love you, love others, myself, and accept your love for me." It took years, years beloved, for me to accept His love for me and truly love and like myself. Today, I am confident and fully persuaded and convinced of God's perfect wisdom, love, and forgiveness for me. I know without a doubt I am loved by God and called to minister the Gospel of Jesus Christ to the Kingdom: men, women, youth, singles, couples; the body of Christ and people in general. I am clear of my call, my purpose, and the gifts God has given me and the Gift I am to the Body. Today, I am sold-out for and too Him. I cannot go back to weak and miserable ways. I know that His grace is sufficient. Even now,

I am remembering the lengthy study I did on love, forgiveness, mercy, and grace. His Word won me over and continues to keep me. Though His gifts and calling are without (His) repentance but mine (ours) should be (is) daily. Had you caught me some years back…my attitude about standing behind the Holy Lectern and declaring God's Word was full of fear and self-judgment. Today, there is still a fear, but it is a love fear – a reverence. Changing my perspective freed me to love Him more and caused gratefulness and a desire to please Him at all cost to grow.

In Fellowship

The fellowship that can come is the waiting is powerful. Fellowship goes beyond the relationship. It is the enjoyable time and memories created shared and created in the relationship while in fellowship. John 14, admonishes us to abide in Christ. Here in this scripture, abiding is a state of waiting. It means to: wait in submission, reside, dwell, remain in until, to stay behind, to sink deeper into. Hmm, why does that make me think about someone who is or has fallen in love with someone? It is the waiting on a friend or someone you love not out of obligation but an enjoyable expectation and anticipation of who that person is and what the bring as a part of who they are: their nature, personality, and character.

Matthew 25 tells the story of the 10 bridesmaids; five were wise and five were foolish. What made the five wise and the five foolish was that the wise waited right. They actively waited. They were ready when Jesus came. They were prepared. Though the groom delayed in coming, the wise stayed focused on the purpose. They stayed awake, alert, and ready for His arrival. They had what they needed in their waiting place to fellowship with Him when HE arrived. The unwise bridesmaids only wanted the social experience of being with Jesus. To have true fellowship,

Christ must be the focus. Through fellowship with God, abiding in Christ, and in His Word you learn Him; what HE likes and expects. You become more familiar with His will.

In your waiting place, the reward of fellowship with God establishes a stronger and more sustainable relationship with Him. You have the opportunity to go from "have to" to "want to" to be with. So how do I fellowship with an invisible God? Through prayer, reading and meditating on His Word, spending time with Him, sitting in His presence with Him, listening to Him to hear Him, sharing with Him; these are the blessings of waiting in fellowship. In our fellowship with Him, we gain knowledge of Him and His wisdom to do things His way – the right way. Because our relationship with the Father is personal, our fellowship through that relationship will be different. Because our purposes are different our experiences will be different. Therefore the results and outcomes will be specific to our individual purposes. It will be based on what God desires to reveal to each personally and according to your purpose and assignment. Who HE is to you becomes better defined through fellowship. What we each discover about ourselves and Him will be different. Yet, how we wait should be the same. Your place of fellowship in waiting is useful for obtaining and gaining what you need to know about you and God. It has been set, defined, and made for you to perfect you. It is your waiting place. Furnish it as you like. Make it comfortable, but do not plan on staying there forever. If you want to know what Jesus would do – wait on Him in fellowship with Him and He will reveal.

Without Worry

I know it is hard not to worry, nearly impossible for some. Yet, God's Word tells us in Matthew 6, *"to not worry, let worry worry about itself."* What time in a day can you add to your life or your situation by worrying? Worry is elevated when (it appears) our prayers are not being answered or at least not in the time we need them answered. Worrying expands and grows with octopus arms the longer we wait. We are commanded to not be anxious, to pray about everything, to rejoice always, and to pray without ceasing (1 Thessalonians 5:17). Sylvia Gunter remarks in her study that "Nothing tries our faith like waiting on God for answers to prayer. Waiting tests our submission to Him as our trustworthy Authority."

Worry is a belief (mind) and trust (heart) issue. We continue to come back to trust because it is critical in the waiting place. Guard your heart and keep your mind stayed on Jesus. Philippians 4:8 tells us that *"whatever is true, whatever is noble, whatever is right, whatever is pure, whatever is lovely, whatever is admirable—if anything is excellent or praiseworthy—think about such things."* Your mind is the enemy's only direct means of access to you. If you let him, he will make it his play ground. Where he comes to mess with, confuse, and deceive your soul; your thoughts, will, and emotions. That same chapter in Philippians, tells us to focus and mediate on things that are true, noble, just (right), pure, lovely, and of a good report. It is imperative that with all diligence you guard our heart and mind in Christ Jesus against worry and all it tentacles in the waiting place (Proverbs 4:23).

The process to be changed, matured, and made ready for the world that awaits you to fulfill your purpose requires waiting but does not include worrying. No need to worry about what will come. God's got it and you. HE has your reward and it will be great! Your promised end will be better than your beginning.

Without Fear

If worry is a belief and trust issue, then fear is a faith and love issue. I believe it is more a love issue than faith. Remember we discussed that faith was spiritual, belief was mental (mind), and trust was emotional (emotional). We know that without faith it is impossible to please God. We must believe that HE is and that HE is still a rewarder; a giver of gifts (Hebrews 11:6) of those who diligently – intentionally resolve to seek Him. Waiting is a test that perfects our faith in Him, love towards Him, and trust of Him. Every test is given to determine, measure, and assess how much we have learned and retained. This is also true with learning to wait right and how to wait without fear. It is said, no test - no testimony. It is after the test; after successfully waiting and coming through that you have your testimony. Be mindful that success does not mean you did everything right. It means that you learned from the things you experienced and from that you have gained and applied truth and knowledge which is wisdom.

Fear comes to cancel out our faith and paralyze our hope. It causes us to question God's love for you. For years I have heard people say, "Fear is false evidence appearing real." And that is good. Yet, what can also be true is that what you are facing is not false. It is real. It cannot and should not be ignored. We must face it to deal with it. After Moses' death, God had to tell Joshua over 10 times "Do not fear – fear not." Throughout the Old Testament these words "do not fear" are declared over 180 times. Fear is real. But let us be clear, it does not come from God. To live in fear, be led, controlled, or influenced by it is not what the accepted in the beloved and righteousness of God are to do. We must face fear, and let the perfect love of God cast out fear. We should not be entrapped, snared or bond by it.

One of my mentors and the author of "Spiritual Warfare: the Myth Exposed", Dr. Dora Sanders Hill gave me something a little different to consider as it relates to fear. She says it this way, "The opposite of fear is not faith. The opposite of fear is love...When we fear we are rejecting or misunderstanding and not trusting in God's love for us...When we do not trust we are operating in or out of fear." The first time I heard her say it, I pondered it for many days and then it came to me. God so loved that HE gave us the Prince of Peace. A sinless Savior. We never have to fear, because HE is with us and for us. Paul said it this way in Romans 8 that if God is for me (us) who can be against. He goes on to say that nothing can separate him (us) from the love of Christ. God has not given us the spirit *(lower-case 's')* of fear, but of power, of love, and a sound mind (2 Timothy 1:7). God loves you because HE is Love. You being in this place, season or time of waiting is not because HE does not love you. It is because HE does love you.

Paul goes on to say, *"Hold fast the pattern of sound words which you have heard from me, in faith and love which are in Christ Jesus. That good thing which was committed to you..."* What was the good thing? It was God's love. 1 John 4 tells us that *"there is no fear in love; but perfect love casts out fear, because fear involves torment. But he who fears has not been made perfect in love."* Ready for a new perspective that is absent of fear? It is not faith that overcomes fear but the perfect love of God as God and for you. Yes, we receive His love and love by faith but it is His perfect love not faith that overcomes fear. God goes before you, His rear guard of goodness and mercy are behind, He is for you, you are in Christ and HE is in you and Christ is in the Hand of God and at His right hand. On top of all this you are the apple of His eye and your name is written in the Lamb's Book of Life and in the palm of His hand. We have no need to fear of the enemy, circumstances or people.

It was His perfect love that sent His son Jesus who is the manifestation and demonstration of that love that came to die for you and me. Commit this truth to your heart, mind, and memory. Be and remain encouraged. It is important that you know and keep the love of God in view; always before you. This will help you in the waiting place as you work towards keeping and having the right perspective and waiting without fear. Yes, fear maybe the opposite of faith and certainly a blocker but I submit that our willingness to love by faith and receive God's love is what overcomes fear. Maybe that is why we are not victorious in overcoming fear because we have not completely accepted God's perfect, complete, and lacking nothing love.

Fear is real, but it does not have to become your truth or a bondage or gage for how you live your life and love. When we fear we will not, cannot and do not love or receive freely or right. When we live in and out of fear, our earthly and spiritual relationships suffer and lack authenticity, truth, transparency, and freedom. This is true in our relationship with God as well. According to The World Book Dictionary, truth is what is constant. It does not change. It is a fixed or established principle. Truth is not science nor is it your feelings. Unlike science truth does not change nor can it be added to. To add to a truth is to create or speak another thought, opinion, fact or possible a genuine truth. Thoughts, opinions, and facts change. The truth is the Word of God. It changes not. Jesus is the Word. HE is Truth, HE is the Way, HE is Life (John 14:6). Believe the Word of God. Believe Jesus. Hide His Word in your heart, so you do not sin against Him or others. Keep your mouth filled with His Word and speak truth. You have nothing to fear. Let the perfect love of God cast out – put out - snuff out – suffocate every fear in your life. Do not fear. God is with you and for you.

With Praise and Worship

Finally, waiting right is sealed with praise and worship. It is the outward demonstration of our anticipation and appreciation of what God has done and will do. A grateful heart produces right waiting and praise is the natural outflow. Oh that man would give thanks with a grateful heart from even their waiting place. Giving thanks is praise. Worship is praise from a grateful heart. Praise God in your waiting place and season. We praise to celebrate God for what HE has done and has promised to do. We worship; give Him worth and value Him because of who HE is. Truly if HE never does another thing, I worship Him because of who HE is; just for being God my Father and my Daddy.

Worship puts your mind and soul on Him; it sets and conforms (knits) your heart to His. Praise takes your attention off your issues and puts them on God. For out of the heart, the mouth speaks. It behooves us to praise and worship Him. Like prayer, fasting, meditating, praise and worship is a diligent seeking of Him. When you choose to worship and praise God in your wait, you will be reminded, refocus, and reset. Through our praise and worship a confident rest, hope, and peace comes. Expectation and anticipation resurfaces in times of weariness. In all things, even in your waiting, give thanks. You will begin to see that your wait is worth it. We can wait right and even longer as we let praise and worship become our source of sanity and rejuvenation. Do not wait to be happy. Be happy now. Enjoy life now. Praise Him now...in advance. Take your prayer life and worship to the next level. Build an altar to Him. Establish a place of prayer and worship. Worshipping God while you wait is of great benefits.

Praise will silence your pressures, frustration, fear, and hurts of waiting and loss; while worship will soothe and remove them. Suffering will subside as we worship. One at a time or all at once, your worship will sanctify you through the stages of waiting. Impatience will implode on itself. You will be free from frustration. Praise will put to rest loneliness and doubt. Praise and worship will center and ready you for resurrection. As you give God His glory, His honor, HIs worth, His due; your resolve will be noted and rewarded. Due season will be close at hand. Praise Him and celebrate your waiting place as you expect and anticipate the reveal of your promise(s) and reward. In-spite of what it looks like and feels like, His promises for you are yes, and Amen in Christ Jesus. HE is not a man that would nor could HE lie; nor is HE a son of man that must repent. HE has been commanded to bless you (Numbers 23) and bless you HE will.

WHAT I LEARNED

My waiting right is still being perfected. As I look at each of the waiting right teachings, I discovered that most of these I do well in…that is why HE called me to write the book but the part I need to still work on are the moments that I start to get anxious. As I write this, I am in transition. Put in a place by the insecurities and personal issues of a person, but God allowed it. He allowed His anointed to be touched and His prophet to be done wrong. What and how it was done was wrong. Through it I learned that God is not only my Source, but my Resource. A new understanding for me. He is I AM (Source) that I Am (Resource) – whatever I need Him to be HE is that! Thank you Jesus! My attitude in the waiting place is key. Bishop Walker's McDonald's story encourages me in the wait for my desire for marriage, and the manifestation of the call and vision for my life, ministry, and business – for my Kingdom purpose. So, I seek Him to know His plan – my next. I am confident that He who began a good work in me will perform and complete it. His plans for my life will not be halted, stopped, or left undone. He has a purpose and a plan for it all. What the devil and his imps' means for evil, God will turn it all around for my good – vengeance is Mine says the Lord. So, here I am again, waiting – being still, actively listening (waiting) to hear to know my next. What happen I had never experienced before, but I am determined to master. What I need I have, and God will bring me through on the other side to and with better and greater – with much more than what I had going in. I love You Lord even more today than I did on yesterday. In my waiting season, I have learned at another level to lean not to my own understanding but to acknowledge Him in all my ways, and He has promised to and HE will direct my path. HE is truly ABLE.

To you God my Father, I ask in Jesus name, that you help me Lord not to worry, doubt, fear, or be anxious for anything. Sustain and keep me as you have always done. Protect and guide me. Show me and perfect that which concerns me. Show me what concerns You Daddy, I want to be found doing Your will. My prayers and supplications are to you and I anticipate and wait daily for Your peace, joy and provision to overshadow me. As you lead me, I will follow. Make known and clear to me Your path and plan. You know what was done, by who, how, and why. Vindicate me Oh Lord and bring my reward. Make all grace abound to me that I lack nothing. Supply all my needs according to your riches in glory through my Savior Christ Jesus. I praise you and give you glory, honor, and worship. In Jesus name, I say yes and Amen.

I have learned that...

_____

_____

_____

_____

_____

Scripture or Statement for Meditation

_____

What waiting means to me...

_____

_____

_____

_____

_____

_____

EIGHT

Mastery

By definition, to master a thing means to become skilled or proficient in the use of it and to gain a thorough, undeniable understanding of that thing. In the business world, there is a concept known as the "10,000-Hour Rule". It states that the key to success in any area is the consistent practicing of a specific task for a total of 10,000 hours. That equals about 417 days, a little less than 14 months. Based on this concept, I just might be a master of waiting as I continue to develop and grow in the practice of waiting right. Waiting right is truly what defines mastery. Recalling that waiting right is to wait patiently without complaint, speaking the Word, seeing it done, serving with a promise, giving towards the request, expecting and anticipating the day of receipt, praising Him until, working towards wholeness, and preparing to receive. Waiting right is 'active waiting' not sitting unless directed by the Lord to be still.

How does that look? Once, the Holy Spirit instructed me not to make any debt, and I waited right for 18 months before He cause someone to provide a debt free car into my life. And God did it - twice. I have been waiting on God for over 16 years for the manifestation of a good love and marriage. HE allowed a resemblance of it to come a couple of times and HE removed them all. I have waited for nearly 15 years for the vision of ministry, business, and all that HE has placed in me to come forth. This book being one of those. I have waited close to one hundred thousand and five hundred (131,500) hours on LORD for the vision HE gave me and the promises HE has spoken over my life and in His Word to come to pass. To see a return and the restoration of bigger, better, greater, and more of all I walked away from in obedience to Him. By definition of the "10,000-Hour Rule", my mastery has happen thirteen times over. It has come at a great cost. Yet, today my joy is (becoming) complete. All the while, still learning, growing, and practicing waiting right.

The continued practice of an applied thing brings understanding to the knowledge of that thing, which becomes wisdom and wisdom equates to mastery and the ability to help, coach, train, and equip others. Practice still makes perfect and produces Master Teachers, Topic or Subject Experts. To make one a master learner or master teacher, God will allow us to be stretched to our capacity and sometimes beyond. From the experience; whether positive or negative, prayerfully, we (hopefully) learn, apply, and grow. The challenge is where you put and focus your hours. In this case, your hours of waiting. When you know better you do better. The goal is to overcome and master the thing(s) that has been (or trying to) overcoming and mastering you.

We must master 'the little' so that we can have access to and experience the much. The Word of God says, be faithful over a little and HE will reward you with much (Matthew 25). God desires to not only give us much, but to use us greatly by preparing us to do good work (2 Timothy 2). One of those methods or tools of preparation HE uses is waiting. Though waiting is a big thing for most of us; once mastered, it will become a manageable and minuet thing. Mastery comes with opportunity, practice, and experience. Consistent, applied knowledge from each experience increases our ability to be successful at it and produces understanding and wisdom. This warrants the title of Master. Jesus was and is the Master; not because HE was God in the flesh but because HE knew, experienced, applied, and practiced (lived) all the Word in His life. In and from wisdom, patience, applied practiced, HE taught what HE knew to others through His actions.

To master this discipline, it is important that I insert this reminder and explanation: Waiting is for you. It comes to perfect (mature) you and your character before the promise is obtained. Mastering waiting, demands that you learn to respect and trust the timing of the Lord. Ecclesiastes 3 infers that it is possible for you to wait and it be your time but it not yet be your turn. To everything there is a season and a time to every purpose under the heaven.

When our waiting is called by God, it is always tied to something greater and better. Waiting is not to be confused with procrastination. Though procrastination is a type of waiting; it is waiting wrong. It the absent of confidence, trust, and hope. It is rooted in fear, doubt, and confusion. Waiting in and or on God is the exact opposite. Hebrews 6 tells us that the Father does not want us to become lazy (procrastinate), but to imitate those who through faith and patience (continued to do as the Lord instructed, worked their faith – actively waited) inherit what had been promised.

Waiting on the (weighted - heavy) promises is where the real stretching begins. You must believe that your promises are worth the weight and the wait. God is not a man that HE should, could, or would lie. HE has promised to restore. HE has promised to bless you. And when HE does it will be bigger, better, greater, and more. Your end will be better than your beginning. You, the call on your life (no matter what it is), what you are purposed to do will be is be tested, perfected, and must be authenticated.

Your next level and undeniable anointing comes as a part of your making and making it through your waiting and weighed seasons. Faith encompasses what you believe, shows that you trust, and demonstrates your willingness to wait on God. Without it (faith), it is impossible to please God. It must be perfected. HE is a Rewarder and your reward. Beloved again I say, *"Don't grow weary in your well doing, due season is nigh and you will receive greatly if you do not faint – stop – give up...Hold on – don't go back to weak and miserable way"*(Galatians 6:9).

One of the best examples of waiting mastered is a fisherman. I do not fish but I know a few people who do. What I got from them was how early they go to fish and how long they are willing to stay and wait at a lake or pond to get a catch. Then to hear them (a true fisherman) say, "If what I caught is too small for the time I have been out there, I will throw it back in and wait for the right catch." Mastering waiting says, "I can wait on what is for me – what I deserve. I do not have to grab or run to the first thing that comes my way. God desires what is best for you. I can and I am willing to wait. Even if that means by passing or not jumping at or taking (the first thing) what looks good."

In the waiting place, we must learn to master our emotions, grow our faith, trust and believe Him without question or doubt. We must learn the difference between your wants, needs, hopes, and desires. In Hebrew, the word "desire" breaks down like this: "de" means "from" and "sir" means father...Psalm 37 verse 4, says, *"Delight yourself also in the LORD, and HE shall give you the desires of your heart."* A desire is a strong deep feeling of wanting, longing craving, yearning to have something or someone. Seeking God and delighting ourselves in Him in the waiting place and seasons, welcomes Him to deposit His will – His desires into our heart. This is so that we might know Him and not sin against Him. Knowing His will and having His desires in our heart, helps us to not grow weary, and get (stay) frustrated in the waiting. God is not bothered by our weariness. Jesus was wearied at the thought of the Cross. HE just does not want us to grow – get planted – rooted in weariness, heaviness, and worry. Desire is more than just wanting, wishing, and hoping for something to happen. It is more than a feeling. A desire has truth attached.

The thing about desire is that it stays with you. It can lay dormant for days, weeks, months, years, but a true heart desire will come back. It is more than a hope or a want. However, if left unfilled, it can have a negative impact. A want will dissipate but a true longing or desire from God will remain. Even when you are not thinking about it or believe you are long past it; it will come back. God is seeking to change our desires to His desires and to give them to us. God desires are good things. They are often tied to purpose and destiny. There is an urgency to see what you desire to come to pass. God placed desires are His will and are meant to be fulfilled. When it is from God, it is goes past the soul and flesh and connects and agrees with your Spirit. In its original intent it is not tainted or unwholesome. It is not a lust tied to our flesh or our selfish gain. A true God desire is distinctively different from a want which is soulish. .

Weighing your Wait

In your waiting place, how do you measure or count your wait? Do you weigh it by your attitude, what you achieve or accomplish in the wait, how you serve others, your tears, how long you have been there, if you receive a blessing in the wait or if bad things happen while you're waiting? I submit to you the only way to weigh the success of your wait is to align it against the Word of God. Mastery requires that we lay aside the weight and the sin. The things that so easily come to disturb, worry, draw you away, or entangle you and get you caught up in fear, doubt, and worry. God has a plan for you and your life. Though weighty, our waiting seasons come to perfect and ready us. While you wait, allow Him to perfect the things that concern you. HE has promised to put no more on you than you can bear.

Train 'em up

As we seek to master waiting, the opportunity will present itself to be an example for others; particularly your children. The scripture says to train them up in the way that they should go (Proverbs 22:6). News to most is that this training is not exclusive to taking them to church. Training children in life, education, health, social, and spiritual disciplines is important in helping them develop good character. Waiting is a discipline that is never too early to start training. Unaware, you may already be training them when you tell them to wait their turn, be patient, say excuse me, etc. Training children in the mastery of waiting will help them avoid many of life's frustrations that come as a result of never learning and or practicing waiting and waiting right. It is the statement that I made earlier that it is good to sometimes tell your children; 'no' even when you can and they are ready. It teaches them patience and that delay does not always mean denial. Then the wonderful teaching moments of grace; when you give them what they do not deserve. Mastery passes on what you have learned and becomes a teacher through your testimony.

WHAT I LEARNED

Since waiting is inevitable for everyone, mastering this unavoidable disciple is not only possible but necessary. In my walk as a believer, I have experienced many seasons of waiting. Over the years, I have overcome great challenges of despair, lack, fear, dreams deferred, desires not yet fulfilled, questions not yet answered, restless, frustration, and alike to grow in my trust of Him. The longer I waited the more challenging consistency to believe and trust became. I realized that I had to get control over my emotions and thoughts. I had to flip this. The Father needed me to get in line with His will and rest in Him and trust Him no matter what it looked like, felt like, or seemed. I began to commanded my soul to believe and my mouth to declare: I CAN DO ALL Things - everything…this and that…I believe in the greatness God has for me and in me – I will wait on the Lord and I will be of good real cheer. My faith grew; my dreams became even bigger, trust expanded to believe the ridiculous. His desires became my desires – His will - promises began and continue to manifest. Not always when I wanted it but surely they came and shall come to pass. What peace I have gained in the wait – in the hallway – dreaming and expecting and anticipating the manifestation of EVERY promise – my purpose fulfilled – my special order – the great and awesome things HE has awaiting me. I may not yet be a Master of Waiting but I am darn near there. The Master created me for good work. HE is calling me to greatness.

I have learned that...

_____

_____

_____

_____

_____

_____

Scripture or Statement for Meditation

_____

What waiting means to me...

_____

_____

_____

_____

_____

_____

NINE
Back @ Wait

Handling Waiting...Again

We must resolve that since waiting is evitable, the possibility of waiting again is a given. Yes, even waiting again on the same or a similar thing. You thought he or she was the one but like John the Baptist you are now saying "Are you the one or should I look for or wait for another..." They are (were) not the one. That job was not it. That which you thought was yours; you knew that you knew this is it but here you are back at wait. I believe sometimes the most disappointing and challenging part of waiting is the return to the waiting place...particularly, for the same thing.

I recently found myself back at wait. My assignment here is not to speak directly the role of the other party that caused me to be back here at wait. Never to demean a person or persons I once loved and cared a great deal about and for. My desire is to help you and provide comfort to others when they find themselves back at wait. What I will share are the circumstances on my part that brought me back to wait. Like many of you, I thought, believed, knew..."This is it, my dreams, wants, desires, my prayers have come true. God did it. HE answered and (it looked like) HE had even exceeded." Could it really be true...My special order was delivered to me in a chance meeting while I was mining my own business...Doing what I was sent and created to do...Living on purpose. It all started out great...amazing even.

As the relationship continued, I prayed and continued to pray throughout..."God show me if there is anything in me or them..." Once revealed, it was emotionally, mentally, and spiritually devastating. Both regrettably and thankfully, my seventy-nine year old mommy was here to watch the travesty. With all that was good and great, I suddenly found myself painfully back at wait. As many of you can testify, what brought you back was not your doing or your fault. It was circumstances beyond your control. How disheartening and painful this was. This was my truth. For others, perhaps it was your issues or the sins of another, and or the unhealthy negative influence of others or disobedience to do something, have something, or get something God told you not to do but you did it anyway.

Whether the loss was a 'dream' job; a dream relationship, dream home, the death of love one, a business closing – loss is loss and back at wait is not a good feeling. The journey back was breathtakingly painful. However, one is brought back to wait, and back at wait is difficult and can bring with it a great ache and frustration particularly, when you did not see it coming or understand why it happen or the big picture. Ultimately, and often a necessary critical part, God needed to show you and give you your way of escape. For many of us, the gentle nudge or peek into the truth past reality does not work. With reality, we can excuse or convince ourselves or be convinced what is true is a lie. So HE will blast us with the truth; unchanging and undeniable truth that changes not. HE knows how to get each one's attention. The challenge is will you pay attention, listen, and obey. Whether your way to truth is logic, practical, principle, or systemic; it is all strategic.

After faithfully waiting on God for over fifth-teen years; working on and examining me to be ready to be found, I found myself back at wait. It was a bitter pill to bite into, chew, swallow, and digest. The totality of why this test and trail visited over time became clear. Through this, God was allowing my faith, trust, and belief in Him to be tested and strengthened. I had to trust that when I returned from this, I would be used to go and strength others. I quickly identified that I needed to get an understanding of what God desired for me to learn and get from this. I could not linger here too long in the pain, sadness, back and forth conversations, and hurt. I needed to be brought back to the joy and peace I had prior to the encounter. Before I could be given to bless someone us, I had to purge, cleanse, and be set free from it all; including the residue. I recall the day the Holy Spirit charged me to add this chapter to the book. I had gone through sooooo much to get this book written, to the publisher, edited, and to print. I had said to God, "I cannot believe I am back at wait." I resisted because I did not want to write from a place of pain, hurt, and unforgiveness. Of course, I was telling Him how unfair it was and HE responded. "Pull it back…Write…You are not finished….Help someone else…Your breakthrough and healing is in your helping…" I know my response was because I was not ready to deal with the pain and the truth.

Once I resolved to say, "Yes." My questions became *"What did I learn about me, how had I grown, what have I learned about what I wanted, desired, deserved, needed, what did I now know about what I was not ok with, what was unacceptable...what were my deal breakers, my boundaries and standards."* Listen, to be brought back and you haven't learned, grown, or examined yourself is a wasted test, trial, heartbreak. Let your obedience not only grant you reward from God but for you to take time to grow in your character, spirit, and soul. Until now, I had not asked myself what drew this type of person to me and why did I allow them to remain? Without a doubt the journey back confirmed God's love and care for me and who I was in Him. It made me love and appreciate Him and His wisdom more. I experienced God in a new way. HE truly is Super. The Omni of all. What I desire, deserve, and need in and from the man of God and relationship HE blesses me with became crystal.

I recall asking God what I missed. What did I overlook or ignore? The analogy HE gave me was: Often look at the outward appearance and hear the words and all seem to be lining up but it is surface. You must watch, listen and pray and keep doing it not only when you feel there is something amidst or because you have trust issues but even when everything is great. I was reminded of Jesus and the fig tree in Matthew 24. We see the fig tree and think it is in full bloom; ready, ripe for picking and living out purpose. But it was without figs. The leaves or outward dressing were there but no figs. It was without substance. It lacked what was needed to sustain. It was all superficial.

This does not make it a bad true but a tree misrepresenting and deceiving none the less. Remember, it was the leaf of the fig that was used to cover Adam in the Garden. So at a minimum, the superficial person needs to be able to cover that which comes to it for what it needs spiritually and naturally. Unfortunately, people are guilty of presenting the same falsity. But with them it is often intentional. All dressed up, talking, looking, and acting ready but deceiving. Very good pretenders; actors if you will. They have lived and existed in this place of denial, pretending and mask their own hurt and pain for so long, they have mastered deception; deceiving themselves and others. Like the tree, they perpetrated a fraud.

Well, you are in good company; Jesus and I made the same mistake. Jesus, the discerning all wise Savior in Matthew 24 got tricked by the tree too. Often what we encounter is their representative; not the real man or woman but their proxy. HE thought it had just what HE needed and was the answer to His prayer but upon closer examination HE discovered it was not ready; therefore it was not for Him. It was not capable of satisfying Him or meeting His basic short or long-term needs. It had a form but no substance, no power. It was good at pretending to be and presenting to the world they wanted or needed it be. But underneath it lacked what was necessary to produce in season and out of season and maintain healthy fruit. This angered Jesus greatly and HE (not us) cursed the tree. But before HE did that HE extended grace and gave it time to get it together. Jesus said it could produce and be what it was portraying and created to be. HE gave it time to change.

This was a way I had never been before. I had experienced hurt but I cannot recall a pain like this. Maybe it was because I had waited so long. Maybe it was because of the world-wind love of it all, complexities, multiplicities, and the constant compounding of issues that came out of the blue and blindsided me. Or maybe it was because of the impact it had on my mom and other family members. This was a pain I had never experienced. God allowed them to find me, and sweep me off my feet. Yet, when things took a turn, God had to make it without question plain to me. I only had one choice…halt everything and evidentially end everything. I had to let it and all things that came with the relationship go; car, house, ring, the wedding and dress of my dreams. But my obedience did not make the decision to halt, end, and walk away any less painful or difficult. I had to accept the experience (good and bad) with them, the escape from them, and my return to wait was all His will. And His reward for my obedience would be great.

Experience has taught me that no longer what I have heard or thought, and no matter how big the house, how pretty it is decorated and furnished, the fancy cars, tones of clothes, lots or some money, big wedding, lots of gifts, expensive trips, gorgeous jewelry…If there is no peace, there is no rest, and probably minimum to no trust and certainly not a good healthy love; God's love...To live without peace, love, joy, trust and rest of mind, spirit, body, and soul would be most miserable. This is not the abundant life. It would not be living only existing. People in a coma and those on ventilators exist. They are alive. They have life but they are not living. I chose to have life and life abundantly.

I was asked by several gentlemen pursuers; new and few from my past how did they get me. I took a moment to reflect. In the beginning, they were encouraging, kind, and loving in word and deed. Their support of me, my vision and purpose was something I had never seen. If chivalry and charm was a middle name, they represented well. There were undeniable amazing demonstrations of acts of love. We are taught and teach that love is action and men (real men) take on responsibility to provide, to meet need, to pamper, shower...make their woman feel like they are the only woman in the world. And that they did. They knew what it takes to win but not sure if they knew what it takes to keep. They had learned all these steps and methods to win the heart of whom and what they wanted. Any woman would have and will be won over. Even without a great deal at their access when we met, his ability was without competition. The beginning was without argument or complaint. Disagreements were met with sound judgment and discussion. Then something changed. It was sudden. For me, it was out of nowhere. Though the cause I was unaware and or I did not understand, anger, argument, and rage presented itself. The first time I deflected and chalked it up to the many many things that were going on in their life. I could not ignore the Word of the Lord that clearly tells me what love is and that His blessings come to make me rich (brings peace, prosperity, joy and happiness) and adds no sorrow, sadness, fear, doubt or worry to me.

I interject this for someone's encouragement. Though things turned and ended horribly; if you experienced a time and season that was loving and good do not discount that or beat yourself up or take on guilt or shame because you did not see the negative in them before it manifested. Some would say the love you experienced was not real because it was with motive or tainted. Or it was possibly used to manipulate you to get or keep you. Because of what happen, how they behaved, what they did; someone may say, you cannot count that as love. I would say not necessarily or always so. From the portion of their heart that had been sanctified and purged, they loved. In many moments of quietness, reading and meditating on His Word and in prayer, the Lord brought me great comfort that it was love and what was good was real. Yet, whether good, bad or indifferent, people can only love and give from their capacity, willingness, experience, and understanding. However, we cannot excuse what is done that is disrespectful, irresponsible, unkind, or abusive. Your love will not ever be enough to change a person to good and right.

The Bible says, the heart is desperately wicked and deceitful. It is only the love of God that can cast out, deliver, and make whole. Nowhere in 1 Corinthians 13 does it say, love puts up with and accepts bad behavior and abuse. That is not what patience or love means. Healing or at least being on the way to healing and wholeness is critical for people to have a healthy, good, godly relationship. If God has released you to walk alongside the person you love as they get the help (spiritual, clinical, mental, medical, etc.) they need that is ok and that is love…It doesn't mean you marry them as you may need to postpone until change is evident. And if married, this may mean you get to safety while they are getting help. However, if and when they stop, are no longer committed to the getting the help, their heart changes about what they need or what you need to have healthy marriage that is not love.

All that is good in you and from you; your love, patience, loyalty, commitment, support, nurturing, sex, staying in it and taking it hoping they will change; unfortunately beloved without God or help, all you do – nothing you do will never be enough. You can't fix or heal them. Only the love of God, His Word, His Spirit, (and when need counseling or therapy) can heal and bring change. If you are already married and feel you are in danger, get to safety. Allow them to get counseling and start walking in their healing and freedom. As stated, as God leads, walk alongside as best as you can; if at all possible, show – communicate your support and give them time to demonstrate their commitment to their change and being better for themselves, you, your family, and their future (purpose). If you are not married, flee. In these extremes, whatever the relationship dynamic, if you can separate yourself until it is (if ever) safe. Do not buy into or believe that marriage can or would change manic, sociopath, pathological, or patterned bad behavior.

Often the deeper the soul issues that challenge people who have been affected mentally, emotionally, physically and or psychologically requires counseling (clinical and or spiritual) and or medication. It is not time for marriage and sometimes not time for a relationship. If this is you or a loved one, I encourage you (to encourage them) to seek out what is needed to be healthy, healed, and whole. These deep life challenges and their behaviors need correction, counseling, therapy, healing, accountability, and sometimes medicine but not marriage. Healing is God's business. Can healing come as a blessing and benefit from a healthy love covenant relationship? Yes, but it is not where we should go to obtain get it. That is not the purpose of it. Marriage is not (should not be) the method or mechanism used for fixing or provoking lasting, sincere, and permanent change in our hearts, habits, or behavior. Do it for yourself, then for others, and for your future. Do your best to seek and get your healing before you say "I do" or at least know what your stuff is and be on your way to healing and wholeness. If you cannot, will not admit to, take responsibility for or say what your issues are and be honest about them; you are not ready to get (be) married. Use your waiting season to be honest with yourself and ones you love and care about and for and who love you.

God revealed to me that HE gives each one of us a span of grace – of time to obey, to repent, to do the right thing, to receive with grace the blessings HE sends our way and gives us. When we will not or cannot do right by the gift – the blessing God give us, HE will take His gift back and bless someone else with it who will do right by it; remember Matthew 25 and the talents. Though at the time none of it made sense to me and it was painful, I am grateful that HE continued to nudge me and set it up to confirm that I was in His will and what HE was requiring of me; to let it and them go was His will. Hurt people really do hurt people. It is neglectful and short of a sin for someone to know (believe) they have emotional, spiritual, mental, psychological issues and throughout their adult life never to have sought and obtained help for it. To continued on in that behavior and expect others to just accept and put up with them and it because they had a hard (bad) childhood or life is unacceptable and irresponsible. When I was a child, I acted childish and was careless, but now that I am old (an adult), I put away childish things and stop blaming others and take responsibility for my actions.

Allow me to interject this thought. It is equally irresponsible for those who say they love and care about a person whom they have witnessed patterns of blaming everyone else. Watching them not taking responsibilities for their actions and demonstrating abusive, unhealthy, unwise, bad choices and behaviors against themselves and others, and you overlook it and them or pacify them and their actions. The Bible tells us to warn people who are in danger, in trouble, and correct (in love) those whose behavior is ungodly; hurtful to them and others (2 Timothy 3). When we do not, His Word says we will be held accountable (Ezekiel 3, and 33). This is not about judging or being hard on people. It is what is necessary. It is love. This is about holding persons accountable and helping those we say we love and care about. Though this can be difficult, it is very necessary. Pray. Ask God to give you the time, space, and words to say and that they have an ear to hear and to receive. They may not accept it or you. That is not your responsibility. By love, faith, and obedience, you do what you know to do and or have been instructed to do and God will do the rest.

No, you didn't get it all right the first, second, or third time. Now that you know, this time – the next time you will. Use your return to the waiting place to heal and be made whole. I feel you; I really do. You prayed and believed you heard God to take the job and quickly grew to hate it. Or they hired you and let you go; last hired first fired. Ok, they hired someone else, and you thought you were made for that job. You believed you heard God to move away and sought wise counsel on your decision. Only to now find yourself without a job or headed back to where you left. They started dating someone or married someone shortly after your relationship ended. Someone else is already living in your house, driving your car, reaping the benefits of your work of labor…but God. You obeyed God even though it hurt and looked how things turned out but your end is going to be better than the beginning. I hear the questions. Seek God to let all that; the pain, the hurt, the loss, the thoughts, questions, and the memories go. Ask Him to cast them and the situations and all parties as far as the east is from the west that you will not remember them (even the good) anymore. Let God deal with them and every situation as you let Him heal you. Continue to pray, ask, petition. Forgive. If you need too, do a committal service. No more beating yourself up. That is the enemy and his footmen's job. God allowed it or HE did it. There was a reason. Will you allow Him to heal you and to make you whole?

Being back at wait can be painful. Even though you know God did it, it still hurts. But, when you allow God to let you see it His way, the pain of your present suffering will be nothing when you compare it to the glory of your future. When you allow Him to comfort you in His presence, in His truth, the pain and hurt will subside. When we let Him, God will get in the middle of your misery moments and turn them around for your good. You may not see it, understand it or feel it now but all things will and are work(ing) together for your good. If you love the Lord and are the called according to His purpose, it is going to work in your favor. Do you believe? Can you believe there was a purpose in the job loss, the relationship ending, in the divorce, the house you so faithful kept, your business closing, etc.? Know that your end will be good and even better than your beginning.

In my return to waiting, I have learned many things about God, myself, them, others, etc. I am solely convinced that God loves me. I am equally confident in what I know HE has for me is His absolute best and I deserve nothing less. I know that I am a good, no, great woman and I am ready to be wife to the man God has for me who is ready to be a husband to me. I am clear about my deal breakers. I use to think they it was being demanding to say what I needed, wanted, and expected, but my standards were not crazy, not burdensome, unrealistic or unreasonable. Then I heard Jakes teach on this and my dear spiritual big brothers and natural brothers gave me wisdom in this. They are basic human desires: do not lie to me or on me, do not abuse me in any way (physically, verbally (curse me or at me), emotionally, psychologically, financially, spiritually or mentally), do not cheat on me (sexually or emotionally), and do not make (or try to make) me look like a fool of or embarrass me in private or public. Pretty basic stuff.

Needs and desires pretty much line up with the Word concerning a man of God and godly holy relationships as it relates to healthy, good love relationship, dating, a man pursuing a woman, seeking to find a wife, to be a husband and certainly me as a wife. I know you are thinking, "There must be others..." sure, but those are for private discussion in courtship considering marriage. Coming back to wait caused me to know and better define things. As I became more concise, and able to easily communicate what I desired, wanted, and needed, I grew to know me better and learned a bit more about men and relationships. I know better definition comes once you meet and are with someone as you share your personal needs, wants, and desires but this waiting state has been good to clearing out the fluff. My boundaries without compromise and avoidance became clear. My desire to be not only a good woman, but a great woman, wife, and mother to his or our children, be it his will. Solidifying these things brought a great joy, peace, and hope of what I believe God has for me.

I encourage you to use this time to get clear and know beyond a shadow of turning what you desire and deserve. Whether it is in a relationship, a job, a doctor, a church, a business partner, your education, purpose, goals, a house, etc. define your standards. Align them to the Word of God, and what is best for you and your future, and hold to them. No comprise, no settling; nothing less than His best. Notice I did not say, "Your best." Always, declaring His will be done on earth (in us) as it (already) is in Heaven. Remember, in Heaven there exists His absolute grand and supreme best! And we can ask for His will to be done on earth; in us and all that is a part of us as it already is in Heaven. I declare at least double for your trouble. Believe that best is yet to come for you. Pursue God's will for you to be the best you. Enjoy your time with Him. Make this time beneficial. Fall so in love with Jesus that when HE does send someone they are bought jealous of your relationship with Him. I am not talking about being so spiritually minded you are not earthly good. What I am speaking of is your commitment and love for God being evident in all you do, for all to see. Let the love and the light of God in you, draw them to you.

As unbelievable as it may sound, sometimes your return is not because you have done something wrong but because God simply needs to continue His perfecting in you. What if it is to spend (more) time with you? What if there is something HE desires to reveal to you and HE needs you to be still to do it? In the days that you find yourself returning to the waiting place; rest, trust, and steady yourself and your heart to hear and know. Maybe that man or woman, the relationship, friendship, the job, house, car, money, gifts, the stage, the mic, your name, became your primary focus. Did these any of these become what you idolized? Did you lose sight or balance? Putting all your attention on the blessing, did you forget who blessed you? This may challenge some of you, but maybe your neglect of your spouse and family in pursuit of your purpose or call caused God to bring things to a halt, you to a waiting place, loss or back at wait.

Whether this is the first or the second or the eighth time, be still until you hear God. Do not allow the emergencies of life and people to cause you to move you before your time. Let God completed His finished and planned work in you. Declare your 'never return' to this place for this thing. Deal with you and the issues (past and present), challenges and secrets that keep bringing you back to this place. That keeps you stuck, behind, loosing good things. Figure it out and get it together. Get it right this time. Do not go AWOL (absent without leave – permission). Do not leave your waiting place without permission or before time. An unofficial release will only delay you, hurt you and maybe others, and certainly delay your progress and process. Do not be found missing in action.

So you ask, "Tuesday, what did you do when you found yourself unexpectantly back at wait?" I prayed, I prayed, and I prayed. I cried out to God for my Daddy God to heal my heart, take away the hurt and the pain and then I prayed some more. Whatever it takes for you, do it. If it is therapy, writing a letter that you mail or never mail, take a trip, go on a sabbatical; do what you need to do for your healing, breakthrough, and deliverance. I took an extended trip to a couple of friend girls' homes that just let me be. I remember asking God to take all memories (good and bad) of the experience and person away. What came to my remembrance 38,000 feet in the air was the Word that God would cast our sins (*wrong doing that is against God and painful to Him to see us do*) as far as the east is from the west and HE will remember them no more. So I ask the same, that HE cast the memory of this as far as the east is from the west that I remember it no more. As I was headed back from my trip travel literally from the east coast to the west coast, HE said, *"I will do just that."* My breakthrough began thirty thousand plus feet in the air. Though, the complete purging and healing took a few months, it soon came. And for it all I am grateful. In all things, I give thanks. For this, I give Him praise.

When you hold on to any part of the experience and allow them to keep coming back even in your thoughts, it keeps you connected to the person, the pain, and a false hope. For me, back at wait had a minute of back and forth with numerous attempts on their part to come back and work out, talk through it, including a four-hour counseling session, rings back and forth, promises to get help, starting personal counseling but stopping and not telling me. At some point you have to love yourself more than feeling like you do not want to give up on them or a false hope of 'us'. God spoke expressively to me."*Time and turn was given to commit to healing and they rejected it.*" I would have taken the journey with them but not without their full commitment to their own work of victory. Love you enough and more to say no and no more. You cannot accept loss or take on reject when someone else changes the rules or their mind.

Guard every part of you. How do you that? Your eye gates, delete every picture. Even the ones you really like and would love to keep. Guard your ear gates. Removed every means of contacting and communicating with them and them being able to contact you. Delete those saved voice mails This I suggest you do sooner than later. To be free in your heart and soul, you may have to do the unthinkable…Like ask them to block you from FB so you can stop looking at their page. Some of that stuff they are putting on there is for you to see. Knowingly or unknowingly you do not want to hold on to any part of it that might stand in the way and overshadowed the blessing God would and will send. Choose to be healed and whole and made ready for when HE sends the real, ready, healed, and whole reward and blessing. Declare today, "I will be – I am back at 100%'. Whatever it took, I had to get back to where I was before I was blindsided.

I found Scriptures that were related to my situation. I spoke the Word, I meditated on them, and I prayed the Word. I wrote, I sang, I sat quiet to hear God. I sought wise counsel. I talked to those I trusted as confidants. I guarded my heart. It took a very wise woman to speak a truth to me about me; something I had never considered. Actually, she caused me to see many truths about me through self-examination. What she revealed was that I do not get angry (outward demonstration of my hurt) with people I love and care about. I tend to extend a great deal of grace and mercy and wait to address hoping the God in them will bring the conviction. When it is clear, God has released me to speak in love. Though done may take me a minute, but not unto abuse, when done comes, my done is all the way done! Two extremes.

Beloved let me help you. It is ok to get angry, but do not sin. I finally let myself get angry (without sin). I learned to distinguish my response to hurt verses when I am upset. Though many things got back to me; that was said about me and my family that were lies. I did my best to keep my mouth off of them. I quickly learned who to trust and the messiness of non-invested people. I highly suggest in the ending of any good or bad thing, sow no seed you are not willing to reap the harvest from. Practice subtly and quiet discretion. Do not lower yourself to personal attack or retaliation. Let God deal with those who misused, dishonored, mishandled, or disrespected you. God said vengeance is mine and HE will repay and will contend with those who contend with you.

Keep your hands and mouth clean and your heart pure. How do you do this when you are hurt and angry? Pray. Meditate on the Word. Seek wise, confidential, and spiritual godly counsel. Whenever possible do your best to keep the peace. Even if you have a moment of letting them have it and I did; after months of back and forth craziness, Gods grace is sufficient towards you. He honors the times you could have and did not. You must let all the unanswered questions go and rest in God's wisdom. HE knew and knows what is best for us. I was reminded that resting in God is synonymous with trusting Him and waiting right. Keep yourself up in spirit and appearance and even stepped it up a bit. Continued to serve, work, go to church, work to advance my vision – be purposeful. Go back to doing the things that ware good before it happened. As I went, I realized the pain left before the hurt. Eventually, the hurt subsided and healing came and wholeness prevailed. Forgive them. Speak well of them and if are not quite able to do this yet, just keep your mouth and mind free of negativity concerning them. This can only happen through the washing of the Word, prayer, and the love of God. Without the love of God in your heart and a desire to please you, you cannot truly forgive with pain, hurt, and residue being washed.

Unless God tells you differently or until HE says stop, pray for them. Not God get 'em; though you may start there or want to pray that, I encourage you to simply pray something like, *"God let*

Your will be done, show them them as You (have) show(n) me, me,
heal the part of them (the hurt, the pain, etc.) that causes them to
behave in this...Heal me Lord and help me to forgive...I make my
mind up to forgive - now help me walk it out until my heart
agrees." First peace will come, then the pain will go, which
means your breakthrough and healing is on the way. In time,
wholeness will come and victory will be yours. How do you know
you are healed and whole? When you no longer have good or
bad thoughts, feelings or words concerning them or the situation.
When you can speak well of them, wish them well, or say God
Bless you (them) and mean it. When you no longer do things in
hope that they see or hear about it to rub in your good fortune
(blessing) or you want to be seen with the new...When you are
past these types of things, you are healed and on your way to
wholeness. You have the victory. These were my indicators that
you are being or have been reset; moving from pain and hurt to
healing, freedom, and wholeness.

I know some people say, replace the love lost with new love
(lust) found. I tend to disagree with rebound, settling for, place-
holder and or replacement love. Why? Because we take the last
and accumulative hurt, pain, disappointment, anger, bitterness,
unforgiveness, etc. into the next relationship. Which is unfair to
the new one; particularly, when they don't know. Some would
say deserving if the new one knows but walks in any way with
their eyes wide shut. Very few take time to work on themselves to
be healed or at least on their way before the next. That is
probably why so many people and relationships are so jacked up.
Once all the gilts and smoke cleared, in my reflection and honest
assessment, I had to admit, it was not my special order. All the
material, complimentary components, amenities, and acts of love
were ever present but the spiritual and emotional maturity and
stability was not. They presented enough that many women
would overlook and keep their fingers cross that they would grow

up into their representative. I truly wish them well. All that was good in and from them for the season and time I experienced it was good. I take none of that from them or our time together. As I would often say to them, "...and God desires to make you great..." HE did then and prayerfully HE still does.

I think in my youth I may have tried the rebound love thing but at this age, I only desire what is real, true, for me, and purposed. I am not interested in space holding temporary fixes. Even in that; your emotions can get caught up and you or them can get even more messed up. Let me say this, stop putting and adding more junk on top of junk. Deal with you and your issues; whatever they may be and go somewhere and sit down and get healed. Stop hurting and damaging people because you are selfish and just do not want to get the help you need or do not want to or cannot be alone. God wants you healed and whole. I truly believe HE will not (continue to) allow those who are guilty of continuously and repeatedly causing the hurt and brokenness of people...Leaving others hearts, emotions, trust, and dreams shattered in their wake. I do not believe HE will allow them to go undealt with. What the consequence will look like is on God but HE cares about the heart and soul condition of His children; all that HE created and HE will not allow the abuser, deceiver, or manipulator to go unpunished...Even if they say they are a Christian. Parents do punish and discipline siblings. Who did it and Who started it were common questions in our house...but rest assured, our father would finish it. And so will your heavenly Father. His discipline and correction is perfect. HE does not miss. Whatever is in you (them) that causes you (them) to behave this way, seek God to stop hurting others and yourself. Be set free, healed, and made whole. HE loves you just as much as HE loves those whom you have hurt. From a sincere place, repent and ask God and those you hurt for forgiveness. Chase after God. Cry out to Him and HE will come with your recompense.

I have come to understand that the things that can come out of a person are what were already in them. Sure, some things can come out of nowhere (upon you) but most of our manifested behavior; good or bad come from within. Without the presence of God living in us and the core of our fruit being the love of God and a desire to change; there will not be change or growth. Without this, consistent and repetitive bad and unacceptable behavior will remain and always manifest. We all have moments on occasion that we bump our head; for all have and will sin and have or will fall short of God's glory. But a mindset and life style of this with damaged people left in your way is not God or acceptable. From God's perspective, it is about each person individual salvation, character, and soul. In matters such as this, your perspective and concern must become about you and God's will for you. This is not about them or them being bad people. Nor those it mean or make you selfish, heartless or disloyal. It makes you a lover of you and God, wise and obedient.

Several months after, healed and on my way to wholeness, I allowed myself to receive the return, pursuit, and advancement of a previous love interest. We had crazy chemistry and a great deal in common. My respect for them was to be admired. I leaned to the good and allowed them back in. Something I had never done before. They certainly thought the rise and fall of my pending marriage was a blessing for them and us. They took great care with persuasive conversation over a couple of months to convince me of the same and that they had changed. Back at wait, I was painfully cautious. All the while, remaining prayerful. Same pray as the last, "Lord, show me…" In time, with an eyebrow raised, I agreed to give it a try. Unfortunately, I soon realized why we did not work the first time and why going back does not work in most instances…It is not what I do. What happens in each person during your time away is telling…Has change for the better occurred? Has self-examination and correction taken place? Have you (both) grown matured for the better? Has godly sorrow brought true repentance to make things right no matter what it takes? Has what caused the initial downfall been corrected? Are you both willing to talk about it and identify what you need to do differently and commit to that? What is the purpose of coming back together? Is (was) the apology just to get you back or does it bring with it a witness of good, lasting, sustainable, creditable, viable fruit? Did they ask forgiveness and commit to do better and not do it again? Great questions to consider in your return to seasons. Well if the answer is no, stay clear. Oh, back at wait made my value clear.

It was through this grave disappointment and reality of truth to these questions that three things occurred: 1) I solidified my deal breakers, wants, desires, and needs and 2) I sought God in prayer and wise counsel to identify patterns in the hearts of men who were drawn to me and 3) what was in me that drew them. So very unlike but similar…There was a common behavior in them that God revealed and I had to examine. I had to ask myself and find the answer to 'what was it in me that drew them to me'. That revelation and truth was eye opening, refreshing, and freeing. The answer however is reserved first for private discussion with my future boa and for my next book "I Tasted My Tears Today". I am forever grateful for what this and these experiences have brought and taught me. To get to this point and place that I can say I am free. I love being me. I like me and it is the truth…I give all praise, glory, and honor to God. I am back at 100. I asked Him to reset me back to where I was before we met and HE has done just that. Actually, if possible, I think HE has caused me to surpass that. I believe I am better in spirit, character, as a woman, and Believer overall. I am grateful to have come into the knowledge of me.

What else did I do you ask? Well, what else was I made to do…I distinctly remember the day God told me to forgive them. I thought I had done that but there was still a place in my heart where hurt resided and a place in my soul that was still connected. In tears, I spoke aloud several times; "I forgive you _____ (their name)" and finally it broke. I ran in that sanctuary in 5 inch heels. I was free! Fo'real back at 100. You may never get the apology you want or deserve but you cannot let that hold you in bondage because you did not get it or you are not willing to give it. Whether they receive it or not, forgiveness is a process and it is for you. Sometimes the fullness of that forgiveness comes quickly and other times it takes time. It happens as you go. As you continue to live life without regret, without blame, without meanness or spitefulness in your heart towards the other person, situation or entity, forgiveness comes and puts a seal on you and your impending blessing can be released. It was and is God and His love in me that prompted and caused me to forgive. Forgiveness requires the love of God. His love alone has power to change and make us do what we may not want to do or think we should (have to) do. It was truly the love of God for me that healed me, set me free, and made me whole. His love truly lifted me out of my hurt, pain, and disappointment.

I recall being in prayer one morning and the Spirit of the Lord directed me to contact them to apologize. How painful that was…Why? Well, in my mind and heart I felt I had done nothing that warranted me apologizing. I prayed and travailed to not have to. Once I surrendered, I asked God to search my heart purge me where needed that there be nothing in me that would hinder and make my apology insincere or of ill effect. If I could not say God Bless you and mean it, that was my indicator that my heart was not yet whole and I was not ready. In the meantime, I unblocked one means to contact them. I created the message and it sat. Once released, I obeyed and sent it. I never received a response, but that is well. Forgiveness became God's good pleasure for me. I quickly accepted it in order to obtain and walk in wholeness and victory and sent the other. I had to not only forgive, but communicate my forgiveness and ask for it from and with a clean heart. First step in the process of forgiving is to decide to forgive; set your heart and mind to forgive and start walking it out. Then as led and God brings it to you, ask for forgiveness. This is key our healing and being made whole. Walking it out is not just in word but in applied action and deed. My obedience speeded up my return to better, my release, and my reward.

There was another instance where HE led me to pray for someone who hurt me deeply. They never apologized for the hurt and still have not to date. They accepted my apology but never took responsibility for what they did and said that was mean, nasty, and ugly. The tongue of the learned in combination with the street unreformed and untransformed part of them can be (is - was) more vicious when not tamed by God, His Word, and the Holy Spirit. Bringing with it a scaring and damaging at a whole other level. This act of forgiveness made me check in with God to make sure this was perhaps what HE meant by seven times seventy. What made this so difficult was because of their place in and time with Christ and His Word. My thought was they should do and be better because of who they are and what they know. They (should) know better. It was a situation where I extended grace upon grace upon grace because I certainly thought they would allow the Spirit of the Living God to bring conviction to them. It was very hard. I remember, I could not say their name in pray. I truly agonized over this. In my mind I prayed for them but aloud, I could not.

I did not want to open my spirit and soul to them again. Long ago, I became very aware of the power of prayer for the opposite gender that was not strictly platonic or a family member, spouse, and spiritual leadership. Particularly, someone your heart and or soul and for many their flesh is or was still open to. Prayer is a very powerful. It is an intimate encounter with God and the

Spirit. Then HE reminded me, "I Am requiring this of you…The Spirit that you pray from and with is My Spirit and your soul also belongs to Me…I got you." Once I surrendered, I prayed fervently for their childhood and heart hurt and the remaining pain of their past. The prayer was not for me or us but for their soul and life purpose. The prayer the Father had me pray for them was very strategic to release them from where they were to their next level. I know that was God. How and what all God will do to get them ready to be released to the next is up to Him but for me to be able to pray for them was major. Only God and His love could cause me to do this. Only HE could bring me to a place of freedom through forgiveness and pray and cause me fervently pray for someone who intentionally hurt me in word and deed. But God and only God! His love is powerful. Without it we can do nothing and all our works and efforts are like clanging symbols to Him.

In obedience you must make a decision to forgive. That decision starts in your heart. Though it is a process; it is one we all will be faced to go through. It is a decision we make and then let the Lord do the rest in and through us as we go. One day you will look up and your soul will have caught up with your heart and your forgiveness will be complete. Much like what I shared, I have known God to require of the innocent, the inflicted, and the injured person to ask the person who caused the hurt for forgiveness. This was and is a very humbling and difficult task. I tell you this and shared my story so you will be ready if and when HE requires this of you. Forgiveness is more for you and about your relationship with God then about the other person.

Scripture tells us in Matthew 18 that unforgiveness is torment. Forgiving the other person releases you to let it go, be healed, set-free and made whole to receive what God has for you. We are commanded to forgive. It seals our healing and I believe speeds up our processing to receive. What is important in all of this is that we obey God, His Word, and the leading of the Holy Spirit. Whether they respond or not, say they are sorry or not, ask you to forgive them or not, accept your apology or not, what matters to God is that you obey from and with a pure heart and without motive. Certainly in a committed and or covenant relationship, we pray that response is present and sincere and brings about change for a healthy lasting relationship. However, if you are not in covenant and if God requires, let it go and you go. Pray and obey God no matter the relationship, partnership or situation. I wish everyone would make it easy to forgive them but if they did, forgiveness would not be necessary. My Lord God. Forgive them before they have to be forgiveness…because they will need to be forgiven just like you and me.

The journey back to wait and wholeness required a reset back to Me. Victory came, was, and is now mine. It was by His power and strength that I overcame and learned. Now back at 100%, I believe God has approved and stamped me again as ready. Able to receive the good; the best HE has for me, not only in love but life. I am confident it will be better than I could have every asked for, dreamed, or imagined. If what you thought you had was good; even if only for a season or a reason, imagine what the real thing will be and bring? I get excited thinking about it. It will truly be the special order and delivery that will come with extra blessings. I encourage you to take time to be by yourself and with yourself to learn, know, and understanding you. Learn to love and like you. Use your return to wait wisely. Take time to learn God in a new, different, and precious way. Fall back in love with Him. Can you imagine God feeling like a jilted lover? How…Why? Because we let other relationships, jobs, businesses, pursuit of wealth and riches, and status quo interfere with our time and relationship with Him. Turn back to Him; your first love. Delight yourself (again) in Him and HE will give you the desires of your heart. HE knows and will send exactly what you need, want, desire, deserve, and have dreamed about. The ideal is a partner, mate, love, lover who is just as in love with God as you are. Now that is some serious love and lov'n. Trust Him and His timing. Both are perfect and without fault. God never misses His moment. If we stay close Him to hear and walk in obedience according to His leading and will, neither will we.

Consider the next relationship and final good love that is coming that will lead to holy matrimony; it will be nothing to compare. The next house, job, business deal will bring to shame what the enemy tried. You trusted, looked over your shoulder, and checked your mirrors but somehow he maneuvered and you were sideswiped. For this sneak attack, your pay out shall be great. You will forget the former things of the past. The last house is nothing to be compared to what is to come. The new job will put you in awe. The next relationship will in every way bring fulfillment of desire, joy, peace, love, and satisfaction. The next business, deal and contract will put you in a league of your own. Can you see that? Can you believe? (1 Corinthians 2:9) Even this hit, this loss God had and has a purpose. God knew what could happen and or what was coming. HE knew the truth and what was really behind that tree and underneath its' leaves. HE knew where that anger and rage could go and what it would lead too. HE knew what that hateful language, yelling, and screaming and balled up fists would turn into. HE knew how those mood swings, insecurities; childhood unresolved self-hate issues, inability to be monogamous, and their womanizing would affect you, your soul, your life, your womb, your future, and ultimately your purpose. HE has not allowed me or you to wait and sacrifice to wait right; pray, fast, and be obedient and faithful to Him for us to end up in an unhappy, unfulfilled, and unhealthy job, place, relationship or marriage.

Ok, so you thought they were the one and they weren't. Hear me beloved, hear me, it may feel like rejection but it was not. It was God's protection. HE blocked it to protect you. On this side of 'I Do', that business deal, that purchase, that decision…HE said, no…go no further. HE blocked it. I remember watching a football game. As I sat there, I saw player after player being hit, tackled…blocked. When it was a good hit or block everyone cheering for that team would literally scream, 'That was a good hit! Block him, get him!' I heard the Holy Spirit say, *"Have you ever seen block yet that didn't hurt."* No. Why, because, blocks hurt…pads and all…all that protective gear; prayer, accountability, fasting, family, friends…blocks will hurt. Even blocks that are good for you; sent by God can and will hurt. HE knew and knows what you and I do not. HE sees and knows what is up the road. Painful or not HE had to show me. Undeniably, HE let me get a glimpse and see what could be and where things were headed if they continued as is (and they were going to) and I ignored, made excuses, extended grace again. Not forced on us; giving us a free will, HE allows us to make the decision. We can choose to do it our way and go in with our eyes wide shut but God. Stay if you want to for a car, house, ring, dress, the image of marriage, hopefully good intimacy, cause she cute, he fine, money for a moment…Stay if you want but God is saying flee. HE will give you a way of escape. HE will give you signs of His will and what is to come and a way out. You asked Him to show you and He did but you want to play blind. Wake up and run! There is a better love, a better job, a better house, a better car, another city…Get out of that situation that the Father – Mercy has said no too.

For some of you, HE had to force you to make a right choice. In His great love and wisdom, HE kept (and will keep) trying to show you. Still there are many who have not yet decided to obey and will not take the way of escape that God has sent and is leading them toward. Beloved, walk towards and go into the light of truth. It is safe there. I recall a number of people telling me after the engagement and relationship was over what they saw, what they knew, and how they prayed I would see. Though I had no clue and grateful for the prayers and their concern after the fact; prayers (theirs and mine prevailed), I would highly recommend, caution, and encourage if you know something and are concerned enough to pray for and about someone that you obviously love or care about, I would say tell them. Why do I say this? What if I was not a lover of God? Not one who sought Him or desired to please and do His will? What if I was not a praying woman? What if my desire for marriage and children and all that was being given and presented me, drew me away and blinded me now at 47. What if I did not have family, Spiritual mothers, godly sister friends and big brothers in the Spirit or a loving Pastor and First Lady? Thank God it didn't take all them for me to see and flee. But what if I would have gone forth? To God be the Glory! In my weakness, by His Spirit, His love, and truth, I was made strong, and HE kept me. However, a less mature person; spiritually or emotionally could have, would have, and will most likely be drawn away and overtaken. It is not your concern if they believe and receive and obey, just that you come in love and obey and say.

Out of desperation for love, people often act out of fear of being alone, who else will love me or want me, do for me what they do, or 'do' me the way they do. I have a question, 'how are they really doing you if you are questioning if you should stay and insecure about leaving?' Out of a crazy since of loyalty, guilt or 'I can fix him or her' they remain. They stay in abusive, mean, painful, unhealthy, toxic, dangerous relationships or situations with people who are all those things just listed. Knowing that not only has God told you to break camp but those who care about you have (prayerfully) told you (tried to help) you get out This I knew before and I am convinced of now; with all the love that was there, love does not encompass fear or abuse of any kind.

God wants you safe and HE has something bigger, better, greater, more for you. Your obedience is always better, more favorable, and comes with a greater reward than the sacrifice of what you give up, give back or walked away from. I am confident of this.

Back at wait, 1 Corinthians 13 verses 4-8 have become more real to me. That love considers the other person above themselves; through care and sacrifice; not cursing and scare tactics. Yes, you loved them and they loved you but love does not fear or intentionally hurt or inflict pain. It is not abusive or makes excuses and blames you and everyone else for why they do what they do, don't or won't do. Love does not blame their past, their father, mother, their loss and suffering of their life, their stress, the tragedies of their childhood and now adult life for their horrible hurtful behavior. It does not use pity to gain sympathy to excuse what they do or say. Hear me beloved, when and where this is your experience, there is more in operation and at stake than meets the eye. The Scripture shows us a healthy, good, and receptacle love.

If HE allowed you to see, experience, taste what you thought (and probably) was wonderful, amazing, awesome, the answer to your prayers and looked like it was sent by Him from heaven...Then what more will HE give to you for the heartbreak, ache, and pain of having to walk away from it and all that you thought was your answer; particular when it was not of your doing. The Bible says when you catch the thief; he has to give it back seven times. Everything he stole, destroyed or you gave back in obedience and gave up including your peace, your time, your joy, your love, your resources, etc., he (the devil) has to give it back at least double for your trouble. (One Scripture says give it back seven times). God allowed me to identify and catch the thief. I am confident – certain that my obedience and keeping my hands and heart clean in this and toward them that my reward will be amazing and supernatural.

When you are brought back to wait, you must resolve to not start doubting and questioning God or yourself. If you missed God, Ok. The Bible says in Mark 13 that the elect can be deceived if possible. So, you are not the first and you will not be the last. Either way, we know that HE did not miss us. What happen did not catch Him off guard or unaware. The truth is whether HE did it or HE allowed it; there was a reason for it. The hidden treasure of this test comes to allow God to show you you in the situation. Will you, can you humbly accept your role; whether big or small in the demise of the situation? Are you willing to repent, sincerely apologize and ask for forgiveness for your part, and forgive? The blessing for me was that God did not allow me to be deceived and drawn away by my own desires. HE did not allow a momentary affliction to become a permanent lifelong dis-ease. I had to resolve that God is in control. No matter how much I did not like it, understand what happened, how it happened, why it happened, why they behaved the way they did, I had to accept that God knew and knows best. I mean after all…HE is God…All knowing…All powerful…All wise.

If you know in your heart and soul that in this you did right by the person, situation, organization, etc., I encourage you to be released. No more worrying, fretting, rehearsing the past, revisiting the thoughts and memories that allow regret, fear or hopeless to creep in. Be at peace. Let nothing disturb your peace. A good indicator of a present or potential future challenge is the lack of peace. I am a pretty peaceable and thus a joyful person. I enjoy peace and order. I do not do drama very well. I try to keep it far from me. When my peace becomes uneasy and unsettled or my joy starts to wane that is an indicator…Stop, ask, be still to hear and know. God will reveal. If my trust in them is being questioned that affects my peace. Pay attention to peace. Do not feel guilty for loving yourself more than they said they did or do or loving you enough to say no more. The truth is; neither you nor them can or will ever love you more than God (your Creator) and Jesus (your Savior and big brother) does. They want the very best for you. It is full of love and peace, healthy, lasting, and good. I mean really, HE sent His son (Jesus) and HE willingly came to die for you for this very cause to be accomplished and received.

Keep truth at your core. Never regret what God shows you, blocks, and protects you from. Never mourn the loss of that which was not or is not willing to, able to, did not or could not do or be right for God, the relationship, themselves or you. Certainly do not mourn those who are unwilling to love you, honor you, and your love from them, or be a blessing to you. For the blessings; the love of the Lord is still sent to make us rich (bring us joy and happiness) and are never to add sorrow to us. Always remember that God loves you too much to let you go any further than your return stamp. Stop tripping on how far HE let you or you chose to go. Just be thankful you opened your eyes…You looked, saw, heard, received, obeyed, and turned. Don't take that lightly. Be proud of yourself that you obeyed. Never mind it was after the fifth attempt. You obeyed. Do your best to remain righteous. What does that mean? It is doing the right thing God's way; obeying, even when it hurts. When you do not have all the facts to understand or appreciate where you are. This is truly walking by faith and putting your trust in God. By this, you will be RICHLY rewarded. You will not be put or brought to shame.

It is the self-accusation and doubt of why you are back at wait that makes the return and the season more difficult. What did I not learn the first or the last time that I am sentenced again to wait? What did I miss? Beloved, may I bring comfort to your confusion and the series of questions that you may be bombarding your brain with? It very well could not have been anything wrong with you or that you did wrong. You took your medicine, completed your treatments, and got a clean bill of health but here you are back at waiting on the results from a routine test. Does that mean that you did something wrong, absolutely not. Healing is still the children of God's bread? It is simply a part of the process and life. HE still took the stripes and by them you are healed physically, emotionally, mentally, etc. Ok, so what if you did miss it? What if you were led or drawn away by your own heart's desires and emotions. Maybe, your flesh led you astray. They did deceive you and everyone else. You did cast your pearls before that which was not worthy. Leave them there. God will give you more and the next string will fresh water ones and valued by who receives them. In all this, God's grace is still sufficient. His love which encompasses His commitment to you and forgiveness of you still covers a multitude of sins, iniquities, trespasses, mistakes, and wrong decisions.

God allowed me to go into and come out and through this heart break victorious with a healed and whole heart. My testimony is that I am without the stench of smoke. Without the stench of anger, regret, bitterness, fear, desperation, depression, hopeless, etc. I am smoke free with my hands clean and my heart pure. I have been healed to help others deal when they find themselves in an extended wait season and or back at wait. I am more than ever hopeful of the promises over my life; including my Holy Adam. Jesus told Peter (Simon), *"I've prayed for you in particular that you not give in, give up, or give out (that your faith not fail). When you have come through this (your) time of testing, turn to others and give them hope (a fresh start)"* Luke 22:31, 32. The enemy comes to tempt you. If you allow him to remain and get into a discussion with him in your mind or via a person sent to tempt, distract or take you off your assignment or away from your purpose, he will cause you to give up on and change your mind about God, your dreams, and hopes. Despite what has happened, hold-on to your faith and God. Do not give up on and walk away from Him or His Word and promises. HE has promised to never do either concerning you. Do not believe the lies or chase them. Whether HE did it, allowed it or it was all you, HE still loves you and has a perfect plan for you. If it was you, repent. Ask Him and the other party for forgiveness and mean it. Forgive yourself and them. Start the journey. Begin walking toward (letting it) go. Be healed and be made whole.

The other day, I happened to look at the cover of my book. In all my times of picking it up, reading it, and reviewing it, for the first time I saw something I had not seen before. The clock. More specifically, the time on the clock read 7:58. I started to ask myself, "Is it reflecting am or pm? Morning or evening?" I concluded that the time of day was less important to me than the time that was being shown. The clock was showing just before 8 o'clock. Eight. Eight Biblically is the number of new beginnings. My Spirit jumped, "I am right at the threshold of a new beginning! In just a few minutes, my 'new' will begin. My return to wait gives me an opportunity for a fresh new beginning and receive it!" A starting over. A reset. It is exciting to know that God is in the business of "do-overs" and second chance. I love me some Him. And so it shall be for each of you who have picked this book; read it and received. My love and faith in Him grows with every encounter of truth, answered and unanswered prayers, and every confirmation of my future.

With great joy, expectation, and anticipation, I accept the call to wait again and trust that my reward for every area of my life will be bigger, better, greater, and more than I could have asked for or imagine. No more hit and misses. My new shall be better than my old. God has promised to do a new thing and I receive it; now in this time. He who shall come will come with my reward and will not delay. I am grateful for all the things HE has done. HE has certainly blessed me. HE stood between me and the decisions I made that would have not ended in or for my good. HE has kept and held me through my processing. In all things give thanks for this is the will of the LORD in Christ Jesus.

Be grateful for "what could have been – what should have been" had the enemy got his way and the stuff you never saw because Mercy said, "No" and HE blocked before it ever got to you. For all of it, I love Him and today I can earnestly say, "Thank You Lord." HE is blocker and a keeper and a sure restorer to better. I love and appreciate Him for loving me enough to allow me to see and giving me the strength to walk away, let go, and forgive.

HE loves me and so do I. I thank Him for showing me I am a woman that can selflessly love a good man; a man after His heart. I am a ride or die, stick and stay girl but not desperate, foolish or a glutton for punishment. Such loyalty and commitment requires the bestowed to humble themselves under God's hand and to value, honor, and protect the gift of me that HE has given them. I (you) deserve nothing less. Such as you give you should receive. What you sow (good or bad) in love and good you should also receive. And what you desire and work towards being that is good and genuine you also can receive. I truly believe one of the primary necessities for a healthy, happy, satisfying, lasting relationship and marriage is a denying self; dying to self and preferring the other above and before you. This is for both parties. Selfishness and pride; both rooted in fear are the root of most failed relationships and marriages. When our heart and will are surrendered to God, we will always conquer the works of the enemy in us, our life, and most certainly our relationships. The Bible says for us to do our best to keep the peace, to love and treat others the way we desire to be treated. Doing what God calls us to do may not always equal or mean easy. Yet, being and doing His will when we do not want to and even when it hurts places us under His mighty, protective, safe, and loving hand. Whether it is to stay or go, do or don't, give or not; I encourage you to obey and trust God.

The love of God, a heart after and turned to God (humility), and the Fruit of the Sprit (Galatians 5:22,23) must be present and evident in the life of the person you are willing to ride with. It is never His will for us to stay in any situation that is dangerous; that is not good for us or unhealthy. HE wants what is best for you and me. HE said HE would withhold no good thing from those who walk uprightly before Him. This is not about being perfect. What it is about is doing right by others and before God according to His Word. The 'good thing' excludes nothing and includes everything that is good and not just material things. I had all that was material being served to me on a silver platter. It was wonderful and greatly appreciated. I loved them for it but that was not why I loved them. The good things are what you go to sleep with in your heart and keep you smiling while you are sleep. The good thing includes; a sense of security, peace, harmony, joy, safety, free to give and receive, prosperity, health, honesty, commitment, loyalty, truth, trust, good healthy consistent love without fear, lies, deception, abuse or control. What the good thing houses is what I would define as the good life and true success.

In our celebration of success and in our return from mishaps and failures HE is with us. There is a peace and joy in knowing that if you obey and was or are now in His will there is no failure or need to fear in God only recovery and restoration. HE has a plan that no man, enemy, situation, circumstance, sickness or disease can stop. HE can and will give you strength in the midst of your journey. HE will have the last say in your wait. HE knows what is best for you, for me, for us His children. HE sees what you cannot and knows what you do not. Thank God that HE is God. I am His and HE is mine. HE is the lover of my soul. I am thankful for my sister friends, family, the divine and strategic people that HE put in my life and path along the way who HE used gently or directly to say or not say, do or not do exactly what I needed.

So what else remains? For many of us, there is a heart's desire not spoken. It is the thing that you dare not express or speak. It is the seemingly impossible thing that time, facts, and circumstance tells you probably will never be or may not, cannot, will ever be…It's impossible. But we thank God that HE specializes in those. It may be the waiting to know if it is His will for you to receive, conceive, carry, speak life, and birth you and your husband's child. Back at wait has caused me to truly exam this and my heart concerning it. It has pushed my faith and trust to another level. In this…I MUST trust Him. Despite what age, doctors or my body says, I must trust Him. Though Sovereign, I find it challenging to believe that my faithfulness, commitment to honor Him and His Temple in this way for over 15 years will go overlooked…That HE saved and forgave me…righted wrong and healed me and it all be for not. Lord, I trust You. My hope and faith is in You. HE has promised we would not be put to shame when we put our trust in Him. Thank you for the Biblical witnesses of Sari and Elizabeth both carried miracles but Mary carried a supernatural miracle. I still believe and trust God. His will be done. I have been blessed that the gentlemen who I have encountered in the last seven years or so all wanted children; those who already had and those who had none. Be it His will, it will also be the desire of my husband and I believe God. If HE says yes, I (we) say, "Your will be done"…If HE says no, I say, "Your will be done." Issues of concern, worry, fret, doubt, and questions can be resolved back at wait, So you too hold on and trust God. If there is a word in the Word for your situation, it is a Word you can stand on and hope in by faith. We trust and believe God.

Trust in the Lord and allow His grace (His plan, His purpose) and love to be and become sufficient, more than enough for you. Romans 11 says, *"But if it is by grace (His unmerited favor and graciousness), it is no longer conditioned on works or anything men have done. Otherwise, grace would no longer be grace [it would be meaningless] (verse 6, Amplified)."* I encourage you to continue in the Lord by faith with purpose of heart. Fall back in love Him.

Let the Word of Grace, the ministry of His love build you up in your return to and coming out season. I am confident that your next chapter will be better than the beginning and end of (the last) this one! Believe and trust God. Put your faith and hope solely and solidly in Him. Whatever the situation, cause, loss, hurt, or pain, HE knew and knows ALL things and does ALL things well. Victory is yours.

No more sadness. No more questioning. No more mourning. It is time to move on. Let go and live. Ok, maybe you did miss God or dismiss the initial signs. Until you got close you did not see to know what else was there and what was not...You did not see what else came along with the good things. You did not see the anger, the rage, the hurtful mean violent words, the cheating, the plan to deceive, the extreme mood swings. You did not see the initial signs of selfishness, jealousy, manipulation, abusive tendencies or their controlling demanding and hurtful nature. You did not see their insensitivity to your feelings, needs, and wants. You did not see it coming; the late hours at work and the hateful nature of your co-workers. I must add, do not let others and their words; genuine concern or meddling cause you to stay stuck; hopeless - regretting something God has clearly told you to release and walk away from. Allow no one to cause you to question yourself and your decision when you know you heard God. Inform all concerned to dismantle their opinions and updates of what they are doing. Let it and if need be; let them go.

Today is a fresh start. This is your commencement. You are the end of an old thing and the beginning of a new thing all at the same time. Caused by God or not, transition can be painful; particularly when unexpected and undesired. Isaiah 43:18, 19 says, "*Do not remember the former things; neither consider the things of old. Behold, I am doing a new thing! Now it springs forth; do you not perceive and know it and will you not give heed to it – pay attention to see and know? I will even make a way in the wilderness and rivers in the desert."* Receive from God whatever and why HE brought you back to wait. Listen, your past; the former things cannot tell you anything new. It can only tell you what you already know. HE has promised new and better. In your desert, dry, hurt, lonely place God has made you a promise; a refreshing surprise awaits you. Though we may think we know what we want, most often we do not truly and completely know what we need. What HE has for us will meet all our needs, our wants, and our desires; physically, emotionally, psychologically, financially, and spiritually and alike.

There are good men (and certainly good women) out there. It is just a matter of time, place, and space that God will send him to find you...to find me and that divine encounter; not chance will occur. For HE is faithful and certainly for those who have waited and waited right, it will be for His glory and His name sake that divine meetings and connections are coming. You do the work to get ready so you can be ready. Whether never married, divorced, widowed...the first or second time around, it will be for His and your good pleasure and joy. No guilt for moving on and living and enjoying life. You never know, you may have already met, seen or know them. If nothing else, they may have already spotted you. FYI ladies, when a man; a godly, mature, ready man with only good pure intent wants you...has identified you...has discovered you and set his sights on you...He has watched you and observed you for sometime before he approaches you. Get ready so you can be ready to stay ready! Ready or not... He who shall come will come and will not delay.

Armed with these truths of waiting and being brought back to wait; you can now believe again, expect again, and hope again. Whatever you are waiting on take joy in time and season of waiting. Your turn is next. Galatians 4 verse 9 was a true blessing to me in this season. It reminds us that we have experienced God in a new way and we know Him in a new way and HE more importantly HE knows us. Implying, the testing of our faith and our relationship with Him goes through a process of being authenticated and solidified. Your broken heart, your loss, your season of lack, want, confusion or doubt did not cause you to lose heart or walk away from the household of faith. You may have thought or said a lot of things during that time but you are still here with God and in God and HE is still with you and in you. For me, Him knowing me; the truth of me; good and not so good, my heart towards Him is more important, more amazing than me knowing Him. Why? HE knows me and HE still loves, wants, and receives me. HE never changes. HE is never in transition. HE is forever consistent. Me knowing and learning Him is always easy, amazing, and sweet. It is always all good and brings me comfort and peace. But Him knowing me, proving me, and me being found in right standing with Him as His friend and His righteousness is too much to comprehend...HE is an Amazing God. Be set free beloved in your mind and heart. No need to fear, fret or to go back to or keep pondering over, turning back in your heart, mind or actions to weak and miserable ways and forces. God does not want you enslaved or trapped again. Let it go. I declare bigger, better, greater, more. Hold on. Do not turn back or away. Do not grow weary...There is a great reward for you remaining in righteousness, not fainting or giving up or giving in. Continue to come to God. Believe Him. Due season belongs to you. It is your due. Your deserving reward and payment.

WHAT I LEARNED

God knows. There is so much I am waiting on...ministry, business, relationship, family, children, breakthrough, debt freedom, wealth, healing, vision coming to pass, purpose being fulfilled. Finally I am seeing it all come together and earnestly believe it is nigh...closer than I think or know! I trust Him in all things that it is and it will be. HE knows. I am grateful that in all things spiritual; blessings in the heavenly realm, I'm good. I have peace, joy, truth, salvation, forgiveness, His grace and mercy, eternal life, the Holy Spirit, etc. In this, I am good. It is the earthly desires that I wait on God to bring, give, and fulfill. So, I ask you Lord, am I in the way of You blessing me? Is there anything You are waiting on me to do? Is there anything in me that You need me to deal with that stands or is standing in the way of you blessing me. Perfect me...my character for Your purpose for my life...for Your good works and pleasure. If it is simply Your timing, help me to continue to wait and wait right and trust You no matter what it looks or feels like. You know and I know You care. You really do love me. You are my protector. My blocker. Pray at the beginning and during. Keep Christ in the middle. Only what is in a person is what comes out. It may lay dormant until touched but what I need to see that is not of or acceptable to God HE will cause me to see. You give people a space of grace to get it together. You give each one time to obey, to repent, to do the right thing, to receive with grace the blessings You send our way and gives us. Forgiveness, patience, selflessness is key to a healthy loving relationship. When we do not do right by those – who God blesses us with, God will give us time to get it right and if we do not HE very well may take His gift back and bless someone else with if (him/her) -- Matthew 25. My good works or acts of righteousness are not what has kept me in good or right standing with God it my confession, my godly sorrow, my repentance, my desire and cry to do and be right with and for Him and others. To ask God to not let my gifts, talents and abilities take me where my character alone cannot keep me. I need to be right and pleasing to You Lord. So my cry remains, Lord give me and help me to keep my hands clean and my heart pure. Let me do nothing that brings shame to You, Your Name, my family, my church or my future spouse and family. Kill anything that remains in me that is unlike you. Heal and make whole the secret faults that are even hidden from me. He who shall come will come and will arrive soon. He will love, accept, respect, honor, and receive me for and as me; natural, wig, pressed, make-up, no make-up, dressed-up, dressed-down. He sees me and knows me before I have to tell him. He gets me. We will have no pretense with one another. Honesty, authenticity, laughter, transparency, kindness, communication, selflessness, and intimate affection will be the secret to our success. His love will not be divided or shared. A woman desiring his time, attention, voice, affection is not always her being needy but a healthy longing for what she comes from and was created for and given to. He found what was taken from him and she longs to be with what she is to be attached to. If he gives me 100, God has created me to give 1000 - 100 fold. Our relationship and marriage will be according to who we are and what you need and have agreed upon. I desire to be a loving supportive helpmate, a wife submitted to my husband who desires and wants to be a husband, who follows and submit to Christ and honors me, takes care of me, lives with me in peace, harmony and understanding – who will love me as his bride – His good thing and Christ loved and so loves His church. It is important that my husband hears me (my heart), honors, and respects me and my opinions. He is a man after Your heart. He supports me. He speaks into and covers me and the vision and purpose You have given me and called me to. He is willing, able, and ready to commit and accept and receive my good love. I choose to die again today. Not only are Your ways not our ways neither is Your timing. Nothing that I went through or will go through takes You by surprise. There are things we "must need" go through. But go through and come out we will. These things come to test our faith and strengthen us. You will put no more on me than I can bear... I was made for this – all that God has allowed me to experience and come through – it came and does come to make me better – to make me more like You. Through this thing I have become even more determined and clear about what God has for me, my value, my worth and what I deserve. You have taught me to not fear and be at peace, contentment, and satisfied in my season of singleness. You oh God have grown me to be the woman I am. I still have work to do and I am grateful You will perfect everything that concerns me. Thank You for taking away insecurities and fears. It is Your truth and confidence I walk in and given by Your Spirit. I am a damn good woman. I am the full package. I great catch. I am saved fo'real. Loving, lovable, likeable, fun, loyal, committed, flexible, adaptable, supportive, encouraging, peaceable, wise, laid back, can role in most environments, family focused…I can cook, I clean. I am educated and articulate. I know who and whose I am. I am authentic. I am worth the wait, effort, time, energy. I have a purpose and know what it is and a vision that I seek to live out to the fullest – I have the power to gain wealth. I am blessed to be a blessing to every environment and relationship I enter into. I am pretty well put together if I do say so myself. I like me. I am the perfect woman and wife for my godly husbandman God has for me. He is perfect for me. He is God's absolute best absolutely for me. I am fitly and perfectly made for him as he is for me. I look forward to the man who I can be all that he needs to help him get to the next level that knows what it means and how to do it and is willing and able to love His wife as Christ loved(s) the church. God desires for my husband man to be a man after His hearts, a man of peace, kindness, goodness, faithfulness, gentleness, giving, patience and wise – full of love that is good and healthy – bearing much fruit. God made me this way and what HE made is good. My husband will accept me just as I am as I will him – not requiring change to live up to others opinions, a past or a memory. Any change in us is for the good of our soul, purpose, character, marriage and family. My love wants what is best for me. This will be a divine purposeful hook up. God has given me a great capacity to love. HE is responsible for sending my mate to find me. What I desire and need is not burdensome or difficult. He is supportive, responsible, a mature believer in Jesus Christ, respectful, ready, willing, and able. He is a man of commitment, integrity, honesty, humor, honor, truthfulness, patience, selflessness, and trustworthy. His love and commitment is undivided and balanced. He is a man of balance, wisdom and truth. He is spiritually, emotionally, mentally, financially, physically healthy, stable, and mature. He will know upon arrival and will be a man of decision and purpose – living out purpose I've learned that blessings can quickly become a sorrow when you don't keep God first. I have learned how to define what love looks and feels like to me. God may give you a hard truth and choice. I know now what it really means to guard my heart. God has and is yet perfecting the things that concern me; my life, business, ministry, and marriage. You will restore all that I gave up, gave back & what the enemy took in time, money, health, relationships, dreams deferred. I have caught the thief and he has to give it all back 7 times or at least double for my trouble. God You still do and work miracles. . I will be a great mother (be it Your will). Be it His will for me and my husband, HE will touch his seed and my womb to bring forth our perfect blessing. I trust God. HE still specializes in miracles. I will not fear or worry. His will shall be done. Whatever the will and outcome of God, I say, yes Lord I agree...I trust You, I love You. My trust, hope, and faith will not be put to shame. My blessings and reward will be great. For You oh God are my joy and my strength...I will not fear or grow weary. My well doing and labor of love and obedience will not be forgotten. Whether it is our child or his, it will be ours. I declare great healthy respectful loving relationship amongst all including our families on and at every level. I eagerly with great excitement wait on God to be God and blow my mine. Wise counsel is good for me in the matters of love. I look forward to new!

I have learned that...

_____

_____

_____

_____

Scripture or Statement for Meditation

_____

What waiting means to me...

_____

_____

_____

_____

_____

TEN

Conclusion

Grace and Mercy

There is a grace and mercy for the waiting place. The simplest definition I once heard for grace is, "It is what God gives us that we do not deserve (gift of God is eternal life)." And mercy is "What HE withholds from us (wages of sin is death) that we do deserve." Romans 6:23, describes this perfectly, *"for the wages of sin is death (deserve death – keeps it from us) but the gift of God is eternal life in Christ Jesus our Lord (grace – HE gives to us)."* In the waiting place, we receive the grace and mercy of God to wait and to wait right. It is by His grace that we are saved. It is this same grace we can rely on to help us to wait, wait right, have faith, and believe. The Holy Spirit gifts us with the supernatural power to do and be effective in ever (good) work that HE calls us to do. Grace gives us the will, ability, desire, and leading to do. It is this same grace that will help us with every stage and emotion we face in our waiting. If you would give me liberty here to encourage you with this scripture, *"By Him giving us what we do not deserve, we are victorious, we receive grace upon grace"* (John 1:16). The evidence of His love is the grace and mercy HE bestows upon us. We need His grace in the waiting place. We need to experience, know, and be convinced of the love of God (daily) in life and in the wait. Since we have to die and repent daily, I ask for His grace, provision, and favor daily. HE will give you the grace to wait and to wait right.

In your times of discouragement and challenge, remember His loving (merciful) kindness (grace) towards you. It is because HE loves you that HE will drive – usher you into your waiting place. If HE will drive Jesus into the wilderness to be tempted; HE very well may drive us into a waiting place to be perfected. Romans 8, confirms this with a questions that I charge you to answer with the affirmative of "nothing"- *"Who (what) shall separate us from the love of Christ? Shall tribulation, or distress, or persecution, or famine, or nakedness, or peril, or sword?"* It seems as if Paul gets a revelation that brings a greater confidence where he is asking and unequivocally answers his own question. His perspective gets even more solidified. He goes on to say, *"For I am persuaded, that neither death, nor life, nor angels, nor principalities, nor powers, nor things present, nor things to come, Nor height, nor depth, nor any other creature, shall be able to separate us from the love of God, which is in Christ Jesus our Lord."* Yes, sometimes we cause ourselves to wait and prolonged our waiting, but whether by Him or by our own doing, know that God is in control, HE is with and for you, and HE loves you.

Be Confident

When commission by God; waiting has a divine purpose. Strength is found there. Wisdom can be gained there. Beloved, be found waiting on the Lord; expecting and anticipating His arrival with your reward for your faithfulness. Expand your expectation. Build your hope; your confidence on nothing less than Jesus Christ and His righteousness. I know it has been a long wait but I encourage you with Hebrews 10, *"Do not cast away your confidence, which has great reward. For you have need of endurance, so that after you have done the will of God, you may receive the promise. For yet a little while, And HE who is coming will come and will not tarry."* In due season, you shall reap if you do not lose heart (Galatians 6:9). Stay in the life preserver and sustaining presence of God for there is an appointed time for you to be rescued and delivered (Psalm 102). HE will have mercy on you and come to your rescue. Stay in the boat of safety unless HE bids you to come. Be still, and know that the Lord God is your God – your Father who is the great I Am (Psalm 46). Be confident that even when the waves surround you and the floods make you afraid, call upon the LORD. HE will hear your voice from His Holy temple. Your cry will enter into His ears and (2 Samuel 22) and HE will come to your rescue. Wait on the Lord.

Though His timing may seem illogical to us, it is perfect. Remember, HE knows what's in your tomorrow, your next week, your next month, your next year, and years from now. Wait on the Lord and be of good courage. HE can and will strengthen your heart. Listen, Lazarus died and Jesus still waited (John 11). Some would say HE took His time to get to him; his friend and that is why he died. Jesus knew what they did not. HE knew Lazarus would not remain sleep (dead). HE knew he would raise him up back to life. HE not only knew there was plan but what the plan was. HE knew a miracle was in store. HE knew the prayers of Lazarus' sisters and friends would be answered. HE only delayed so that the glory of Father God would be witnessed. And so it is and will be for you. Are you willing to wait on God to bring you your answer – your miracle? Greater the story, greater the glory. Can you imagine the testimony of Lazarus beyond the grave of what being the grave was like and then Jesus! Many of us have grave seasons. Our place of waiting on God; on our change to come and had to wait alone in a dark, cold, dry situation. Rest assured that though you too may be wrapped up, bound, gagged, stuck, restless, frustrated, wanting, desiring life and to live but forced, chosen, commission, and ordained by God to wait; there is a day of release and breakout for you. Rest in your wait. HE is soon to come.

You can wait and you can wait right. You can do this. Say this with me, "I can, I will, I must…for His Glory and Name sake." If Lazarus, Paul, Jesus, Anna, Noah, Abraham, Jesus, and God can wait, so can you. I do not know if God will require you to wait 84 years like Anna, or 25 like Abraham and Sarah, or 23 like Joseph, or 3-days like Lazarus, but whatever HE requires of you – Do It. Galatians 4 verse 4 reminds us that when the set time has fully come, God sent his Son, born of a woman (appointed time of delivery) to do all that was required of Him. Be confident of this, your time and your turn is coming.

Because HE has promised, HE will come. According to His perfect timing, HE will be on time! His Word promises us that in the dispensation of the fullness of the times (when Chronos and Kairos meet) that He will gather together in one all things that are in Christ. What is in heaven and what is in the earth (Ephesians 1:9). Trust in the Lord and do good in your waiting place. HE will send help and strength for your wait, for your journey, your pilgrimage. Do you love God? Do you really love Him? Then trust Him in your waiting place. Build yourself up in your most holy faith. There are many blessings in it and when you come out of it. To be chosen to wait; He anoints you and places a mantle of favor on you and your life when you wait right. If you want your reward, wait for it and expect it.

I found an amazing blessing of waiting in the Word of truth. In Judges Chapter 6 verses 17-19, Gideon asks the LORD if he has found favor in the LORD's sight to show him a sign. He goes on to ask the LORD not to leave but to wait in the place where they were until he brought back an offering. What set me in awe was the LORD's response to Gideon, "I will wait until you come back." The LORD – The I AM that I Am – The Great I Am waited on man.

Because of His love HE waited and waited patiently. Consider 1 Corinthians 13; the Love Chapter starts out saysing "Love is patient…" The love described here is agape love; the God kind of, sacrificial, unlimited, uncompromising love. The first thing God demonstrated through His love for us was to give to us Jesus and then their love for us was and is their patience to even wait on us. To wait on what HE created to come to the truth and knowledge of Him and His love for them. Oh the blessing of understanding waiting.

How awesome was it to learn that God will not only wait with me; HE will for me. God will wait with you in the struggle and the battle. HE will converse and fellowship with you there. HE will answer your prayers and honor your humble requests. You can even ask God for a sign and a confirmation. Ask Him for strategies for your future, your next step, your success, His plan, and how to turn around what we messed up. If you were brought to your waiting place because of financial mishandling or a struggle, give your way out of the hallway. If you were ushered there because of promiscuity; sanctify yourself. If you were brought back because you did get it or chose to ignore His voice the last time, die to you and assassinate pride. Ask for an ear to hear and discern to not be deceived. Humble yourself and HE will bring you out. Since waiting is unavoidable and all you have is time in the waiting place, start practicing perfecting your wait. Though it may be hard, do your best to find time and a place to serve, help others, and give while you wait. Be confident of this; HE who began this good work in you will complete it and will not leave you in your waiting place and seasons.

Be Encouraged

God is your Father, your God, and your Judge. Jesus is your brother, your Savior, and your Advocate – your Defense. The Holy Spirit is your Confidant, your Comforter and your Guide.

You are covered and hedged in all about. You are in the hand of God. Your name is written not only in the Lambs Book of Life but in the palm of His hand (Isaiah 49:16). You are protected on every side. Goodness and mercy follows you. You were made, created, and formed to do the thing(s) that await you. Whether what you face is a challenge or an easy win, you were made for it. In your waiting place HE is equipping you to handle and walk boldly and confidently in all that HE has for you. You are fit and more than capable to do it. Your precious Redeemer is the same One – the One and Only who in Mark 5 rebuked the wind and commanded the waves of sea. Jesus knows you and created you. HE was there in the beginning with God the Father creating everything; including you. HE specializes in sinking things: ships (remember Paul), situations (remember Jonah), people (Peter), and souls (remember you). Everything HE created whether forced or chosen, slowly or quickly; everything must submit to Him, including you, me, and our circumstances. HE is able, willing and can bear it all. HE will put no more on you than you can bear. I know it seems like enough already but HE got you. But be encouraged. HE has promised to never leave or forsake (forget about, cast or set you assign, or dismissed) you. HE is God and HE is love. And guess what, HE is in love with you and loves you. Accept nothing less than the good and perfect healthy love of God and His purpose for your life.

WHAT I LEARNED

God is God – no matter what it looks like – no matter how long it takes – no matter what comes or goes – no matter who understands – likes it – loves it – God is God – whether married, single, with or without children – God is God – no matter what happens – God is God and God is Love and God loves, cares for and about me – He has a plan for me and it will come to pass – I desire to please Him and do His will and be a vessel yielded to Him and to His will and for His good pleasure – He has called me to greatness and I accept the call and the charge – He has promised to go with me and before me and behind me is goodness and mercy – my ministering angels lead and prepare the way – I believe Him for the things He has promised and spoken to me and I believe and declare they shall come to pass – for all the promises of God in and from Jesus are Yes, and in Him (Jesus they are) Amen, to the glory of God through me. I accept and receive my promises and blessings. I resolve that the timing of God is perfect, His plan is ideal, and His purpose for my life is sure. The vision HE has for my life shall come to pass. God reigns. I will let nothing other than God have rule over me or my life. My hope, trust, and belief is in Him and I will not be put to shame. I believe and trust God with my life.

I have learned that...

_____

_____

_____

_____

Scripture or Statement for Meditation

_____

What waiting means to me...

_____

_____

_____

_____

_____

_____

PRAYER OF FAITH

Father God, in Jesus name, I ask that You forgive us for our times of going off and doing our own thing. For being led away by our own lusts, wants, and desires. Forgive us for making that man or woman or relationship, job, material things our god and equal to or more important than you. Forgive us for turning to others concerning Your will for our lives. Help those who struggle with forgiveness to forgive those or who hurt them and forgive themselves. Let Your love teach them and cover them. Grant You sons and daughters peace and joy in their waiting place. Strengthen them for their journey. Give them a heart after You to please You…to be wed to You…for You are the hus-band-man for Your sons and daughters. Teach them how to love right while they are single, so that when you send them their good love, they will be ready to receive, honor and cherish it…treat it right and well. Order their steps and establish their pilgrimage. Be their light and their lamp. Make them not to miss their moment and opportunity to develop, grow, advance, heal and be better to increase their life, relationships, and soul. Perfect everything that concerns them. Teach them how to wait. Help them to watch and pray. Reveal - speak and confirm their purpose their waiting place. Give them quick understanding and application of Your truth as shared here and reveal to them Your will and Your cause for them in this season. Help them us not to grow weary in our well do. Let them believe and trust in and anticipate our due season. Let them add to their faith and grow in their faith. Let someone who does not know You or Your Son come into the truth and the knowledge of You and Him. Let someone encounter the truth of You. Your peace, Your joy. For You are hope, truth, love, and peace. Let them know that all you do is good. Let them be found worthy of their calling, and fulfill all the good pleasure of Your goodness. Show them how to walk by faith, work their faith with power and accuracy that the name of our

Lord Jesus Christ may be glorified and the Kingdom advanced. Grant them, according to Your riches of His glory what they need and have earnestly prayed and petitioned You for. Grant them peace and grace to be strengthened with might through Your Spirit in their inner man, that Christ may dwell in their hearts through faith; that they might be rooted and grounded in (Your) love, and be able to comprehend with all the saints what is the width and length and depth and height to know the love of Christ which passes knowledge; that they may be filled with all the fullness of God. Give them wisdom and patience to wait right. Help them to rest and trust You in the wait. Cause them to expect, dream again, and anticipate. Give them a garment of praise and take away heaviness. Give them hope again. Let the evidence of their expectation be found in their praise. Let their praise and worship come unto You as a fresh aroma of their trust and belief in You. Love on them Lord. Let them experience You like never before. Allow them to see You. Help them do what You have said – to obey You even when it hurts. Make them to believe the promises You have written and spoken to, over, and for them. In their waiting place, give them a love and thirst for You, Your Word, and presence. Let them find You there. Oh, God remind them of Your love for them. Give them an undeniable encounter of Your existence, presence, and love for them. Teach them how to love You, themselves, and others. Cause their faith and reverence of You to grow with every answered and unanswered prayer. Comfort them. Let them somehow know that even in Your times of silence, You are still with and for them. Remind them that their non-release is not because You don't love them – it because You do love them. Thank You that Your silence does always mean "No", sometimes it means "Not yet". Remind them that if You said it and promised it – You will do it. You promised and You are faithful. Your promises are still yes and Amen in Christ Jesus. Speak to their heart Lord and manifest Your glory in and over their lives. Grant them peace and patience in the midst of their trials, challenges, difficulties, and *struggles, hurts, losses, break-up and mistake. Teach them how to guard their heart and mouth in this season. Give them sweet sleep and rest. I declare no worry no fear. Remind them that You are able, willing, and can. You rise to show compassion towards them. Let their cry be to please you, for clean hands, and a pure heart. Give them clear direction and outline the order and plan for their life. Reveal purpose and solidify their destiny. Give them the grace to wait and to wait right. Teach them how to actively wait and to work their faith. Help them to use their waiting time wisely. Teach them how to walk by faith and not by sight and lead them in the path of righteousness for Your name sake. Give them an amazing testimonies "That You did it God." Make them to rest in You. Give them a peace that surpassed their and others understanding. Remove fear, worry, anxiousness, and weariness. Give them signs of their soon release and reward. Help them to die to themselves and live for You. Build them up in their Holy faith. Strengthen them and give them self- control over their flesh. Make their desires become Your desires. Help them to be content and flee from sexual immorality. Only send the person who for them and who will respect and honor their decision to wait.*

I pray a special pray for women between the ages 28-58. Those who are trying and have been waiting and many have been waiting right. Not out of hopelessness but hopefulness. Those who are asking "when". When will my love come? When, if, can marriage be mine? Will I have the honor, the pleasure, the joy to experience marriage ever or for some, again! Can a second chance be mine? There is a longing, a deep desire to be a wife; a helpmate to a loving husband that will love her as Christ love the church. So many are weak, discouraged, hurt, sad, lonely, and dismayed and a few are angry. Not only those who are back at wait, standing the midst of a lost love, an unwanted or needed divorce but those who have yet to experience marriage. They thought they had the love they had believed for, waited on. They waited, they prayed, they trusted, they went into the relationship right, and tried stayed right. Yet, they found themselves left – alone again. "Oh, God heal the hurt of again". Strengthen them in the power of Your might. Comfort them in Your loving embrace. Heal the pain of soul and body abuse that came by cursed and course words, hands raised against them, rejection of their love, kindness, goodness, care and support of them. Their hearts are broken. Restore hope and trust. Lord heal. Heal their mind and emotions. Remove the thoughts and memories of any and all things and people who keep them oppressed and stuck. Cast it as far as the east is from the west and let them remember it and or them no more. Remove the sight of things that causes their mind to wander and wonder. Wipe their late night and early morning tears of pain way and cause them to sing and dance again. Remove anger, bitterness, guilt, shame; embarrassment of the break-up, singleness, and divorce. Let them see the blessing in the block. And cherish this time with you. Show them they still got it and are desirable. Let them be patient in the wait. Let them not be drawn away by their own desires, lust and need to be loved and to love. Let them not be deceived in any way. Give them keen discernment and wisdom. Build them up in the confidence and their faith. Make them to forgive themselves, the person, and perhaps even You. I command your soul to be untied and you let it and them go. Forgive. Let the will of God be done and receive it and His peace. I speak and declare sweet sleep and rest to your soul and members. Hold their mind and thoughts God and wash them clean and make – set them free. Heal their hurts, disappointments. Remove fear and loneliness. Let them not grow weary; get stuck in feeling of negativity in their well doing of waiting on who and what You have for them. Let them hold on to their faith, hope, and love. For those who have done or are doing the work to be healed and whole; send, give, fulfill the desires of their heart. Make them ready for the blessing that You are preparing or have prepared for them. God ordain their divine *encounter. Awaken the holy Adam or the 20th Century Boaz that is for each individual woman – who You have for them. They are men of peace and not of war. Men of strength but not of demand. Cooperative not controlling. Worshippers and lovers not fighters and abuser. Let him be tender in his touch and in his words. Anger, rage, and abuse are not his portion. He is a man of wisdom and passion. Priest, prophet, and her king. Let adoration be their appreciation one to another. Even now, put her name in his heart and on his mind. Give him a seek to find her and a desire for only her. Let him see her as his good thing and know of her favor and what she shall add to his life and purpose. Teach her now how to love and support him and teach him how to love and cover her. Give them to one another as joy and pleasure of their youth. We declare their eye and intimacy is one for another. She is his pleasure and he is her satisfaction. Keep him and keep her until your divine plan orders their steps to each other and in holy matrimony. No more false, incomplete, forfeited starts and miscarriages. Full term, peaceful, painless delivery unto manifestation of their promise. The next will be the best and fit for the finish. No settling just to (say you) have. Let him be what she needs and let her be what he needs. I declare true matches made in heaven that all will know "God did that." Remove and heal any fear, hurt and insecurities, suppressed pain he has. Cause those who have not yet faced, recognized, accepted or are willing to face the need for them to work on them to be still to hear and know. Raise up and make ready strong, confident, humble, giving, loving men of God who are genuinely healthy, mature, and sound; emotionally, mentally, and spiritually. His heart is turned to God and his desire is to please God and his future bride and wife. He understands and respects his responsibility as a man, husband and father. Make him to know and understand what it means to 'love his wife as Christ loved and loves the (His) Church." Let each one examine themselves according to Your Word and Spirit and allow You God to be the change agent of character and behavior.*

Let him not miss his good thing and forfeit his favor. Fitly join them together for Your glory, for Your name sake - as a Kingdom example of love and a godly marriage. Let him be her kinsmen redeemer and her covering. Let her be his reward and his crown. Cause their prayers for their mate to begin now as they seek You and ask You to teach them how to love their gift – their mate. Let only a good healthy love find my sister but let it and him not delay. No impostors. Let the next love that comes be The Love; a healthy, holy, godly, kind, loving, patient, giving, sustaining, nurturing, growing, supportive love that stays and remains til death do them part. Grant 25, 50, 60 years of Holy joyful loving passionate matrimony and marriage. Grace those called to be a witness of Your love and grace in the ministry to other couples. Bless and anoint their ministry one to another. If called to serve together, let him accept, receive, and support her and the call on her life and she do the same unto him. Let them put each other 1st in wisdom, balance, encouragement, love and patience. Thank you that he is a man of power, integrity, humor, kindness, gentleness, faithfulness, self control, accountable, responsible, of a peaceable spirit, supportive, encouraging, loving, full of truth comfort and truth, his worship is genuine in every way, he is a promise keeper, a bearer of fruit. Thank you for sending Your daughter Your best because she is Your best. You God, choose this one. We wait to hear You say, "I do, I give her – My child – My daughter to this man in Holy Matrimony."

I pray the joy of You of Lord be the strength of all those who read and receive. In Jesus name by faith, I pray and believe and Amen.

Scripture or Statement for Meditation

_____

My prayer for me...

_____

_____

_____

_____

_____

_____

_____

_____

_____

_____

_____

_____

APPENDIX 1

Daily Declarations and Confessions

I (your name) _____ am what and who God says, I Am.

I Am _____, that, I Am

I Am _____, that, I Am

I Am _____, that, I Am

I Am _____, that, I Am

I Am _____, that, I Am

I Am _____, that, I Am

I Am _____, that, I Am

I Am _____, that, I Am

I Am _____, that, I Am

I Am _____, that, I Am

I Am _____, that, I Am

I Am _____, that, I Am

I Am _____, that, I Am

I Am _____, that, I Am

I Am _____, that, I Am

APPENDIX 2

Survey

Waiting: Possibly the most difficult discipline you will face

1   Have you ever waited on or for God   ☐ No ☐ Yes

2   Is waiting a challenge for you   ☐ No ☐ Yes

3   If yes, what emotions/behaviors does it invoke, e.g., impatience, restlessness, doubt, anxiety, frustration,worry, impulsive, procrastination, negative words/thoughts, etc. *List at least 2:*

_____

_____

_____

4   Does waiting make you uncomfortable   ☐ No ☐ Yes

5   In your times of waiting, have things been unclear   ☐ No ☐ Yes

6   What challenges you most in wait Is the challenge of waiting because of the uncertainty, for example; uncertainty, fear, doubt, time. *List at least 2:*

_____

_____

_____

7   Are waiting 'on' – waiting 'upon' – waiting 'for' the same   ☐ No ☐ Yes

8   Is there a (right) way to wait   ☐ No ☐ Yes

9   Have you ever witnessed someone wait right   ☐ No ☐ Yes

APPENDIX 2

Survey

a.   If yes, use 3 words to describe their demeanor :

_____

_____

10   Have you ever gained/learned anything in the waiting place   ☐ No ☐ Yes

11   Does waiting require patience   ☐ No ☐ Yes

12   Does waiting require expectation   ☐ No ☐ Yes

13   Does waiting require trust   ☐ No ☐ Yes

14   Does waiting require you to believe   ☐ No ☐ Yes

15   Do you need to know the will of God to wait *(right)*   ☐ No ☐ Yes

16   Is the Word of God important in the waiting place   ☐ No ☐ Yes

17   Are you currently waiting on God for or to do something   ☐ No ☐ Yes

a.   If yes, how long: _____ days _____wks _____ mons _____ years

18   Is what you waiting on: spiritual or natural – medical – relational – financial – situational – emotional – material – psychological or other *(circle all that apply)*

19   Is there a way to show that you believe and trust God to do it ☐ No ☐ Yes

a.   If yes, give 2 examples:

_____

_____

20   Is God waiting on you to do something   ☐ No ☐ Yes

21   Which is easier: **waiting on God** or **waiting on people** *(circle one)*

APPENDIX 3

Prayer of Agreement Grid

Prayer of Agreement Grid

Date:

Prayer Needs/Requests - Promises you are waiting on

Believing God for
(to the right, list things you are believing God for/to do)

Faith/Belief/Trust in:
(for each prayer need, check the box that applies in the affirmative)

Jesus

His Name

The Word

God

His power

Others

Speak what you are believing Him for

My motives are pure/right about this request

I will give God the glory when this comes to pass

APPENDIX 3

Prayer of Agreement Grid

Prayer of Agreement Grid			Date:						
Prayer Needs/Requests - Promises you are waiting on									
Believing God for (to the right, list things you are believing God for/to do)									
Faith/Belief/Trust in: (for each prayer need, check the box that applies in the affirmative)									
I give Him glory now for His blessings									
I praise & delight myself in Him & in the hope of His promise									
I will be a good steward of the manifested promise/blessing									
My stewardship/discipline is good									

APPENDIX 3

Prayer of Agreement Grid

Prayer of Agreement Grid										
	Date:									
Prayer Needs/Requests - Promises you are waiting on										
Believing God for *(to the right, list things you are believing God for/to do)*										
Faith/Belief/Trust in: *(for each prayer need, check the box that applies in the affirmative)*										
My request is God's Will - It aligns w/ His Word										
I will give an offering to thank God for answering this prayer										
I am ready to receive this blessing										
Is there any unforgivness in your heart as it relates to this request/promise										

APPENDIX 3

Prayer of Agreement Grid

Prayer of Agreement Grid

Date:

Prayer Needs/Requests - Promises you are waiting on

Believing God for
(to the right, list things you are believing God for/to do)

Faith/Belief/Trust in:
(for each prayer need, check the box that applies in the affirmative)

Is there any fear associated to this request/promise

Is there any unconfessed/hidden sin(s) as it relates to this request/promise

This is a need/desire that only God can meet

Are there any unresolved issues/unhealed hurts- unforgiveness related to this request

APPENDIX 3

Prayer of Agreement Grid

Prayer of Agreement Grid										Date:
Prayer Needs/Requests - Promises you are waiting on										
Believing God for *(to the right, list things you are believing God for/to do)*										
Faith/Belief/Trust in: *(for each prayer need, check the box that applies in the affirmative)*										
Are there any unresolved issues/unhealed hurts-unforgiveness related to this request										
Do you believe it is time for you receive this										
Are you ok if God does not answer yet - you have to continue to wait										

While you wait – Worship: prayer, serve (keeping going), watch (expect), declare (speak God's Word & what you believe), prepare (be ready), examine again

313

Notes

Introduction

Dr. Seuss, *Oh, The Places You will Go,* (Random House, 1990), 15.

Chapter One: Wait on...Wait for *It*

J. Strong, Strong's Hebrew and Greek Dictionaires, QuickVerse (Findex, Inc., 2005), 21.

The World Book Dictionary, (World Book, Inc., 2001), 21.

The World Book Dictionary, (World Book, Inc., 2001), 27.
Anonymous, Ableever.net, "*Wait_On_The_Lord*", *www.ableever.net/Exhortation/Wait_On_The_Lord/wait_on_the_lord. html,* 28.

Anonymous, Ableever.net, "*Wait_On_The_Lord*", *www.ableever.net/Exhortation/Wait_On_The_Lord/wait_on_the_lord. html,* 28.

Chapter Two: Wait for *It*

David Timms, Sacred Waiting: Waiting on God in a World that Waits for Nothing,

(Bethany House Publishers, 2009), 31.

Charles Nichols, "Questions", *http://www.poemhunter.com/poem/questions-257, 34.*

Richard J. Foster, *Celebration of Discipline,* (Harper, 1978), 40.

Chapter Four: Issue with *It*

David Timms, Sacred Waiting: Waiting on God in a World that Waits for Nothing, (Bethany House Publishers, 2009), 84.

Sylvia Gunter, "Waiting on God - How do we wait?," *http://www.thoughts-about-god.com/biblestudies/sg_waitongod.htm,* 93.

Richard J. Foster, Celebration of Discipline, (Harper, 1978), 97.

Chapter Five: Waiting States

The World Book Dictionary, (World Book, Inc., 2001), 103.

"A Dream Deferred", Langston Hughes Home Page, *http://www.cswnet.com/~menamc/langston.htm (1996,* June), 104.

John Ortberg, The Life You Always Wanted: Spiritual Discplines, (Zondervan, 2002), 119.

"Wait-on-the-Lord", Christian Science Sentinel, www.csmonitor.com: *http://www.csmonitor.com/The-Culture/Articles-on-Christian-Science/2012/0215/Wait-on-the-Lord* (2012, February), 126.

The World Book Dictionary, (World Book, Inc., 2001), 135.

Chapter Seven: Waiting Right

Andrew Murray, *Waiting on God,* (ReadaClassic.com, 2010), 153.

Darryl Harris, *When God says Wait,*(Darryl Harris, 2008), 154.

J.Strong, Strongs Hebrew and Greek Dictionaires, QuickVerse (Findex, Inc., 2005), 159.

Stoelting, S. R., *"Hate to Wait for God"*, *www.cbn.com.*,
   http://www.cbn.com/family/youth/hate-to-wait-for-god-stoelting.aspx,
   160.

Sylvia Gunter, *"Waiting on God - How do we wait?,"*
   http://www.thoughts-about-god.com/biblestudies/sg_waitongod.htm,
   176.

Dr. Dora Sanders Hill, *Spiritual Warfare: The Myth Exposed*
   (Xulon Press, 2004), 177.

The World Book Dictionary, (World Book, Inc., 2001), 178.

About Dr. Tuesday Tate

A Motivational and Inspirational Speaker, Minister, Life Coach, and Author, Dr. Tuesday *(The Vision Coach and Life Advisor)* is a powerful, "real talk" orator. A dynamic and highly sought after keynote and national speaker and Prophetic Teacher. She is uniquely anointed to motivate, challenge, charge, and direct you to your purpose. Her words bring revelation, understanding, and encourages her listeners to action. With a powerful testimony, the call on her life has produced her 1st love and passion of purpose; the Ministry of the Gospel to persons of all walks of life. Her personal mission statement synergizes her passions and solidifies her purpose: *"to share God's love through prophetic teaching and preaching by presenting a revelatory Word of God that is functional, reproducible, applicable, and portable that encourages a more excellent way in relationships, business, ministry, and life. She assists individuals and organizations in identifying their purpose and set a vision and course of action towards success through personal, spiritual, social and/or professional development through teaching, training, speaking, and coaching."*

She has been blessed with multiple gifts for the uplifting and building of people and programs. Using her gifts, skills, and talents, her desire is to bring awareness of the message of H.I.V. (hope, identity, value) to all those who hear may live life on purpose. Dr. Tuesday has achieved great rewards in her work with youth, women, singles, ministries, professionals, leaders, organizations, and the body of Christ.

After years in Corporate America, she concluded that season of her life and separated from all she had been trained and educated in, was supported by, and knew and began to pursue the call that God placed on her life. In the fall of 1999, she surrendered to the service of God and left her corporate position and the fast track and accepted the call to ministry. An ordained minister, she serves as an elder in her local church. She ministers in other churches and arenas across the country; including women's', youth and singles conferences, juvenile centers, and prisons. Through the Word of God as led by Spirit of God; with a clear directive and assignment, she boldly, lovingly, and confidently pursues the call on her life to equip the believer for the work of service and the advancement of the Kingdom of God.

Not limited to public speaking, preaching, teaching, training, and coaching, her other talents have included; TV hosting on local TBN Program, "Joy In Our Town", and her own weekly ministry teaching program on local and internet called "Tuesdays with Tuesday". A published author of two group writings: one titled "How to Survive when Your Ship is Sinking", Tuesdays contribution "The Art of Waiting on God" has received great reviews. Through her involvement in these projects, she discovered her third passion of purpose as an author. And has now published her first self-authored book "Waiting: *Mastering the UnAvoidable*". She continued her education by obtaining a Certificate in Biblical Counseling, a Master of Biblical Studies and a Doctorate of Theology from North Carolina College of Theology (NCCT).

Using her leadership and business skills, she started her Mary Kay business and in less than 5-months, she promoted herself to director and earned her first car. After stepping down as a director, she reignited her fourth passion of purpose certified life coach, trainer, and speaker and established *Vision Focus Coaching and Consulting Group*; a subsidiary of ATK Enterprises, Inc. She combines her spiritual, corporate, and professional training and expertise to help organizations, ministries, churches, professionals, groups, youth, and individuals to identify their "why" and their personality type and gifts. She helps them to define, develop, and document their purpose and vision and to create a personal image. As a Certified Life Coach, she coined the concept of *P.R.I.S.M.* Coaching; where she focuses on *P*rofessional, *R*elational, *I*dentity, *S*piritual, and *M*inistry Coaching. Specializing in helping her clients design and redesign their life through Strategies for Success, she will take them from where they are to where they desire to be. She helps them bring their vision into focus.

Bringing together her four-pillars for life success: coaching, writing, speaking, and ministry, Dr. Tuesday is fully equipped to help others reach their desired goals and connect with their life purpose. She is a gift you will be blessed to encounter, engage, and experience. A faithful, humble, and grateful servant of the Lord, she serves as a member, leader, an ordained minister and Elder. She serves at *Healing Streams Word and Worship Center (HSWWC)*, where Pastor A. Thomas Hill is the Senior Pastor. She is a spiritual daughter of Bishop Joseph W. Walker, III, Senior Pastor, Mount Zion Baptist Church, Nashville, TN. She obtained her undergraduate degree from Wilberforce University. Her professional affiliations and training include Professional Woman Network and Speakers Bureau, Toast Masters International Member and Speech Winner, Alpha Kappa Alpha Sorority, Inc., and many others. Raised in Benton Harbor, MI. She is the youngest of her parents' 6-children.

**To book Dr. Tuesday for book signings
and discussions please contact her at**
atkpublishing@hotmail.com **or** 888.991.0979

Books and other products may be purchased at
http://atkpublishing.wix.com/atkpublishingwaiting